IN PURSUIT OF
WEALTH

THE MORAL CASE FOR FINANCE

Edited by
YARON BROOK and DON WATKINS

With additional contributions by
RAYMOND C. NILES and DOUG ALTNER

AYN RAND
INSTITUTE PRESS

First Printing 2017

ISBN: 978-0-9960101-1-5

AynRand.org

CONTENTS

INTRODUCTION

When Bernie Sanders challenged Hillary Clinton for the Democratic presidential nomination, his core message was that America's greatest challenge was rising economic inequality—and the main villain in this narrative was "Wall Street": the bankers, traders, and other financiers who make up America's financial industry. "The business model of Wall Street," he said, "is fraud."[1]

It was one of the least controversial statements he made.

Throughout history, finance has always been viewed with skepticism if not outright hostility, whether it was the ancient Greeks and early Christians who condemned (and often punished) "usurers," Franklin D. Roosevelt who insisted that the Great Depression was the product of greedy speculators, or Occupy Wall Street which vilified "the 1 percent."

And, to be sure, we have seen real problems concentrated in the financial industry, whether it be massive crises like the Great Depression, the Savings and Loan debacle, and the Great Recession, or scandals like Bernie Madoff's Ponzi scheme, the outcry over high frequency trading that occurred with the release of Michael Lewis's 2014 book *Flash Boys*, or the recent Wells Fargo phony account controversy.

But the fact is that our economic well-being *depends* on a vibrant and innovative financial industry—and that we would all be far worse off but for the productive achievements of this maligned and vilified group of individuals. Even if one is outraged by the behavior of some bankers, to call every member of the industry a participant in fraud is a profound injustice.

Why then does no one speak up to defend finance? Why do statements like Sanders's evoke a yawn rather than a protest? Because what Sanders said was only a crass variant of a belief shared by almost everyone in some form: that finance is *immoral*. Maybe not totally. Maybe it has some redeeming features. Maybe it is a *necessary evil*. But it is an evil nonetheless.

This belief in the immorality of finance can't be explained merely by the specific wrongs committed by specific financiers. Soldiers have

---

1. Sam Levine, "Bernie Sanders: 'The Business Model of Wall Street Is Fraud,'" *Huffington Post*, November 14, 2015, http://www.huffingtonpost.com/entry/bernie-sanders-wall-street-fraud_us_5647fb78e4b08cda3489294a.

committed atrocities without tarring the reputation of the military itself. The special ire directed at finance comes from the recognition that financiers are motivated by the selfish desire for profit—and the belief that the profit motive leads financiers to take short-range, irrational, predatory actions to line their pockets at others' expense.

In this regard, finance is not unique. This same view of the profit motive taints our evaluation of all businessmen. The reason finance gets singled out for special rebuke is, in large measure, because financiers are the most naked in their pursuit of profit. Although all businesses aim to profit through their productive actions, their *primary* concern is (or at least should be) making great products and providing great services. But finance's product *is* profit. A financier's job isn't to make money by making cars or computers—it's simply to make money. (How do financiers make money? In large part by making it easier for others to make products like cars and computers.)

This points to why Ayn Rand's philosophy of Objectivism is indispensable for understanding and defending the morality of finance. If you assume that the profit motive necessarily encourages predatory exploitation, and that self-interest *per se* is immoral, then at best you will see finance as a necessary evil and tend to see any problem or injustice associated with finance as a reflection of its inherent immorality.

Rand's philosophy, however, challenges those assumptions, first and foremost by questioning the conventional understanding of self-interest. Whereas we are taught to equate self-interest with short-range desires for things like wealth, power, and prestige, and morality as a guide for tempering our selfish desires for the sake of others, Rand encourages us to look more carefully at what our self-interest *actually* consists of. Human beings thrive, she argues, not through the short-range, predatory pursuit of our desires, but through living a life committed to the ideals of reason, productive achievement, and the trader principle—seeking to gain values from others through mutually beneficial trade.

This conception of self-interest, which she calls *rational selfishness*, leads to an understanding of the profit motive diametrically at odds with the conventional one. Profit is the economic insignia of production: one profits by *creating value*—and the motive of those seeking profits is to *earn* wealth by creating value. It is a selfish motive, yes—in the sense that the pursuit of one's own happiness is inherently selfish. But it has nothing to do with the short-range, predatory motives that drive cons, crooks, or even the "get rich quick" types who stay within the bounds of the law but have no genuine interest in productive enrichment. The symbol of the profit motive is Steve Jobs—not Bernie Madoff.

In Rand's view, the man who profits through productive achievement is doing something moral. He is supporting his own existence and pursuing his own happiness by using his mind to create values—the values that human beings need to live and enjoy life. And this is as true for bankers, traders, and investors as for any other producer. They use their minds to create wealth—not by taking existing materials and turning them into more valuable goods, but by taking existing wealth and putting it toward more valuable uses. In short, financiers don't create the products that enrich our lives—they help create (and nurture) all the businesses that create the products that enrich our lives.

This book consists of a collection of essays on finance written from the perspective of Rand's philosophy. Part I covers the moral attacks on finance, dispels some of the most important myths that prevent us from reaching a proper evaluation of finance, and lays out the moral framework necessary to grasp the industry's virtues. Part II examines today's most conspicuous attack on finance—an attack that damns finance not primarily for its allegedly immoral *methods* but for its supposedly immoral outcomes: finance, we are told, produces enormous *economic inequality*, and this inequality, the critics say, is unjust and destructive. Part III looks at a few recent controversies surrounding finance, highlighting how Rand's moral perspective helps us make sense of those controversies. We end with an interview with Yaron Brook that summarizes and ties together the key points of this collection.

A key takeaway from this book is that to counter the vilification of financiers requires *moral reframing*. Those who recognize the irreplaceable value of finance must change the terms of the debate. The question should not be whether financiers are "greedy" or selfish or motivated by money. The question should be: Do they profit through creating values that enhance human well-being—or are they parasites who line their pockets through short-range gambling and predatory exploitation? If we ask that question—and if we answer it honestly—then the moral case for finance is undeniable.

Don Watkins and Yaron Brook

PART 1

How Finance Helps Us Flourish

The Moral Case for Finance

By Yaron Brook and Don Watkins

A few passages in this chapter draw upon a shorter essay that the authors contributed to *Goud geld: De staat van de financiële sector* (Deventer, Netherlands: Wolters Kluwer, 2016).

Introduction

The 2016 film *Arrival* starts with a familiar premise: aliens arrive on earth and humanity finds itself struggling to answer the question: Why are they here? Are they benefactors or threats? Driven by fear of the unknown, some people predictably conclude that the creatures have bad intentions, and it is only the intervention of the protagonist—who discovers that the creatures are peaceful—that prevents an all-out attack. As with all good science fiction, the movie isn't really about aliens. It's about human beings, including the fact that we tend to fear, vilify, and persecute things we're unfamiliar with.

So it goes for the financial industry. Two things are striking about our attitude toward members of the industry, whether they be bankers or hedge fund managers or speculators or "Wall Street": the intensity of our opinions—and our almost complete inability to explain what it is these people do. Ask the average American what financiers do and you'll likely get some vague response about how they use stocks and bonds and "complex financial instruments" to make risky gambles. And yet whereas most people don't have an opinion about geochemistry or electrical engineering, nearly everyone has an opinion about finance—and all too often that opinion is skeptical at best and hostile at worse.[2]

These sorts of negative attitudes toward the industry are encouraged by activists, intellectuals, and political leaders who actively work to vilify the industry. Throughout history, they have demonized financiers as greedy, dangerous, and unproductive—as leeches who make money by exploiting the rest of us. Luther declared that "there is on earth no greater

---

2. See, for instance, John Wood and Paul Berg, "Trust in Banks," *Gallup*, 2011, http://www.gallup.com/services/176294/trust-banks.aspx; and Edelman Intelligence, "2015 Edelman Trust Barometer Executive Summary," *Edelman*, 2015, https://www.scribd.com/doc/252750985/2015-Edelman-Trust-Barometer-Executive-Summary.

enemy of man, after the Devil, than a gripe-money usurer."[3] Franklin Roosevelt blamed the Great Depression on financiers, saying that:

> The rulers of the exchange of mankind's goods have failed, through their own stubbornness and their own incompetence, have admitted failure, and have abdicated. Practices of the unscrupulous money changers stand indicted in the court of public opinion, rejected by the hearts and minds of men . . . [We must] apply social values more noble than mere monetary profit.[4]

More recently, in the wake of the 2008 financial crisis, Occupy Wall Street became notorious for targeting America's financial center as enemy number one. During his bid for president in 2016, Bernie Sanders declared that "the business model of Wall Street is fraud."[5] Senator Elizabeth Warren has built her political career on attacking financiers, advocating breaking up the big banks, raising taxes on the industry, and reining in the pay of Wall Street executives.[6] This same attitude can be found even among those who are more sympathetic to free markets. Congressman and presidential-hopeful Ron Paul relentlessly attacked bankers, accusing Wall Street of "stealing from the American people."[7]

But for all the attacks on finance, no one except the occasional Communist crackpot proposes outlawing the financial industry. Unlike the gun industry or the tobacco industry, even the harshest critics of the financial industry view it as a *necessary* evil. There is simply no denying that progress and prosperity depend on a burgeoning financial industry. It's something we each experience in our daily lives: most of us

---

3. Paul M. Johnson, *A History of the Jews* (New York: HarperCollins, 1988), p. 242.

4. Franklin D. Roosevelt, First Inaugural Address, March 4, 1933, http://avalon. law.yale.edu/20th_century/froos1.asp.

5. Bernie Sanders, "Wells Fargo's Business Model Is Fraud," *Medium*, September 20, 2016, https://medium.com/senator-bernie-sanders/wells-fargos-business-model-is-fraud-d19fb6fbe0a8#.l2kp9t58a.

6. Bryce Covert, "Elizabeth Warren Calls On Americans to Fight Wall Street," May 24, 2016, https://thinkprogress.org/elizabeth-warren-calls-on-americans-to-fight-wall-street-4c4ef07f7e9f#.99yhmbfie.

7. David Sherfinski, "Ron Paul: Time for Gov't, Fed, Wall Street to Stop 'Stealing from the American People,'" *Washington Times*, July 22, 2013, http://www.washingtontimes.com/blog/inside-politics/2013/jul/22/ron-paul-time-govt-fed-wall-street-stop-stealing-a/.

keep our money in a bank, use checks and credit cards, buy insurance, invest for our retirement, and have a home mortgage. Finance clearly plays a vital role in our lives and in our world. But what exactly is that role? And are we right to vilify and persecute the people who perform it?

How Finance Enriches the World

What is finance? From one perspective we can think of it as the industry that deals with financial instruments, such as cash, stocks, bonds, and derivatives. Or we can think of it as a set of activities involving those financial instruments, such as borrowing, lending, and investing. We can also think of it as a number of institutions carrying out these activities, including commercial banks, investment banks, insurance companies, hedge funds, stock exchanges, mutual funds, private equity firms, and venture capital firms.

What unites all these different products, activities, and institutions is the assembly and use of *savings*.

Human beings have to consume material values—*wealth*—in order to live and enjoy life, whether it be food, medicine, transportation, computers, or books. But nature doesn't give us the wealth we need to flourish. Even wild berries do us no good unless we first exercise the thought required to discriminate edible berries from poison and the effort required to gather the berries. To consume, we need to produce.

At the most primitive level, human beings can produce enough to meet their immediate needs. But that is a precarious mode of existence. We progress by creating more wealth than we can consume today. That provides us with security and it liberates us to take up tasks that require more time. If you need to eat three fish a day to live, and you catch nine fish in a day, then that frees up two days of your time you can use to build a net that can enable you to catch thirty fish a day, which frees up your time so you can start a garden, which will eventually allow you to feed yourself for months with only a couple weeks' worth of work. Whatever we produce beyond what we consume immediately is *savings*.

Savings is the *master tool* because it gives us the time and resources to make and use every other tool. The more savings we have, the more productive we can be, and the better we can live. On an island, our savings consists of actual material values we can use in the future: stored food, for example. In an advanced division of labor economy like the one we live in, savings refers to *financial* savings. It consists of *money* we can set aside for future use. Instead of setting aside extra food, we set aside money which we can use to buy any other good or service we want, including food.

When we spend our money over a short period of time to meet our immediate needs, we're "living paycheck to paycheck." If our source of income dries up, we're in trouble. We have no cushion. We also lose out on opportunities to advance our well-being through *investing*.

Investing is paying a price now for an expected larger reward later. We invest whenever we forego the use of our savings and put it to *productive use* in the hope of growing our savings. For example, we use our savings to start a new company, or pay for an education, or lend the money, with interest, to a friend who is going to start his own company. We don't just set aside our savings to consume later—we use (and risk) our savings productively in the hopes that it will grow and thereby *increase* our ability to consume later.

But investing our own savings has its challenges. Trying to find investment opportunities and assessing those opportunities takes time. It also takes knowledge and judgment that we might not have. Should I lend my money to my brother-in-law who wants to start a restaurant? Or what about a neighbor I barely know who wants to use it to renovate his house and pay me back out of his salary as a doctor? Which is the better deal and how much interest should I charge to compensate for the risk? And what if I want to lend my money for a month, but I only find people who want to borrow the money for a year? On the other side, what if I'm the one looking to borrow money or to find an investor for my plans? How can I find willing lenders and investors? And how do I know I'm getting a good deal?

These and other challenges are what give rise to the need for the financial *industry*. The financial industry's purpose is to gather and deploy savings in order to maximize the financial well-being of everyone involved in trade. It solves the problem of how to most efficiently assemble savings and put it to its best use, given the wide variety in interests, time horizons, and risk tolerances of people.

Take a commercial bank. In its simplest form, a commercial bank accepts deposits and makes loans. Its job is to channel people's savings into profitable investments, and it profits by paying the savers less interest on their deposits (say, 3 percent) than it charges borrowers for their loans (say, 6 percent). Why would borrowers and lenders tolerate that? Why wouldn't they deal with each other directly and cut out the middle man? Because by dealing with a bank, they end up better off.

As a saver, you no longer have to hunt for people to lend to. You don't have to learn how to assess various investment opportunities. You don't have to worry about how long someone wants to borrow for.

And you don't bear the risk of a particular borrower defaulting on his loan. All you have to do is assess the soundness of the bank itself. (And the bank, since it makes many, diversified loans, is very likely less risky than any particular loan you might make.) Apart from that, your work is done. You get to see your savings grow. And what about the borrower? As a borrower, you don't have to hunt for random people who happen to have savings to spare. You just go down to the local bank and fill out an application. And the bank? It specializes in making loans, learning how to assess loan-worthiness, learning how to price its loans, and so on. Everyone involved is better off.

Similar stories can be told about every financial institution or technology. They all arose to solve a certain problem, enabling individuals to put savings to better and better uses. Stock exchanges, for example, arose to solve a problem created by the Dutch East India Company. Earlier joint-stock shipping companies were established for the duration of a single voyage, after which they were liquidated and their assets were divided up among the owners. But the Dutch East India Company didn't liquidate, and so the owners had to develop a secondary market for their ownership shares. As one writer notes, "Because the shares in the various East India companies were issued on paper, investors could sell the papers to other investors. Unfortunately, there was no stock exchange in existence, so the investor would have to track down a broker to carry out a trade."[8] This was wildly inefficient and expensive, and this difficulty meant that sellers could rarely get a genuine market price for their shares. That started to change thanks to the development of the Amsterdam Stock Exchange, which regularly brought together traders and massively increased the liquidity of stocks: investors could more easily invest and cash out their savings and businesses could, as a result, more easily raise funds from investors, increasing the number and scale of wealth creating projects they could undertake.[9]

One of the perennial attacks on finance has been that financiers are unproductive. They don't create anything. They make paper profits. In Tom Wolfe's celebrated novel *Bonfire of the Vanities*, Wolfe captures

---

8. Andrew Beattie, "The Birth of Stock Exchanges," *Investopedia*, April 24, 2017, http://www.investopedia.com/articles/07/stock-exchange-history.asp.

9. L. O. Petram, "The World's First Stock Exchange: How the Amsterdam Market for Dutch East India Company Shares Became a Modern Securities Market, 1602–1700," *University of Amsterdam*, 2011, https://pure.uva.nl/ws/files/1427391/85961_thesis.pdf.

this view in a discussion between Sherman McCoy, his parents, his wife and his daughter about McCoy's job as a bond trader:

> "A bond is a way of loaning people money. Let's say you want to build a road, and it's not a little road but a big highway, like the highway we took up to Maine last summer. Or you want to build a big hospital. Well, that requires a lot of money, more money than you could ever get by just going to a bank. So what you do is, you issue what are called bonds."
>
> "You build roads and hospitals, Daddy? That's what you do?"
>
> Now both [McCoy's] father and his mother started laughing. He gave them openly reproachful looks, which only made them merrier. Judy was smiling with what appeared to be a sympathetic twinkle.
>
> "No, I don't actually build them, sweetheart. I handle the bonds, and the bonds are what make it possible—"
> "You help build them?"
> "Well, in a way."
> "Which ones?"
> "Which *ones*?"
> "You said roads and hospitals."
> "Well, not any one specifically."[10]

McCoy's wife goes on to explain his job this way:

> "Daddy doesn't build roads or hospitals, and he doesn't help build them, but he does handle the *bonds* for the people who raise the money."
>
> "Bonds?"
>
> "Yes. Just imagine that a bond is a slice of cake, and you didn't bake the cake, but every time you hand somebody a slice of the cake, a tiny little bit comes off, like a little crumb, and you can keep that."[11]

In the same vein, Barack Obama declared that "Too many potential

---

10. Tom Wolfe, *The Bonfire of the Vanities* (New York: Bantam, 1988), pp. 238–39.

11. Ibid., p. 239.

physicists and engineers spend their careers shifting money around in the financial sector, instead of applying their talents to innovating in the real economy."[12]

The notion that finance is unproductive is profoundly wrong and unjust. It ignores the three enormous and unparalleled value-creation activities of the financial industry that follow from its core function of putting savings to its best uses. The financial industry helps us:

1. Boost production
2. Manage risk
3. Increase consumption

Boosting Production

Production requires power. We produce by moving around the raw materials provided by nature and recombining them into a form that is more valuable for human life. That's hard work, and the more power we have to do it, the better off we are. The problem is that human beings aren't particularly strong. For millennia we relied on animals to meet most of our power needs. It was only with the advent of plentiful, reliable, affordable energy—particularly fossil fuel energy—that we were able to increase our reservoir of power and multiple our standard of living many times over. We were able to power machines to do our work for us, and as a result we were able to get far more work done.

The energy industry is a productivity multiplier. Most of the things we do with energy are things we did without a lot of energy: travel, communicate, build, produce and cook food. But the energy industry allows us to do all of that and more on an unprecedented scale. As a result the average human lifespan from birth has gone from thirty to eighty in just two hundred years. One way to think about the *financial* industry is as the *other* energy industry. It provides us with the *financial* fuel that multiplies our productive power.

This is most clear when we look at finance's role in promoting economic progress. There are two ingredients for economic progress: innovation and capital. Financial capital is the savings used to fund

---

12. Barack Obama, "The Way Ahead," *Economist*, October 8, 2016, http://www .economist.com/news/briefing/21708216-americas-president-writes-us-about-four-crucial-areas-unfinished-business-economic.

productive ventures through the purchase of things like factories, raw materials, machines, inventories, and labor, as well as research and development. The basic challenge in an economy is that the people with the best productive ideas seldom have the capital necessary to put those ideas into practice, and the people with the necessary capital do not automatically know who has the best ideas. That's a big problem: failing to put money in the right hands means that we miss out on revolutionary achievements that can dramatically improve our lives—putting money in the wrong hands means wasting our most valuable tool. Finance is the industry that solves this problem by what economist Luigi Zingales calls "matching money with talent."[13]

There are two basic ways of matching money with talent: lending and investment—or debt and equity. In both cases, savers are providing crucial capital to producers. With debt, savers are loaning out funds in exchange for a promise by the borrower to repay the loan plus interest. Savers are effectively taking their economic resources, their savings, and loaning them to someone who can put those resources to more productive use, the way that many people are renting out spare bedrooms on Airbnb. With equity, the saver is buying an ownership stake in a productive venture. Think of a simple partnership to sell strawberries. One party supplies the funds, say, $1,000 to pay for the berries and a booth at a farmer's market; the other party supplies the labor, buying and selling the strawberries, and they split the profits. The same principle applies to more complex financial relationships. When a company "goes public" and issues stock to raise money, it is selling ownership: its stock gives shareholders a claim on the assets and future earnings of the company, and the cash influx allows the managers of the company to grow more rapidly.

Both debt and equity channel financial capital into the hands of producers. The difference is that debt is a promise: whether your venture is successful or not, you have an obligation to repay your loan (unless it's discharged in bankruptcy). But your payment is capped: if you borrow a million dollars at 10 percent interest for one year, you only have to repay $1,100,000—regardless of whether you turn that million into $2 million or $20 million. Equity, on the other hand, allows an investor to take part in the upside. The more profitable your venture, the

---

13. Russ Roberts, "Luigi Zingales on the Costs and Benefits of the Financial Sector," *EconTalk*, Library of Economics and Liberty, February 2, 2015, http://www.econtalk.org/archives/2015/02/luigi_zingales_1.html.

more the equity stake is worth. But on the downside, the risks are larger: equity is the residual claimant—if the venture is a failure and you end up in bankruptcy, he gets only what's left over after all your creditors have been paid off. In either case, debt and equity are the tools that allow financiers to match money and talent.

The most obvious example of matching money and talent is the venture capital industry. In the early 20th century, it was enormously hard to get money to fund speculative ventures. Most capital came from banks and banks largely preferred to deal with established companies and traditional business lines. J.P. Morgan, for instance, was famous for lending only to established businesses (although he occasionally made exceptions, as when he backed Thomas Edison's venture into electrical lighting). To start a new business depended on the ability to scrape together savings from your own work and friends and family, and businesses tended to grow slowly by reinvesting most of their profits. It's impossible to say how many potential ideas never made it to the market, or took far longer to spread. That was changed by Georges Doriot, who almost single-handedly created the venture capital industry—an industry that funds highly risky startups. Unlike many other investors, venture expects that most of its investments will fail, but that the ones that succeed will grow so big so fast that the venture fund will still be profitable. Key to the industry's success, however, is its ability to spot talented individuals with good ideas—ideas that, in almost every case, start out looking like bad ideas. Think, for example, of Airbnb: almost no one believed that people would willingly let strangers stay in their homes. And yet because a small number of venture capitalists saw the potential of the idea—and were willing to put their money where their mind was—Airbnb has become one of the fastest growing companies of all time, changing the way we travel.

But matching money with talent goes far beyond venture capital. Community banks often fund new restaurants and other stores, including those that will have the potential to grow and expand. These banks have to distinguish between which ventures are likely to succeed and which are likely to fail. Or take a less obvious example: the stock market. When companies go public it enables them to raise a vast amount of capital—but which companies will be able to raise capital, and how much? That is decided by financiers based on their estimate of which companies will be able to create the most value going forward. Less obvious still, private equity is in the business of matching talent and money. The core activity of private equity firms is to buy businesses that are underperforming and either make them more efficient or to break them up and sell them to companies that can better use their resources. Another way to put it is that they spot resources that aren't being used in their most productive way and put them into the hands of people who will use them better. Whatever the details, the basic pattern of financial institutions is to aggregate savings (from depositors in the case of banks, investors in the case of the stock market, and large institutional investors like insurance companies in the case of venture capital and private equity), and then find the most productive use for that money by placing productive resources at the disposal of the most innovative and productive thinkers.

Matching money with talent is not the only productive role of finance. Financiers also make possible the existence of the division of labor by creating and improving payments systems, they improve the division of labor by reducing transaction costs and promoting accurate prices, they provide liquidity through well-developed financial markets, and much else besides. Take speculators, for example—probably the most hated actors in the world's most hated industry. A speculator might buy stock based, not on an assessment of the long-term prospects of a company, but instead on the belief he's identified an underpriced stock which he will be able to quickly resell at a slightly higher price. By trading on this opportunity, the speculator helps the market adjust to a price more reflective of the value of the stock and by supplying the market with liquidity, the speculator is creating an enormous value: anyone who wants to sell his stock is able to do so easily, cheaply (i.e., with low transaction costs) and roughly at the stock's market price. Anyone who has ever tried to quickly sell an illiquid asset, such as a house or a car, has probably experienced firsthand the difficulties and frustrations that would abound in a stock market free from speculation. And notice that this *does* indirectly help to match money and talent: businesses would be able to raise far less money in public markets if investors worried about their ability to easily turn their stocks into cash.

What does all of this mean for our ability to produce? Consider the role of finance in the transformation that happened in the U.S. economy during the 1970s and 1980s. By the late 1970s, American corporations were organized into large, sluggish, inefficient conglomerates. They were uncompetitive globally, and partially as a result, the U.S. economy was sluggish. The American business landscape was completely restructured during the 1980s and 1990s, fueled in large measure by Michael Milken's high-yield bond revolution.

Milken's basic insight was to grasp that under specific market conditions, low-rated or unrated ("junk") bonds could perform better than highly rated bonds, even after adjusting for risk. It was an unpopular idea at the time, but after a deep study of the data, Milken was convinced. According to business writer Robert Sobel, Milken "concentrated on a subset of a single market and its implications. His desire was to encompass all knowledge and all business experience relating to this kind of financing. He was the consummate workaholic—intense, humorless, even grim, when on the job."[14] His success depended on more than one basic insight however. "To most traders," notes Sobel, "bonds are paper; they have little interest in the companies behind them except for their ratings. Milken was different. He monitored activities at those firms for which he was a banker and in whose paper he traded."[15]

Slowly, Milken succeeded in creating a market for these high-yield bonds. This meant that many companies unable to get a high rating from the bond ratings agencies—virtually any startup, for instance—could suddenly raise significant amounts of capital, which they had previously been unable to do, at least without giving up a large share of ownership in the company. And it meant that talented entrepreneurs without huge fortunes at their disposal now had the ability to takeover and improve (and often break up) large, poorly run companies. According to Daniel Fischel:

> [T]he dramatic growth of the high-yield bond market made it possible for takeover entrepreneurs who themselves otherwise lacked sufficient funds to make credible threats to acquire firms of virtually any size. The investment banking firm of Drexel Burnham, and particularly Michael Milken, the head of its high-yield bond division, was primarily responsible for this development. Drexel and Milken established contacts with the emerging class of takeover entrepreneurs . . . who routinely came to Drexel to finance takeover attempts knowing that Drexel had a stable of institutional clients interested in investing in Drexel deals. Drexel became known as a firm that could, if necessary, finance a takeover bid by raising billions of dollars within a matter of hours. Its reputation was so formidable that a Drexel-backed deal for billions of dollars could go forward even if no money had been raised. All that was necessary was a let-

---

14. Robert Sobel, *Dangerous Dreamers* (New York: Wiley, 1993), p. 64.

15. Ibid., p. 77.

ter from Drexel announcing that it was "highly confident"
the funds would be available when needed.[16]

It wasn't just that Milken helped unwind the stagnant behemoths
of the 1970s—he helped channel capital into the growing tech and
telecomm sectors of the new economy, helping launch the career of,
among many other business trailblazers, Ted Turner. According to author George Gilder, Milken and other financiers get the credit for taking "the vast sums trapped in old-line businesses" and putting "them
back into the markets," where they could be used to fuel the productivity surge of the 1980s and 1990s.

> Focusing on the turmoil unleashed by the microchip in
> TV, films, and telephony, Milken channeled some $26 bil-
> lion into MCI, McCaw, Viacom, TCI, Time Warner, Turner,
> Cablevision Systems, News Corp., Barnes & Noble, and
> other cable, telecom, wireless, publishing, and entertain-
> ment companies that first began weaving together the ele-
> ments of the telecosm.[17]

Milken, counting on nothing except his judgment that "junk"
bonds weren't really junk and that the entrepreneurs and businesses
he was helping were *good*, led the revolution that would liberate capital from the turgid old boy network so that it could eventually find its
way to Silicon Valley.[18]

Economists have tried to measure the precise connection between
finance and economic progress. After reviewing the literature, banking
and finance economist Ross Levine concludes that

> the preponderance of theoretical reasoning and empir-
> ical evidence suggests a positive, first-order relationship
> between financial development and economic growth. A
> growing body of work would push even most skeptics to-
> ward the belief that the development of financial markets

---

16. Daniel Fischel, *Payback: The Conspiracy to Destroy Michael Milken and His Financial
    Revolution* (New York: HarperBusiness, 1995), pp. 16–17.

17. George Gilder, *Telecosm: How Infinite Bandwidth Will Revolutionize Our World* (New
    York: Free Press, 2000).

18. For the definitive account of the facts surrounding Milken's eventual arrest and
    conviction for SEC securities violations, see Fischel, *Payback*.

and institutions is a critical and inextricable part of the growth process.[19]

Not only is finance as an industry critical, though: we need a *dynamic* financial industry that can rapidly innovate to meet the evolving needs of the rest of the economy.

> [G]rowth itself makes the "old" financial system less effective at screening and monitoring the new, more complex technologies. Without commensurate improvements in financial systems, economies become less effective at identifying and financing growth-inducing endeavors. Laeven, Levine, and Michalopoulos (2011) show that financial systems that rapidly adopt and adapt improved screening methodologies exert a positive effect on growth, while more stagnant financial systems slow economic progress.[20]

All this is true. But it badly understates the importance of finance for economic progress. One way to assess the contribution of any industry to human productivity is to ask: What would the world look like without it? For example, imagine the world without Silicon Valley and the modern computer industry. We would be stuck back in 1970, writing on typewriters, communicating via phone and snail mail, getting our music at the record store and our books at the bookstore. It would mean a massive loss in terms of how well we live. If we didn't have finance, though? Forget the 1970s—try the 1270s. Economic progress emerges from the intelligent combination of capital and innovation. Remove capital from the equation—and the financial markets that accumulate and direct that capital into the hands of innovators—and

---

19. Ross Levine, "Financial Development and Economic Growth: Views and Agenda," *Journal of Economic Literature*, June 1997, http://www.jstor.org/stable/2729790. See also Ross Levine, "Finance and Growth: Theory and Evidence," *Handbook of Economic Growth, Volume 1A* (2005), http://faculty.haas.berkeley.edu/ross_levine/ Papers/Forth_Book_Durlauf_FinNGrowth.pdf and Yongseok Shin, "Financial Markets: An Engine for Economic Growth," *Regional Economist*, July 2013, https:// www.stlouisfed.org/publications/regional-economist/july-2013/financial- markets--an-engine-for-economic-growth.

20. Ross Levine, "In Defense of Wall Street: The Social Productivity of the Financial System," *The Role of Central Banks in Financial Stability: How Has It Changed?*, 2013, http://faculty.haas.berkeley.edu/ross_levine/Papers/defense%20of%20wall%20 street_post.pdf.

the result is poverty and stagnation.

To accuse financiers of "shifting money around" and not contributing to "the real economy" reveals an embarrassing ignorance (or shameful evasion) of finance's contribution to human life and happiness. Without some of our best minds going into the financial industry there is no Apple or Google or Walmart or Amazon or Uber or Facebook, and all the wealth, jobs, and pleasure they create. There would be no small businesses, no real estate developments, no imports and no exports. Everything we buy would be more expensive, including our food, our clothes, and our homes. Our ability to save for retirement would be crippled. Yes, financiers shift money around. But not like a dim-witted dog taking dirty socks to the other side of the room. They shift money around the way a Michelin chef shifts ingredients around— they organize the resources we need to live and enjoy life in a way that dramatically enhances the productive value of those resources.

Managing Risk

In his book *Against the Gods: The Remarkable Story of Risk*, Peter Bernstein tells this story:

> One winter night during one of the many German air raids on Moscow in World War II, a distinguished Soviet professor of statistics showed up in his local air-raid shelter. He had never appeared there before. "There are seven million people in Moscow," he used to say. "Why should I expect them to hit me?" His friends were astonished to see him and asked what had changed his mind. "Look," he explained, "there are seven million people in Moscow and one elephant. Last night they got the elephant."[21]

Just as we enhance our lives and happiness by boosting our productivity, we also enhance our lives and happiness by managing the risk we are willing to face. But assessing and coping with risk is not easy. The financial industry plays a key role in both reducing risk and in transferring risk from those who don't wish to assume it to those who do. Four examples are worth noting.

---

21. Peter L. Bernstein, *Against the Gods: The Remarkable Story of Risk* (New York: Wiley, 1998), p. 116.

Insurance. Insurance companies allow individuals and companies to protect themselves against risks such as death, property damage, or legal liability. By agreeing to pay a predictable, affordable fee they can guard against a potentially catastrophic loss. Take life insurance.

We human beings structure our lives around the assumption that we will live a full lifespan. We buy homes based on the assumption that we will be able to continue working and pay them off over the course of thirty years. Our spouse may make certain career choices based on our ability to pay the majority of the bills. We have children, knowing that they will depend on us to provide for their material well-being for several decades—hopefully no more than two! And yet all these decisions are risky: people can and do die unexpectedly, and the financial impact on the people who depend on us can be painful if not catastrophic. Life insurance companies allow us to limit or eliminate that risk. For a relatively small premium, we can guarantee that the people who matter to us will be taken care of in a worst-case scenario.

And why would total strangers be willing to assume such risks? Because insurers are able to use their ingenuity to make sure that the claims they pay out are less than the premiums they take in. Although it's impossible to know when any given individual will die, the use of complex mathematics and statistics makes it possible to accurately estimate the average lifespan of a large population. Through their use of actuarial science, life insurance companies can set premiums large enough to cover their costs and earn a profit and low enough to remain attractive to their clients. (Most of their profits come from investing part of the premiums they collect in financial assets such as securities and real estate: as a group, insurers are the largest providers of capital in the economy.)

Credit. Just as credit can be used by companies to finance growth, it can also be used to mitigate risk. On an individual level, we often maintain a cash reserve to deal with unexpected costs that fall outside of our budget. Credit can perform the same function. If our car breaks down, we can pay for the repairs out of pocket, but we can also cover the cost with our credit card or by asking a friend for a loan.

Companies do the same thing. Short-term credit can be used to deal with cash flow and other challenges. For instance, a business may expect a million dollars from one of its customers in the next ninety days, but not have the $100,000 to meet payroll for the month. Short-term credit of the sort offered on the commercial paper market or banks give the business the ability to cope with such risks. By making credit available and affordable, the financial industry gives value-cre-ating businesses (or potentially value-creating businesses) *a longer run-way* so that fewer businesses crash and burn unnecessarily.

Diversification. How should you invest your money? One meth-od might be to look for the best investment you can find and put all your money into it. But that is super-high risk. If you're wrong or cir-cumstances change, the loss can be crippling. So how can you gain the benefits of investing while minimizing the risks? Through diversifica-tion—for example, buying a lot of different stocks, so that any losses are likely to be more than covered by offsetting gains. And finance not only makes this possible—it continually invents new ways to make di-versification easier.

Take index funds, like those pioneered by Jack Bogle's invest-ment management company, The Vanguard Group. Bogle created the first index fund individual investors could access, enabling them to easily and cheaply diversify their stock portfolios. Instead of buying hundreds of different stocks, investors could put their money into a Vanguard fund that would automatically track a benchmark, such as the S&P 500. Although index funds lack the allure of investments that promise to outperform the market, they protect against the risk of un-derperforming the market.

Diversification doesn't simply provide protection to individual in-vestors, however. As Ross Levine points out, it also "promote[s] growth and expand[s] opportunities": "When securities markets ease the diver-sification of risk, this encourages investment in higher-return projects that might be shunned without effective risk management vehicles."[22] In other words, investors are more willing to put money into promis-ing but risky ventures when they are able to mitigate that risk through diversification. If they had to put all their eggs in one basket, they would be less willing to fund potentially transformational businesses.

Derivatives. Derivatives can seem intimidatingly complex. But the basic idea is straightforward. Suppose you bought a couple tickets to see a famous boxer in a highly hyped match only to discover that you will have to travel out of town that day thanks to an unexpected work obligation. So your friend agrees to stop by on the day of the fight and pay you $200 for the tickets. It's a good deal for you—you'll get your money back—and it's a good deal for him, since the event is now

---

22. Levine, "In Defense of Wall Street," http://faculty.haas.berkeley.edu/ross_levine/Papers/defense%20of%20wall%20street_post.pdf.

sold out and scalpers are selling tickets for twice that. A few days later, though, the fighter everyone wanted to see drops out of the fight and now scalpers are lucky to get $50 per ticket. But you're a pretty lousy a friend so you tell your buddy "a deal's a deal," and demand your $200.

Congratulations, you've just dealt in derivatives. A derivative is a contract whose value is based on an underlying asset, like a stock or a bond—or, in our example, the tickets to the fight. You sold your friend a type of derivative called a forward contract: he agreed to buy the tickets at a set price in the future, and the *value* of that contract depended on the value of the tickets.

Derivatives perform many functions, but one important one is to allow a business to transfer certain risks. Again, consider a forward contract. A farmer may be excellent at growing corn, but not at predicting what the price of corn will be at the end of the season. A forward contract allows him to lock in a price for his corn, which means that although he won't profit on the upside if the price of corn rises at harvest time, he will also be protected from the downside if the price of corn collapses.

More complex derivatives do essentially the same thing: they allocate risk from parties that don't want to bear it to those who do. This means that riskier, but potentially more valuable, investments are made possible, since investors have the power to hedge their risk through derivatives.

Increasing Consumption

The ultimate goal of production is consumption, and finance not only helps us maximize what we can produce, but it helps each of us as individuals consume more effectively over the course of our lives.

First of all, both of the functions of finance we just mentioned—maximizing production and minimizing risk—help increase our ability to consume. We can consume more because finance helps fuel the businesses that turn out more, better, cheaper goods year after year. At the same time, finance also increases our income by supplying the capital that increases the demand for labor and the productivity of labor. In other words, the fact we make far more than our grandparents and great-grandparents did is owed in large part to the fact that financiers have supplied us with machines that make us more productive and supplied the financial capital that bids for our productive effort. On the risk minimization side, we can consume more because, for instance, if our new car is totaled in a wreck, insurance protects us from eating a $20,000 loss.

But there are two other ways that finance contributes to our ability to consume: *return on savings* and *consumption smoothing.*

We achieve a return on savings thanks to banks and investments. The most obvious example is retirement savings. Imagine that you saved $100 each month from your paycheck but instead of investing it or even putting it in a bank you literally just stuffed it under your mattress—from the time you were 21 until you were 65. By the time you were ready to retire, you'd have amassed $52,800. But now let's say instead of hoarding cash you invested that same $100 in an index fund that earned a return of 6 percent a year. You would end up with $253,000 by the time you retired. And that's not the end of the story. Without relying on the financial industry, every time you spent your $52,800 nest egg, your wealth would decrease. But if you instead kept your money invested, you would be able to spend more than $15,000 a year from interest payments on your $253,000 without ever touching your principal.

In short, finance gives you the opportunity to dramatically increase your consumption by doing nothing—or, more precisely, by choosing not to consume everything you produce today, but instead providing the productive economy with savings that can be used to generate additional economic value with minimal effort on your part. For all of the demonization of financiers, this is as close to magic as you can get.

Increasing the raw total of what we can consume over the course of our lives is not the only way finance helps us maximize consumption. Human beings face a *time mismatch* between our desire to consume and our ability produce. Our ability to produce—to generate income—tends to start out low when we are young, to rise as we grow in experience and skill, to peak somewhere around middle age, and to decline as we reach old age. But our consumption preferences don't usually follow that same trajectory. When we're young our consumption goals likely outstrip our earning power, whereas that is typically reversed when we hit our peak earning years.

Finance solves this problem by giving us the tools to engage in what economists call "consumption smoothing." Instead of consuming only what we can afford today, we can consume more than we can afford today so long as we consume less tomorrow, leading to a less volatile standard of living over the course of our lives. What makes this incredible achievement possible? *Credit.* In his book *Smart Money,* journalist Andrew Palmer describes the power of credit this way:

> The acts of savings and borrowing are both forms of time travel: they are transactions that we undertake with our future selves. We save in order to fund the older us—the retirement from the job we do not yet have or the tuition fees for the children we do not have with the partner we have not met. The more connected we feel to our future selves, the more likely we are to save for "them." . . . Similarly, young people are able to borrow now by unlocking the earnings power of their future selves. When a lender gives you a thirty-year mortgage, it is in effect contracting with the higher-paid, grayer-haired edition of yourself.[23]

Thanks to credit, you are able to buy things today with money you'll earn in the future. By smoothing your consumption you can actually *increase* the lifetime value of what you can consume from a given lifetime income. Think of a house. What's more valuable: waiting twenty years and buying a house that you'll live in for another twenty years—or being able to live in that same house for forty years? That's what a home mortgage does. Credit effectively lets us make buying decisions, not on the basis of what we happen to be able to afford today, but on what we will be able to afford over the course of our life.

There's simply no question that finance is an enormous and almost unrivaled force for good. It helps us flourish by making us more productive, more secure, and prosperous. And *this*—the creation of value, rather than fraud, theft, recklessness, or exploitation—is how financiers profit.

Profit: The Insignia of Productive Achievement in Finance

The 1987 movie *Wall Street* perfectly captures the conventional view of how financiers profit. "It's a zero sum game. Somebody wins, somebody loses. Money itself isn't lost or made, it's simply transferred."[24] Building on the assumption that financiers are unproductive and simply "shift money around," the zero sum argument claims that since financiers don't create wealth they must profit by "shifting money" into their own pockets at others' expense—often resorting to shady tactics if not

---

23. Andrew Palmer, *Smart Money* (New York: Basic, 2015), pp. 6–7.

24. *Wall Street*, directed by Oliver Stone (Twentieth Century Fox 1987).

outright fraud. The financial industry's profits, in other words, are the result not of value creation but economic exploitation.

To parse this claim we need to start by looking at the broader phenomenon of profit.[25] In an economic context, profit is a company's revenues minus its expenses. What determines its revenue? The economic value of what it creates, as judged by the voluntary decisions of buyers.

To the extent a company is operating in a free market, it cannot force anyone to buy its products. It offers them for sale at a given price, and others are free to buy or not. Think of a company like Apple. It doesn't make money by rounding people up at gunpoint or getting a grant from the government. Its revenue reflects the choice of millions of buyers to make purchases from Apple. Why does someone buy an iPhone from Apple? Because the phone is more valuable to them than the $600 it costs. The buyer gains: she values the phone more than the $600. Apple gains: it values the $600 more than the phone. It is a win/win transaction.

And what about a company's expenses? These too are determined by voluntary transactions, with the company in this case acting as the buyer—the buyer of productive resources. Apple has to pay its employees and its suppliers in order to be able to sell phones and other products to its customers. Its salaries, for example, are based on an agreement between the company and a worker to work for a given amount of compensation, and that agreement only takes place if Apple thinks it will benefit (the employee will contribute more to the company than his compensation) and if the employee thinks he will benefit (Apple is compensating him better than his alternatives).

Profits, then, reflect the *gap* between the economic value consumed during the productive process and the economic value obtained through voluntary trade. A company profits by using resources in such a way as to produce something more valuable. Profits, in short, are not *extracted* but *created*. Profits are an insignia that a business has made something economically valuable—it has brought new wealth into existence.

What enables a company to create economic value? It is not physical labor. Profit has nothing to do with how "hard" people work, in the sense of how much physical effort they've exerted or how much discomfort they've endured. It is primarily an intellectual achievement.

---

25. See also Yaron Brook and Don Watkins, *Free Market Revolution: How Ayn Rand's Ideas Can End Big Government* (New York: Palgrave, 2012), chapters 8 and 10.

Apple's profits reflect the enormous amount of *thinking* Apple's founders, managers, and employees did to design and run a company that can provide cutting edge technologies that buyers love.

What needs to be emphasized here is that, although Apple's staff by necessity exerts an enormous amount of effort to build the company, Apple's profit is not a reward for effort as such. We can easily imagine a company that works "harder" than Apple, assembling each phone painstakingly by hand rather than using machines. But far from being more profitable, this company will be less profitable: its costs will be higher, its products will arrive later, its customers will be less satisfied. Profits, in other words, reflect not the physical effort that went into producing them but how much more value a company creates than it consumes. We pay people for helping us achieve our goals or solve our problems. The better the job they do, and the fewer resources they use to do it, the more profitable they will be. And that depends not on muscles but on the mind.[26]

In sum, to the extent economic transactions are voluntary they tend to be win/win. To earn money through voluntary exchange you have to offer value—value you create not primarily through physical toil but intellectual effort. Hence, profits reflect, not exploitation, but value creation: to earn a fortune is to support your own life by *adding* to the wealth in existence, not by subtracting from it.

Returning to finance, we see that the pattern is the same. Financiers profit by doing something valuable: fundamentally, by putting savings to productive use. This requires using their minds to discover the most valuable uses of savings, with the voluntary nature of economic transactions ensuring that they cannot profit at others' expense over the long run.

Take the bond market. As we've already noted, financiers help companies raise money by facilitating the sale of bonds. The company benefits—it raises the money it needs to finance its productive endeavors, at a cost (interest) it can afford. Financiers can benefit either by earning a commission on the issuance and sale of the bonds (matching investors with businesses in need of capital), or by buying and holding the bonds, profiting off of the interest payments or potentially by a rise in the price of the bond. Savers benefit from the expected return they will get on the bond. Similarly when a financier sells a bond: the sale occurs when both

---

26. See also Don Watkins and Yaron Brook, *Equal Is Unfair: America's Misguided Fight Against Income Inequality* (New York: St. Martin's, 2016), chapter 4.

parties believe they will benefit. The financier may think the price of the bond will go down, the buyer may think the price will go up (or simply wants to hold the bond to maturity). Each gains from being able to act on his own (and different) estimate of an uncertain future.

This last point requires elaboration. To say that a transaction will only take place when both sides gain is to say that both sides believe *ex ante* that the transaction is to their interests. *Ex post* it is possible to regret a transaction. If you purchase a security with the expectation that it will be worth more in the future and it turns out to be worth less, you may be disappointed and even lose money. But that doesn't mean that you were exploited or that someone else gained at your expense. It is in the nature of many financial transactions that they are risky (they involve estimates about the future)—and this is something both parties know going in. Just as we aren't robbed by an author when we buy a novel that turns out to be boring, so we aren't robbed by a seller when we buy a financial instrument that turns out to be unprofitable. Assuming there was no actual fraud involved in the transaction, you did in actual fact get what you paid for: you obtained the security you wanted at a price you thought was justified based on your best assessment of its future value. It just turned out you were wrong. You knowingly accepted that risk when you made the purchase.

The same principles apply to every other financial transaction: to the extent the market is free, and to the extent all parties abide by the law, they are win/win and any profits are an insignia of value creation. They are not earned at others' expense.

But what about what commentator Noah Smith calls "asymmetric information" in his article "The Dirty Little Secret of Finance"?[27] According to this claim, the fact that different parties to a financial transaction may have very different amounts of information can make it possible for one party to exploit the other, robbing voluntary transactions of their win/win nature. To take a non-financial example, if you are selling a car, you know much more about the car than the potential buyer, which might allow you to take advantage of the buyer (or, since the buyer knows you have more information, asymmetric information could lead him to avoid buying a car that—if he had more information—would be to his interest to buy). The existence of asymmetric

---

27. Noah Smith, "The Dirty Little Secret of Finance: Asymmetric Information," Bloomberg.com, August 11, 2016, https://www.bloomberg.com/view/articles/2016-08-11/the-dirty-little-secret-of-finance-asymmetric-information.

information is often seen as proof that voluntary trade is not sufficient to guard us against exploitation: the financial industry can profit by taking advantage of this imbalance of knowledge.

Asymmetric information is seen as leading to numerous different problems in financial markets. For some, the sheer fact that financial transactions involve information asymmetries is viewed as wrong. The Securities and Exchange Commission, which regulates securities, has at various times insisted that investors have a right to *equal* information. This is ridiculous. As Daniel Fischel explains:

> Differences in knowledge and insight of buyers and sellers are universal in all markets, not just securities markets. If someone wants to buy farmland because he believes the land contains valuable mineral deposits, he can do so without saying anything about it to the farmer. The law imposes no duty on him to disclose his knowledge or belief. The no-disclosure rule allows the farmland to be purchased cheaply and thus facilitates the transfer of assets to higher-valued uses. If the law prohibited informed trading, requiring the buyer to reveal the probable existence of mineral deposits, the incentive to search and innovate would be effectively eliminated.[28]

Virtually all transactions involve asymmetric information, but one of the major ways that individuals create value in financial markets is by discovering and acting on superior information. For example, much of what made Milken successful was his superior knowledge of the bond market and of up-and-coming companies and industries like the telecommunication industry. His actions influenced market prices in a way that communicated his superior knowledge to the market: the value of telecom stocks went up (and their borrowing costs went down), signaling to the rest of the market that this was a burgeoning industry worthy of the capital investment it needed to grow. To treat actions like that as immoral, let alone a crime, is to condemn people for the very activity that makes financial markets powerful tools for human welfare. Yes, all fraud counts on asymmetric information but the reverse is not true.

More sophisticated arguments point to various "conflicts of interest" that can emerge due to information asymmetries, allowing and encouraging some people to profit at the expense of others. For example,

---

28. Fischel, *Payback*, p. 44.

one 2003 report described conflicts that could emerge in investments banks (prior to changes in SEC regulations), explaining that:

> The information synergies from underwriting, research and market making provide a rationale for combining these distinct financial services. This combination of activities leads to conflicts of interest, however. The conflict of interest that raises the greatest concern occurs between underwriting and brokerage, where investment banks are serving two client groups—issuing firms and investors. Issuers benefit from optimistic research while investors desire unbiased research. If the incentives for these two activities are not appropriately aligned, there will be a temptation for employees on one side of the firm to distort information to the advantage of their clients and the profit of their department. When the potential revenues from underwriting greatly exceed brokerage commissions, there will be a strong incentive to favour issuers over investors or risk losing the former to competitors. As a result analysts in investment banks may distort their research to please issuers, and the information they produce on securities will not be as reliable, thereby diminishing the efficiency of securities markets.[29]

Although such potential conflicts are real, what most accounts of conflicts of interest ignore or downplay is that market participants have the power to spot these conflicts and adjust to them. That's what happened in the case of the investment banking conflicts just described. As economist Eugene White (one of the authors of the above quote) observed:

> Boni and Womack (2002) found that 86 percent of the professional money managers and buy-side analysts said that they discounted the recommendations and reports of analysts when there is an investment banking relationship between the bank and the company analyzed.[30]

---

29. Andrew Crockett, Trevor Harris, Frederic S. Mishkin, and Eugene N. White, *Conflicts of Interest in the Financial Services Industry* (Geneva: International Center for Monetary and Banking Studies, 2003), p. 9.

30. Eugene N. White, "Can the Market Control Conflicts of Interest in the Financial Industry?," May 24, 2004, " https://www.imf.org/external/np/leg/sem/2004/cdmfl/eng/enw.pdf.

This points to the wider lesson about asymmetric information. It is not only an inevitable fact about virtually all trades—it is one that people are aware of and have the power to take into account when they make decisions. Not only can buyers or sellers adjust the decisions, but there is also typically a strong incentive to try to reduce or eliminate these conflicts in order to safeguard their reputation.

This does not mean that financial markets are free from such conflicts. They are an intractable part of a division of labor economy where individuals engage in a complex web of specialization and association. And yet they are also a *minor* part of the economy, including financial markets: the evidence is that because people are aware of their existence and can adjust their behavior accordingly conflicts of interests are extremely hard to exploit, and because win/win relationships are to the long-term *interests* of those involved in trade, most traders seek to minimize rather than capitalize on such conflicts. Conflicts of interest can best be thought of as a rounding error when it comes to assessing their role in the profitability of financiers.[31]

To fully appreciate the principle that finance profits through value creation and mutually beneficial trade, let's look at a few cases where the win/win nature of financial transactions may not be obvious.

Private equity. Private equity firms, as we noted, make money by putting the capital resources of a company to better use. Their actions benefit private equity managers, who earn fees and returns on their investments (what's called "carried interest"). Their investors, typically institutional investors like pension funds and insurance companies, benefit through higher returns and through diversification. But private equity is often criticized because part of its strategy for making companies more profitable often involves laying off workers. Private equity firms, many claim, profit at the expense of workers, not by creating value. But that analysis is wrong in two basic ways.

First, laying off workers will only profit the company if those workers are not (sufficiently) profitable workers—that is, if their work isn't creating enough value to justify their compensation. Thus, in firing

---

31. Viewed from a wider perspective, the interests of market participants *don't* conflict. Every productive individual benefits from living in a society ruled by voluntary exchange, where no one has the power to compel them to act against their own judgment. See Ayn Rand, "The 'Conflicts' of Men's Interests," *The Virtue of Selfishness* (New York: Signet, 1964); and Watkins and Brook, *Equal Is Unfair*, pp. 95–98.

the workers, a private equity firm *is* creating value: it is helping to make the company use resources more wisely.

Second, it is wrong to see laying off a worker as win/lose. Rather, the situation is one where a win/win relation *is no longer possible.* The principle of win/win says that both parties should benefit from the relationship or else go their separate ways. In laying off workers who are not adding enough value to justify their employment, the company is ending a *win/lose* relationship—leaving the worker free to find employment where his work will genuinely add value.

Despite the myths, private equity can be enormously profitable because it's an enormous value creator. One study of nearly 5,000 U.S. IPOs, from 1981 to 2004, "found that the stocks of private equity-backed companies did better than comparable companies."[32] Even the notion that private equity is a net job-killer is wrong.

> The most exhaustive survey of the impact of private equity ownership on employees, which looked at more than forty-five hundred investments from 1980 to 2005, found that private equity-backed companies tended to slash jobs at a slightly higher than average rate in the first two years after a buyout but over time created more jobs than they eliminated.[33]

Hedge funds. Hedge funds are investment funds that offer a diverse array of services, but as a general rule, they try to offer investors higher returns or returns that are less correlated to the stock market than they could get through simple investment strategies, like buying an index fund. Their main productive function is to contribute to price discovery—to engage in research and analysis that most other investors do not in order to discover under- and overpriced assets, profiting whenever they help correct their valuation. (This can take many different forms, including arbitrage, which corrects price discrepancies across different markets and thereby makes markets more efficient.)

Hedge funds grew enormously during the 1990s and 2000s. But despite their popularity, hedge fund managers have often been accused of profiting through heads-I-win, tails-you-lose compensation

---

32. David Carey and John E. Morris, *King of Capital* (New York: Crown Business, 2012), p. 303.

33. Ibid., p. 304.

arrangements, which come at the expense of the investors whose wealth they manage. Namely, they get a management fee (typically 2 percent of the financial resources managed by the fund, regardless of how profitable they are) and they get a percentage of the fund's profits (typically 20 percent), assuming they are profitable.

There's nothing unusual or nefarious about a guaranteed fee for service, however. A lawyer gets a fee even if he does a lousy job. But if he does do a lousy job, he will also get fired and find it harder to gain new clients. The same thing holds true for hedge funds. Hedge fund managers perform a crucial service: helping investors grow (and protect) their savings. As for gaining a share of the profits, this acts as a powerful positive incentive for hedge fund managers to do a good job for their customers.

What's important is that no one *has* to pay these fees. They exist only because enough investors value the services provided by hedge funds. But it's a fickle business, and if an individual hedge fund manager does a bad job, he loses his reputation and investors will quickly move their money away from him and to managers who have a better track record. If the industry as a whole underperforms, hedge funds will close and fees will drop. In fact that's exactly what's happened in recent years. Investors have *not* been impressed with hedge fund returns of late, and many hedge funds have been shrinking or closing, and fees are generally falling.[34]

Voluntary trade doesn't guarantee success. But, by leaving us free to enter and *avoid* any contractual relations we choose, it does reward success—and punish failure.

Investment banks. Prior to 1970, Wall Street investment banks were private partnerships, where the partners had virtually their entire net worth tied up with their banks. This led them to be relatively risk-averse. We have already noted, for instance, that J.P. Morgan avoided speculative ventures in favor of relatively safe, established businesses. But in the decades following 1970, all of that changed, as most investment banks went public. According to some commentators, this has been disastrous. As William D. Cohan argues, "bankers were rewarded to take outsized risks with *other* people's money and with very little financial accountability when things went wrong, as happens with far more frequency and severity than anyone cares to acknowledge." After

---

34. Jeff Cox, "Hedge Fund Fees Are Falling as Shutdowns Hit a Post-Crisis High," CNBC, March 17, 2017, http://www.cnbc.com/2017/03/17/hedge-fund-fees-falling-as-shutdowns-hit-a-post-crisis-high.html.

the transformation to public firms:

> [f]irms had much easier access to capital—in the forms of
> both debt and equity—and that capital largely came from
> outside investors, often leaving the original partners of the
> firm very wealthy and with little of their own capital left
> at risk in the firm. The idea of essentially playing with the
> house's money and being rewarded for it would lead Wall
> Street's numerous critics to refer to it as a casino, where the
> house always finds ways to win. It forever altered the reward
> system that had been so carefully calibrated over the cen-
> turies to encourage prudence over wanton risk taking and
> emphasize long-term profitability over short-term greed.[35]

It is by no means obvious that public investment banks, even with
their increased risk, have been a net-negative for their owners. Indeed,
it would be surprising if that were true, given that these banks are now
far better capitalized and the trend has been for financial firms to continue to go public and at quite remunerative prices. (This picture is
complicated by government bailouts, which insulate some investment
banks from risk, though "too big to fail" institutions have hardly been
the only successful publicly owned investment banks.) But even so,
there is nothing inherent in a value-creating industry that guarantees
that decisions will always be right, especially in retrospect. A market is
a discovery process, and it may very well be that we will look back and
decide that publicly owned investment banks were a bad idea—that
they led to misaligned incentives that rewarded managers for actions
that were not to the interests of shareholders.

The fact that transactions are voluntary doesn't eliminate the possibility of mistakes. What it does do is leave people free to avoid those mistakes (and to try to correct them once they're made). Any investor who
did not approve of the behavior of publicly owned investment banks was
free not to buy shares (or to sell them if they owned them). To describe
the situation as allowing bankers to "risk *other* people's money" wrongly
treats investors as helpless, powerless victims. In reality, those investors
gave the bankers capital to risk. That has nothing in common with excessive risk-taking resulting from the belief that taxpayers would be *forced*
to bail out failed institutions. That is truly gambling with other people's

---

35. William D. Cohan, *Why Wall Street Matters* (New York: Random House, 2017), pp. 80–81.

money—money that was not turned over voluntarily.

To say that the financial industry is rewarded for creating value is not to say that each and every transaction always and unerringly benefits all of the parties. It is to say that, to the extent the market is free, financiers have a strong incentive to create win/win relationships and they lack the ability to impose win/lose relationships.

Does Finance Create Instability?

We've repeatedly stressed that when we describe the productive, win/win nature of financial deals we are talking about legal transactions in a free society, where the government protects voluntary interaction. But the government can also interfere with voluntary interaction: specifically it can subsidize and control the industry in ways that create opportunities for win/lose relationships. And it turns out that many of the legitimate concerns people have about finance today stem from the existence of widespread government interference in finance.

One example of the power of government to interfere with voluntary interaction—and of the costs of such interference—is the phenomenon often referred to as cronyism: government privileges bestowed upon the industry or some of its members, including subsidies, bailouts, special loans, and protection from competition. Cronyism severs the connection freedom establishes between profit and value creation, allowing favored companies to reap unearned rewards at others' expense.

Historically, finance and government have usually been deeply intertwined. Banks, for example, were often granted special privileges by the government, such as protection from competition, in exchange for supporting the government—helping it fund wars and other ventures.[36] This (not any supposed need for economic "management" of the economy) was the origin of the first central bank in history, the Bank of England.

In the U.S. a more recent example of cronyism in finance is government subsidization of the big banks through the policy of "too big to fail." This policy not only puts smaller banks at a competitive disadvantage by raising their cost of capital relative to bigger banks, but it also allows big banks to reap undeserved profits in good times and to impose the risks of their decisions on taxpayers in bad times. (It is

---

36. Charles W. Calomiris and Stephen H. Haber, *Fragile by Design* (Princeton, N.J.: Princeton University Press, 2014).

worth noting that there is a strong correlation between spending by financial firms on government lobbying and campaign contributions and how much bail-out money they received.[37])

Cronyism, clearly, is a problem *created* by government intervention (even if financiers sometimes actively pursue special favors from government). Only when the government goes beyond its role as the protector of freedom can it grant special privileges to private institutions.

The larger lesson is that when we want to evaluate any problem or challenge associated with finance, we must ask not only whether that problem or challenge is *real*, but whether it is the product of the free, voluntary actions of financiers—or whether it emerges from incentives, distortions, and constraints created by government intervention.

Nowhere is this more important than when it comes to the most compelling criticism of finance: that it makes our economy *unstable*, unleashing catastrophes like the financial crisis of 2008. This is a large, complex subject that Don treats in detail in his essay "Finance Isn't Free and Never Really Was" (see Part 1). But a few observations are worth making here.

It's true that we see economic crises concentrated in finance. But even if such crises were an intractable result of the financial industry, there would still be no grounds for condemning the industry as immoral, any more than the inherent risks of driving make the auto industry immoral. The positives are so enormous that even such very real negatives can't compare.

Think about it this way. Nothing is more unstable than a pre-industrial society, where your ability to eat depends on the vagaries of the weather. Finance played an instrumental role in helping us rise from living on a dollar a day to more than a hundred dollars a day. The fact that we may at times see our incomes fall and temporarily struggle with finding employment can be incredibly painful, and in some cases truly catastrophic. But even then, we are still better off living in the advanced economy made possible by finance, with all of its wealth, security, and opportunity, than we would be living in a world without finance. People may have avoided the risks of driving in the era before automobiles—but how many of us would want to go back to the days of the horse and buggy?

---

37. Vuk Vukovic, "Crony Capitalism and the Financial Crisis," *Don't Worry, I'm an Economist!*, January 11, 2012, http://im-an-economist.blogspot.com/2012/01/crony-capitalism-and-financial-crisis.html.

That said, there is no obvious reason why production and voluntary trade in finance should unleash financial catastrophes.

There are two sources of financial instability, what we might think of as macroinstability and microinstability. Macroinstability consists of the risks of inflation and deflation, and their effects on the rest of the economy. Microinstability consists of bad decisions and excessive risk-taking that lead to bank runs, which turn contagious, spreading to otherwise healthy institutions and potentially bringing down the entire financial system. But when we look at the freest financial systems, these problems are virtually absent. During the period of the classical gold standard, money's purchasing power remained remarkably stable, with no protracted, harmful inflationary booms or deflationary contractions. It was only when the government interfered with sound money that we got things like the Great Depression, the high inflation of the 1970s, and the financial crisis of 2008. Similarly for microinstability. If we look at the countries that came nearest to having free banking systems—Scotland and Canada for example—we do not see widespread excessive risk-taking by financial institutions nor do we see bank runs affecting healthy banks. During the Great Depression, Canada—which had neither deposit insurance nor a central bank—experienced zero bank failures.

As Don discusses in "Finance Isn't Free and Never Really Was," financial instability is *created* by government intervention in finance. Macroinstability is the result of government control of money and credit (and interference in wages and prices), while microinstability is the result of the government restricting financial freedom and subverting market discipline in financial institutions. The financial crisis of 2008, for example, was the product of *both* kinds of interference.

To summarize a complex story. During the early 2000s, America's central bank, the Federal Reserve, cut interest rates to unprecedented lows. The cheap credit made its way largely into residential real estate, which—with an assist from the government's affordable housing crusade—created a bubble in housing. Some of Wall Street's biggest banks (following the lead of the two government-sponsored housing entities, Freddie Mac and Fannie Mae) loaded up on securities created out of these new, riskier home loans, using enormous amounts of leverage—a situation made possible by the government's long-standing subversion of market discipline in finance, as through the policy of bailing out large financial institutions ("too big to fail"), and by a false belief that these mortgage-backed securities were safe, in part because the three government-approved ratings agencies declared them to be safe. The crisis occurred when the housing bubble burst and these investments (and the home loans they were built on) were revealed to be of far lower quality than people had believed. In short, although private market participants made their share of errors in the lead up to the crisis, absent government monetary policy, housing policy, and financial regulation, the financial crisis *could not have occurred.*

The Collectivist Attack on Finance

Imagine an alternative version of *Arrival*, where it turned out that the aliens were just really curious about life on earth, and at some point the discussion turned to finance:

> **Alien:** So let me get this straight. You give someone your money, and then later on they just give you back a bunch more money?
>
> **Human:** Right.
>
> **Alien:** And then there are complete strangers who will give you hundreds of thousands to buy a house or a car?
>
> **Human:** Yep. You just have to promise to pay them back later.
>
> **Alien:** Man, on my planet you can't even get a friend to loan you money for a pizza. And you say there are actually people who will give you tens of millions of dollars to start a business—and if it fails, you don't even have to pay them back?
>
> **Human:** Sure.
>
> **Alien:** Wow. These must be the most popular people on your planet!

By any objective measure, finance is an incredible force for good in the world. Along with energy, it is one of the fundamental industries that make every other industry possible. And yet it is arguably the most vilified and persecuted industry in history. Why? At one level, it's not much of a mystery. If there is one word most closely associated with Wall Street it is: *greed.*

To be greedy, in common parlance, is to want more than you "need." It's to seek to pile up as much wealth for yourself as possible in disregard of the privations, unmet desires, and well-being of others.

According to Catholic philosopher Thomas Aquinas, it is "a sin directly against one's neighbor, since one man cannot over-abound in external riches, without another man lacking them, for temporal goods
cannot be possessed by many at the same time."[38] This blind desire for
"more" and indifference to the needs of others encourages the greedy
to make short-range, predatory, irrational decisions. And nowhere
is this pattern thought to be more prevalent than in the profit-seeking business world. As one Occupy Wall Street protester explained,
"Behind the profit motive, there is the big G: greed. And this greed has
become a disease across the planet."[39]

Business in general is viewed with moral suspicion—its activities
are seen as tainted *because* they are driven by the profit motive. The desire for profit, we've been taught, is dangerous because it tempts us
to use people as pawns in our pursuit of personal gain. Unless kept
in check, the desire for profit can lead us to engage in unscrupulous,
predatory behavior—behavior that can ultimately damage our colleagues, customers, employees, and society at large. "Greed" may lead
one person to start a software company in the hopes of making billions—and it may just as easily lead another person to concoct a Ponzi
scheme to bilk people out of billions.

All of this goes double for financiers. In every other industry, the
primary concern of a producer is to make a great product or to provide
a great service: he wants to profit, yes—*by* making a valuable product. It
is only in finance that the primary goal of a producer is to make money. Although it is true, as we've seen, that a financier's money-making
activities result in the creation, growth, and maintenance of every other productive industry, the financier himself is not focused on that. He
is focused purely on profiting through the act of exchange, and the degree of his profit is the measure of his success or failure.[40]

This is what explains what you might call the high-frequency
smearing of finance: no matter what happens, whether financiers suc-

38. St. Thomas Aquinas, "Question 118. The vices opposed to liberality, and in the
    first place, of covetousness," *The Summa Theologiae of St. Thomas Aquinas*, 2nd and
    rev. ed., trans. Fathers of the English Dominican Province, 1920, http://www
    .newadvent.org/summa/3118.htm.

39. "'Occupy Wall Street' Protests Give Voice to Anger Over Greed, Corporate
    Culture," *PBS NewsHour*, October 5, 2011, http://www.pbs.org/newshour/bb/
    business-july-dec11-wallstreet_10-05/.

40. Michael S. Berliner (ed.), *Letters of Ayn Rand* (New York: Plume, 1997), pp. 143–44.

ceed wildly or fail woefully, commentators will run those facts through
an "avarice algorithm":

1. When we see greed, look for the needy victims.
2. When we see need, look for the greedy villains.
3. Solve every problem and injustice through subsidizing
   need and restraining and penalizing greed.

For example, each year reports of high pay on Wall Street are met,
not with a celebration of financial wealth creation, nor even a fair and
balanced investigation into why some bankers earn so much. No, instead the immediate reaction is to denounce the pay as "too high" and
to itemize the alleged victims: shareholders, workers, and even the government (which allegedly "needs" more of their money than it currently taxes away).

Or take the case of Michael Milken. During his junk bond revolution of the 1980s, ambitious government officials, such as then-New
York attorney general Rudolph Giuliani, waged a vendetta against
Milken, targeting him long before any crime was "uncovered," simply
because of the scale of Milken's success.[41]

Or take the financial crisis of 2008. Ignoring the complex chain of
choices, incentives, regulations, monetary policy, and macroeconomic forces that added up to perhaps the worst economic catastrophe in
living memory, commentators began pinning the blame on "free markets," "unregulated banks," and "Wall Street greed" before Lehman's
corpse was even cold.

Treating financiers and other businessmen as guilty until proven innocent simply because they are driven by the profit motive is not a well
thought-out conclusion but a *prejudice*—and like any prejudice it is based
on assumptions. In particular is based on a particular view of *morality*.

Morality guides our assessments of what is good and what is bad—
what is right and what is wrong. Is the automotive industry good?
What about the computer industry? What about the tobacco industry? Our answers to these questions depend, not just on the facts about
those industries, but on our *moral standard* for evaluating them. A moral standard identifies the ultimate *goal* we're trying to achieve through
our actions—a goal that allows us to distinguish the good (things that

---

41. Fischel, *Payback*.

move us toward the goal) from the bad (things that move us away from the goal) that so that we can pursue and promote the former and avoid and discourage the latter. For example, many religions hold obedience to God as their moral standard, leading some sects to reject modern technology as worldly and immoral.

The moral standard *we* use to evaluate things as good or bad is *individual human flourishing*. Something is good if it contributes to the long-term intellectual, emotional, and physical well-being of the individual. What *does* contribute to the long-term well-being of the individual? Fundamentally, two basic virtues: *rationality* and *productiveness*. Human beings flourish by thinking and producing the material values we need to live and to enjoy life, whether it's food, clothing, shelter, cars, computers, music, or medicine. We can also gain enormous value from dealing with other people, including knowledge, trade, and friendship. But to gain the benefits of dealing with others while avoiding the threats that other people can pose, we have to treat them *justly*. Importantly, that includes following the trader principle: to gain values from others, we must offer values in exchange, trading value for value—mutual consent to mutual advantage. By contrast, a basic vice is *parasitism*: seeking the unearned through physical force, fraud, or emotional manipulation. Parasitism not only hampers the ability of others to flourish, but corrodes our own well-being as well. (See, for instance, the account of the inner life of Bernie Madoff in the chapter "Steve Jobs, Bernie Madoff, and Wall Street Greed.") You can call this the *individualist* moral framework.

How do we morally evaluate an *industry* according to the individualist moral framework? We need to ask whether the individuals involved in an industry are promoting their own welfare by creating and trading life-enhancing values—or whether they are unproductive, parasitical, and destructive. Every industry has concerns, challenges, and risks, of course: airplanes can crash, food can carry disease, computers can leave us vulnerable to hackers, police can abuse their legal authority. The question is whether, looked at in the full context, the industry is *overall* beneficial or detrimental to human well-being (including: Does the industry work to minimize its problems?). It should be clear why, on the individualist framework, we conclude that finance is not an evil, or even a necessary evil, but an enormous force for *good*.

Not everyone is an individualist, however. Many people accept a *collectivist* framework. For collectivists, the moral standard is not individual flourishing but "social welfare": individuals exist to serve the group, and they have a moral duty to sacrifice themselves for the group whenever the group's welfare demands it. Just treatment of others, on this approach, doesn't consist of dealing with others through mutually beneficial trade. Wealth, according to collectivists, belongs not to the individual but to society as a whole, and should be used to make society as a whole better off. This means ensuring that people get what they "need" regardless of what they've earned—no less *and no more*. Think of the Marxist slogan, "From each according to his ability, to each according to his need." On this view, parasitism is not a vice, but a virtue. The central vice, on the collectivist view, is *greed*: wanting more than you "need" (a word that is always left conspicuously undefined). To ambitiously pursue more than you "need"—even if you intend to *earn* your success honestly and productively—is seen by collectivists as immoral.

Very few people today label themselves collectivists. But most people hold collectivist assumptions to one degree or another, and these assumptions are what lead them to look at financiers, and businessmen more generally, with a jaundiced eye. Do we regard finance as a moral industry? How could we? Its purpose is private profit, not social welfare. Financiers profit through mutually beneficial trade, not serving the need of those who have nothing to offer in trade. Financiers often become wealthy far in excess of what they "need."

But notice that on this view finance is immoral, not for any predatory "excesses" but for its *productive essence*. Although collectivism leads people to assume that the greed and selfishness of profit-seekers will lead them to lie, cheat, steal, and act recklessly, it is not lying, cheating, stealing, and recklessness that they oppose but the self-interested *motives* of those involved in finance—even the overwhelming majority of financiers who earn their money honestly and productively. Using "greed" to damn a Bernie Madoff who steals billions and a Jamie Dimon who creates billions is, to paraphrase William F. Buckley, like equating someone who pushes Grandma out of the way of a speeding bus and someone who pushes Grandma into the path of a speeding bus since both like to "push old ladies around."

Collectivists, in short, revile finance, not for any of its alleged crimes or excesses, but because they do not genuinely value economic progress and its role in enhancing individual flourishing. They are unmoved by arguments that finance is productive: their entire concern is with making sure that individuals sacrifice for society—and they regard it as superior that we all suffer equally than that we prosper unequally. (See Part 2 of this book, which discusses the crusade against economic inequality.)

Recognizing that finance is essential to economic prosperity, numerous thinkers including economist and moral philosopher Adam Smith, utilitarians such as Jeremy Bentham, as well as virtually all contemporary economists and moralists have sought to defend finance and financial markets. Whatever the nuances of their views, all share a common feature: they *accept* the collectivist moral standard and appeal to the beneficial *social* consequences of profit-seeking by financiers.[42]

Yes, these thinkers concede, profit-seeking per se is morally dubious (at best), but allowing financiers to pursue profits can make society better off: businesses can grow and hire workers, banks can help individuals purchase homes and cars, the stock and bond markets can allow people to retire with dignity. Such "defenses," while encouraging us to tolerate finance, have not changed the culture's negative evaluation of financiers, and thus have only tempered the belief that finance needs to be strictly controlled by the government.

By failing to challenge and dismantle the collectivist framework, these nominal defenders of finance leave our basic assumptions about the profit motive unchallenged. And so even people who *do* genuinely value individual flourishing, but who have (often unknowingly) accepted the collectivist framework, remain skeptical of finance. So long as most people view the profit motive as immoral, they will blame "greedy" financiers for any problems (real or imagined) in the financial sector, and demand that the profit motive be reined in through greater government regulation. This is precisely what has happened every time an economy faces a financial crisis. And it is no accident that even most of the so-called champions of finance do not themselves support complete financial freedom, but instead contend that some level of government control is necessary in order to protect us from the dangers of financial greed.

But the conventional picture of the profit motive, despite its ubiquity, is false: it rests on three errors. First, it treats the motives of businessmen as fundamentally similar to the motives of criminals on the grounds that both seek material rewards for themselves. Such a parallel, however, is superficial—as superficial as saying that everyone is a potential rapist because both rapists and law-abiding citizens desire sex. There is a universe of difference between someone who desires to profit through *trade* and someone who desires to *plunder* other people's profits. The obvious

---

42. For an overview of moral thinking about finance, see Yaron Brook, "The Morality of Moneylending: A Short History" in this book.

joy that businessmen get from creating great products or building great companies or making great trades—the joy of earning rewards by producing new wealth—bears no important relationship to those who get "joy" from suckering suckers out of their money. (See essay "Steve Jobs, Bernie Madoff, and Wall Street Greed" in this book.)

Second, this notion that the profit motive is dangerous and immoral ignores the fact that the only way to profit over the long term *is* to be a value creator—not a manipulator or an exploiter. In a system of voluntary trade, where the government punishes force and fraud, it is not possible to succeed for any significant length of time without offering positives to those one deals with. As we've seen, and as is obvious when we look at the economy as a whole, a business that mistreats its employees will lose its employees—usually starting with its best. A business that mistreats its customers will lose its customers—and either reform its ways or go out of business.

The third and most profound error is to equate morality with selflessly serving society. The notion that selflessness is a moral ideal depends on a false alternative: callous exploitation of others vs. selfless sacrifice for the sake of others. But, there is a third alternative: the pursuit of one's own long-term well-being through thought, production, and win/win trade. This is what the philosopher Ayn Rand calls *rational self-interest*: pursuing your own long-range material, mental, and emotional well-being, neither sacrificing yourself to others nor others to yourself.[43] It is true that a Steve Jobs or a Warren Buffett doesn't selflessly serve others in his business activities—but he does not gain at their expense either. He prospers through productive achievement. And, it can be added, he does more genuine good for others than those whose claim to virtue is self-denial and self-sacrifice—because he spearheads human progress, which is the only thing that has liberated humanity from poverty, sickness, and suffering.[44]

But the moral justification for prospering through one's enormous productive achievement is *not* that it serves society or makes others better off. It is that each individual *has* to produce wealth in order to live and to enjoy his own life. To condemn someone as immoral because he is good at producing wealth is to condemn him for making the most of his life. To condemn him as immoral unless he spends his

43. Rand, *The Virtue of Selfishness*.

44. See also Brook and Watkins, *Free Market Revolution*, esp. chapter 6; and Watkins and Brook, *Equal Is Unfair*, pp. 83-91.

wealth (and his time) serving the "needs" of those who have failed (or refuse) to support their own lives is to declare we deserve rewards only to the extent we don't earn them—and that by exercising the thought and effort required to earn them, we surrender any moral claim to them. On the collectivist view, individuals are to be penalized to the extent they succeed in improving their lives and rewarded to the extent they don't. On the individualist view, that policy is recognized for what it is: a profound injustice.

Night and day there are businessmen out there thinking of ways to feed us, to entertain us, to keep us healthy, to help us communicate—all out of a desire for profit. The profit motive is the *producer's* motive. It is the desire to prosper by creating and offering for sale the values we need to live and enjoy life—and to spearhead the invention of new values that raise our standard of living. The profit motive is the foundation of human happiness and human progress. In short, if individual flourishing is our goal, then profit-seeking is an enormous force for good. By that standard, financiers *are* an enormous force for good.

The Morality of Moneylending: A Short History

By Yaron Brook

This essay was first published in *The Objective Standard*.

It seems that every generation has its Shylock—a despised financier blamed for the economic problems of his day. A couple of decades ago it was Michael Milken and his "junk" bonds. Today it is the mortgage bankers who, over the past few years, loaned billions of dollars to home buyers—hundreds of thousands of whom are now delinquent or in default on their loans. This "subprime mortgage crisis" is negatively affecting the broader financial markets and the economy as a whole. The villains, we are told, are not the borrowers—who took out loans they could not afford to pay back—but the moneylenders—who either deceived the borrowers or should have known better than to make the loans in the first place. And, we are told, the way to prevent such problems in the future is to clamp down on moneylenders and their industries; thus, investigations, criminal prosecutions, and heavier regulations on bankers are in order.

Of course, government policy for decades has been to *encourage* lenders to provide mortgage loans to lower-income families, and when mortgage brokers have refused to make such loans, they have been accused of "discrimination." But now that many borrowers are in a bind, politicians are seeking to lash and leash the lenders.

This treatment of moneylenders is unjust but not new. For millennia they have been the primary scapegoats for practically every economic problem. They have been derided by philosophers and condemned to hell by religious authorities; their property has been confiscated to compensate their "victims"; they have been humiliated, framed, jailed, and butchered. From Jewish pogroms where the main purpose was to destroy the records of debt, to the vilification of the House of Rothschild, to the jailing of American financiers—moneylenders have been targets of philosophers, theologians, journalists, economists, playwrights, legislators, and the masses.

Major thinkers throughout history—Plato, Aristotle, Thomas Aquinas, Adam Smith, Karl Marx, and John Maynard Keynes, to name just a few—considered moneylending, at least under certain conditions, to be a major vice. Dante, Shakespeare, Dickens, Dostoyevsky, and modern and popular novelists depict moneylenders as villains.

Today, anti-globalization demonstrators carry signs that read "abolish usury" or "abolish interest." Although these protestors are typically leftists—opponents of capitalism and anything associated with it—their contempt for moneylending is shared by others, including radical Christians and Muslims who regard charging interest on loans as a violation of God's law and thus as immoral.

Moneylending has been and is condemned by practically everyone. But what exactly is being condemned here? What *is* moneylending or *usury*? And what are its consequences?

Although the term "usury" is widely taken to mean "excessive interest" (which is never defined) or illegal interest, the actual definition of the term is, as the *Oxford English Dictionary* specifies: "The fact or practice of lending money at interest." This is the definition I ascribe to the term throughout this essay.

Usury is a financial transaction in which person A lends person B a sum of money for a fixed period of time with the agreement that it will be returned with interest. The practice enables people *without* money and people *with* money to mutually benefit from the wealth of the latter. The borrower is able to use money that he would otherwise not be able to use, in exchange for paying the lender an agreed-upon premium in addition to the principal amount of the loan. Not only do both interested parties benefit from such an exchange; countless people who are not involved in the trade often benefit too—by means of access to the goods and services made possible by the exchange.

Usury enables levels of life-serving commerce and industry that otherwise would be impossible. Consider a few historical examples. Moneylenders funded grain shipments in ancient Athens and the first trade between the Christians in Europe and the Saracens of the East. They backed the new merchants of Italy and, later, of Holland and England. They supported Spain's exploration of the New World, and funded gold and silver mining operations. They made possible the successful colonization of America. They fueled the Industrial Revolution, supplying the necessary capital to the new entrepreneurs in England, the United States, and Europe. And, in the late 20th century, moneylenders provided billions of dollars to finance the computer, telecommunications, and biotechnology industries.

By taking risks and investing their capital in what they thought would make them the most money, moneylenders and other financiers made possible whole industries—such as those of steel, railroads, automobiles, air travel, air conditioning, and medical devices. Without capital, often provided through usury, such life-enhancing industries would not exist—and homeownership would be impossible to all but the wealthiest people.

Moneylending is the lifeblood of industrial-technological society. When the practice and its practitioners are condemned, they are condemned for furthering and enhancing man's life on earth.

Given moneylenders' enormous contribution to human well-being, why have they been so loathed throughout history, and why do they continue to be distrusted and mistreated today? What explains the universal hostility toward one of humanity's greatest benefactors? And what is required to replace this hostility with the gratitude that is the moneylenders' moral due?

As we will see, hostility toward usury stems from two interrelated sources: certain economic views and certain ethical views. Economically, from the beginning of Western thought, usury was regarded as *unproductive*—as the taking of something for nothing. Ethically, the practice was condemned as *immoral*—as unjust, exploitative, against biblical law, selfish. The history of usury is a history of confusions, discoveries, and evasions concerning the economic and moral status of the practice. Until usury is recognized as both economically productive and ethically praiseworthy—as both practical and moral—moneylenders will continue to be condemned as villains rather than heralded as the heroes they in fact are.

Our brief history begins with Aristotle's view on the subject.

Aristotle

The practice of lending money at interest was met with hostility as far back as ancient Greece, and even Aristotle (384–322 b.c.) believed the practice to be unnatural and unjust. In the first book of *Politics* he writes:

> The most hated sort [of moneymaking], and with the greatest reason, is usury, which makes a gain out of money itself, and not from the natural use of it. For money was intended to be used in exchange, but not to increase at interest. And this term Usury which means the birth of money from money, is applied to the breeding of money, because

the offspring resembles the parent. Wherefore of all modes
of making money this is the most unnatural.[45]

Aristotle believed that charging interest was immoral because
money is not productive. If you allow someone to use your orchard,
he argued, the orchard bears fruit every year—it is productive—and
from this product the person can pay you rent. But money, Aristotle
thought, is merely a medium of exchange. When you loan someone
money, he receives no value over and above the money itself. The money
does not create more money—it is barren. On this view, an exchange of
$100 today for $100 plus $10 in interest a year from now is unjust, be-
cause the lender thereby receives more than he gave, and what he gave
could not have brought about the 10 percent increase. Making money
from money, according to Aristotle, is "unnatural" because money, unlike an orchard, cannot produce additional value.

Aristotle studied under Plato and accepted some of his teacher's
false ideas. One such idea that Aristotle appears to have accepted is the
notion that every good has some *intrinsic value*—a value independent
of and apart from human purposes. On this view, $100 will be worth
$100 a year from now and can be worth only $100 to anyone, at any
time, for any purpose. Aristotle either rejected or failed to consider the
idea that loaned money loses value to the lender over time as his use of
it is postponed, or the idea that money can be invested in economic activity and thereby create wealth. In short, Aristotle had no conception
of the productive role of money or of the moneylender. (Given the relative simplicity of the Greek economy, he may have had insufficient evidence from which to conclude otherwise.) Consequently, he regarded
usury as unproductive, unnatural, and therefore unjust.

Note that Aristotle's conclusion regarding the unjust nature of
usury is derived from his view that the practice is *unproductive*: Since
usury creates nothing but takes something—since the lender apparently is parasitic on the borrower—the practice is unnatural and immoral.
It is important to realize that, on this theory, there is no dichotomy between the economically practical and the morally permissible; usury is
regarded as immoral *because* it is regarded as impractical.

Aristotle's economic and moral view of usury was reflected in ancient culture for a few hundred years, but moral condemnation of the

---

45. Aristotle, *The Politics of Aristotle*, trans. Benjamin Jowett (Oxford: Clarendon Press, 1885), bk 1, chap. 10, p. 19.

practice became increasingly pronounced. The Greek writer Plutarch (46–127 AD), for example, in his essay "Against Running in Debt, or Taking Up Money Upon Usury," described usurers as "wretched," "vulture-like," and "barbarous."[46] In Roman culture, Seneca (ca. 4 BC–65 AD) condemned usury for the same reasons as Aristotle; Cato the Elder (234–149 BC) famously compared usury to murder;[47] and Cicero (106–43 BC) wrote that "these profits are despicable which incur the hatred of men, such as those of . . . lenders of money on usury."[48]

As hostile as the Greeks and Romans generally were toward usury, their hostility was based primarily on their economic view of the practice, which gave rise to and was integrated with their moral view of usury. The Christians, however, were another matter, and their position on usury would become the reigning position in Western thought up to the present day.

The Dark and Middle Ages

The historian William Manchester describes the Dark and Middle Ages as

> stark in every dimension. Famines and plague, culminating in the Black Death [which killed 1 in 4 people at its peak] and its recurring pandemics, repeatedly thinned the population. . . . Among the lost arts were bricklaying; in all of Germany, England, Holland and Scandinavia, virtually no stone buildings, except cathedrals, were raised for ten centuries. . . . Peasants labored harder, sweated more, and collapsed from exhaustion more often than their animals.[49]

During the Dark Ages, the concept of an economy had little meaning. Human society had reverted to a precivilized state, and the primary means of trade was barter. Money all but disappeared from European

---

46. Plutarch, *Plutarch's Morals*, trans. William Watson Goodwin (Boston: Little, Brown, & Company, 1874), pp. 412–24.

47. Lewis H. Haney, *History of Economic Thought* (New York: The Macmillan Company, 1920), p. 71.

48. Anthony Trollope, *Life of Cicero* (Kessinger Publishing, 2004), p. 70.

49. William Manchester, *A World Lit Only by Fire* (Boston: Back Bay Books, 1993), pp. 5–6.

commerce for centuries. There was, of course, some trade and some lending, but most loans were made with goods, and the interest was charged in goods. These barter-based loans, primitive though they were, enabled people to survive the tough times that were inevitable in an agrarian society.[50]

Yet the church violently opposed even such subsistence-level lending.

During this period, the Bible was considered the basic source of knowledge and thus the final word on all matters of importance. For every substantive question and problem, scholars consulted scripture for answers—and the Bible clearly opposed usury. In the Old Testament, God says to the Jews: "[He that] Hath given forth upon usury, and hath taken increase: shall he then live? he shall not live . . . he shall surely die; his blood shall be upon him."[51] And:

> Thou shalt not lend upon usury to thy brother; usury of money; usury of victuals; usury of anything that is lent upon usury.
>
> Unto a stranger thou mayest lend upon usury; but unto thy brother thou shalt not lend upon usury, that the Lord thy God may bless thee in all that thou settest thine hand to in the land whither thou goest to possess it.[52]

In one breath, God forbade usury outright; in another, He forbade the Jews to engage in usury with other Jews but permitted them to make loans at interest to non-Jews.

Although the New Testament does not condemn usury explicitly, it makes clear that one's moral duty is to help those in need, and thus to give to others one's own money or goods without the expectation of anything in return—neither interest nor principal. As Luke plainly states, "lend, hoping for nothing again."[53] Jesus' expulsion of the money-changers from the temple is precisely a parable conveying the Christian notion that profit is evil, particularly profit generated by moneylending. Christian morality, the morality of divinely mandated altruism, expounds the virtue of self-sacrifice on behalf of the poor and the weak; it

---

50. Glyn Davies, *A History of Money: From Ancient Times to the Present Day* (Cardiff: University of Wales Press, 1994), p. 117.

51. Ezekiel 18:13.

52. Deuteronomy 23:19–20.

53. Luke 6:35.

condemns self-interested actions, such as profiting—especially profiting from a seemingly exploitative and unproductive activity such as usury.

Thus, on scriptural and moral grounds, Christianity opposed usury from the beginning. And it constantly reinforced its opposition with legal restrictions. In 325 AD, the Council of Nicaea banned the practice among clerics. Under Charlemagne (768–814 AD), the Church extended the prohibition to laymen, defining usury simply as a transaction where more is asked than is given.[54] In 1139, the second Lateran Council in Rome denounced usury as a form of theft, and required restitution from those who practiced it. In the 12th and 13th centuries, strategies that concealed usury were also condemned. The Council of Vienne in 1311 declared that any person who dared claim that there was no sin in the practice of usury be punished as a heretic.

There was, however, a loophole among all these pronouncements: the Bible's double standard on usury. As we saw earlier, read one way, the Bible permits Jews to lend to non-Jews. This reading had positive consequences. For lengthy periods during the Dark and Middle Ages, both Church and civil authorities allowed Jews to practice usury. Many princes, who required substantial loans in order to pay bills and wage wars, allowed Jewish usurers in their states. Thus, European Jews, who had been barred from most professions and from ownership of land, found moneylending to be a profitable, albeit hazardous, profession.

Although Jews were legally permitted to lend to Christians—and although Christians saw some practical need to borrow from them and chose to do so—Christians resented this relationship. Jews appeared to be making money on the backs of Christians while engaging in an activity biblically prohibited to Christians on punishment of eternal damnation. Christians, accordingly, held these Jewish usurers in contempt. (Important roots of anti-Semitism lie in this biblically structured relationship.)

Opposition to Jewish usurers was often violent. In 1190, the Jews of York were massacred in an attack planned by members of the nobility who owed money to the Jews and sought to absolve the debt through violence.[55] During this and many other attacks on Jewish communities, accounting records were destroyed and Jews were murdered. As European

---

54. Jacques Le Goff, *Your Money or Your Life* (New York: Zone Books, 1988), p. 26.

55. Edward Henry Palmer, *A History of the Jewish Nation* (London: Society for Promoting Christian Knowledge, 1874), pp. 253–54, and www.routledge-ny.com/ref/middleages/Jewish/England.pdf.

historian Joseph Patrick Byrne reports:

"Money was the reason the Jews were killed, for had they been poor, and had not the lords of the land been indebted to them, they would not have been killed."[56] But the "lords" were not the only debtors: the working class and underclass apparently owed a great deal, and these violent pogroms gave them the opportunity to destroy records of debt as well as the creditors themselves.[57]

In 1290, largely as a result of antagonism generated from their moneylending, King Edward I expelled the Jews from England, and they would not return en masse until the 17th century.

From the Christian perspective, there were clearly problems with the biblical pronouncements on usury. How could it be that Jews were prohibited from lending to other Jews but were allowed to lend to Christians and other non-Jews? And how could it be that God permitted Jews to benefit from this practice but prohibited Christians from doing so? These questions perplexed the thinkers of the day. St. Jerome's (ca. 347–420) "solution" to the conundrum was that it was wrong to charge interest to one's brothers—and, to Christians, all other Christians were brothers—but it was fine to charge interest to one's enemy. Usury was perceived as a weapon that weakened the borrower and strengthened the lender; so, if one loaned money at interest to one's enemy, that enemy would suffer. This belief led Christians to the absurd practice of lending money to the Saracens—their enemies—during the Crusades.[58]

Like the Greeks and Romans, Christian thinkers viewed certain economic transactions as zero-sum phenomena, in which a winner always entailed a loser. In the practice of usury, the lender seemed to grow richer without effort—so it had to be at the expense of the borrower, who became poorer. But the Christians' economic hostility toward usury was grounded in and fueled by biblical pronouncements against the practice—and this made a substantial difference. The combination of economic and biblical strikes against usury—with an emphasis on the latter—led the Church to utterly vilify the usurer, who became a universal symbol for evil. Stories describing the moneylenders' horrible deaths and horrific existence in Hell were common. One bishop put it concisely:

---

56. Byrne is here quoting Jacob Twinger of Königshofen, a 14th-century priest.

57. Joseph Patrick Byrne, *The Black Death* (Westport: Greenwood Press, 2004), p. 84.

58. Sidney Homer, *A History of Interest Rates* (New Brunswick: Rutgers University Press, 1963), p. 71.

> God created three types of men: peasants and other labor-
> ers to assure the subsistence of the others, knights to de-
> fend them, and clerics to govern them. But the devil creat-
> ed a fourth group, the usurers. They do not participate in
> men's labors, and they will not be punished with men, but
> with the demons. For the amount of money they receive
> from usury corresponds to the amount of wood sent to Hell
> to burn them.[59]

Such was the attitude toward usury during the Dark and early
Middle Ages. The practice was condemned primarily on biblical/moral
grounds. In addition to the fact that the Bible explicitly forbade it, moneylending was recognized as self-serving. Not only did it involve profit; the
profit was (allegedly) unearned and exploitative. Since the moneylender's gain was assumed to be the borrower's loss—and since the borrower
was often poor—the moneylender was seen as profiting by exploiting the
meek and was therefore regarded as evil.

Beginning in the 11th century, however, a conflicting economic reality became increasingly clear—and beginning in the 13th century, the re-
surgence of respect for observation and logic made that reality increasingly difficult to ignore.

Through trade with the Far East and exposure to the flourishing cul-
tures and economies of North Africa and the Middle East, economic activity was increasing throughout Europe. As this activity created a greater demand for capital and for credit, moneylenders arose throughout
Europe to fill the need—and as moneylenders filled the need, the economy grew even faster.

And Europeans were importing more than goods; they were also importing knowledge. They were discovering the Arabic numerical system,
double-entry accounting, mathematics, science, and, most importantly,
the works of Aristotle.

Aristotle's ideas soon became the focus of attention in all of Europe's
learning centers, and his writings had a profound effect on the scholars
of the time. No longer were young intellectuals satisfied by biblical ref-
erences alone; they had discovered reason, and they sought to ground
their ideas in it as well. They were, of course, still stifled by Christianity,
because, although reason had been rediscovered, it was to remain the

---

59. Sermon by Jacques de Vitry, "Ad status" 59, 14; quoted in Le Goff, *Your Money or
    Your Life*, pp. 56–57.

handmaiden of faith. Consequently, these intellectuals spent most of their time trying to use reason to justify Christian doctrine. But their burgeoning acceptance of reason, and their efforts to justify their ideas accordingly, would ultimately change the way intellectuals thought about everything—including usury.

Although Aristotle himself regarded usury as unjust, recall that he drew this conclusion from what he legitimately thought was evidence in support of it; in his limited economic experience, usury appeared to be unproductive. In contrast, the thinkers of this era were confronted with extensive use of moneylending all around them—which was accompanied by an ever-expanding economy—a fact that they could not honestly ignore. Thus, scholars set out to reconcile the matter rationally. On Aristotelian premises, if usury is indeed unjust and properly illegal, then there must be a logical argument in support of this position. And the ideas that usury is unproductive and that it necessarily consists in a rich lender exploiting a poor borrower were losing credibility.

Public opinion, which had always been against usury, now started to change as the benefits of credit and its relationship to economic growth became more evident. As support for usury increased, however, the Church punished transgressions more severely and grew desperate for theoretical justification for its position. If usury was to be banned, as the Bible commands, then this new world that had just discovered reason would require new, non-dogmatic explanations for why the apparently useful practice was wrong.

Over the next four hundred years, theologians and lawyers struggled to reconcile a rational approach to usury with Church dogma on the subject. They dusted off Aristotle's argument from the barrenness of money and reasserted that the profit gained through the practice is unnatural and unjust. To this they added that usury entails an artificial separation between the ownership of goods and the use of those same goods, claiming that lending money is like asking two prices for wine—one price for receiving the wine and an additional price for drinking it—one price for its possession and another for its use. Just as this would be wrong with wine, they argued, so it is wrong with money: In the case of usury, the borrower in effect pays $100 for $100, plus another fee, $10, for the use of the money that he already paid for and thus already owns.[60]

In similar fashion, it was argued that usury generates for the lender profit from goods that no longer belong to him—that is, from goods now

---

60. See St. Thomas Aquinas, *Summa Theologica*, part II, section II, question 78, article 1.

owned by the borrower.[61] As one Scholastic put it: "[He] who gets fruit from that money, whether it be pieces of money or anything else, gets it from a thing which does not belong to him, and it is accordingly all the same as if he were to steal it."[62]

Another argument against usury from the late Middle Ages went to a crucial aspect of the practice that heretofore had not been addressed: the issue of time. Thinkers of this period believed that time was a common good, that it belonged to no one in particular, that it was a gift from God. Thus, they saw usurers as attempting to defraud God.[63] As the 12th-century English theologian Thomas of Chobham (1160–1233) wrote: "The usurer sells nothing to the borrower that belongs to him. He sells only time, which belongs to God. He can therefore not make a profit from selling someone else's property."[64] Or as expressed in a 13th-century manuscript, "Every man stops working on holidays, but the oxen of usury work unceasingly and thus offend God and all the Saints; and, since usury is an endless sin, it should in like manner be endlessly punished."[65]

Although the identification of the value of time and its relationship to interest was used here in an argument *against* usury, this point is actually a crucial aspect of the argument in *defense* of the practice. Indeed, interest is compensation for a delay in using one's funds. It is compensation for the usurer's time away from his money. And although recognition of an individual's ownership of his own time was still centuries away, this early acknowledgment of the relationship of time and interest was a major milestone.

The Scholastics came to similar conclusions about usury as those reached by earlier Christian thinkers, but they sought to defend their views not only by reference to scripture, but also by reference to their observational understanding of the economics of the practice. The economic worth of usury—its productivity or unproductivity—became their central concern. The question became: Is money barren? Does usury have a productive function? What are the facts?

This is the long arm of Aristotle at work. Having discovered Aristotle's

61. Ibid.

62. Frank Wilson Blackmar, *Economics* (New York: The Macmillan Company, 1907), p. 178.

63. Le Goff, *Your Money or Your Life*, pp. 33–45.

64. Jeremy Rifkin, *The European Dream* (Cambridge: Polity, 2004), p. 105.

65. Le Goff, *Your Money or Your Life*, p. 30.

method of observation-based logic, the Scholastics began to focus on reality, and, to the extent that they did, they turned away from faith and away from the Bible. It would take hundreds of years for this perspective to develop fully, but the type of arguments made during the late Middle Ages were early contributions to this crucial development.

As virtuous as this new method was, however, the Scholastics were still coming to the conclusion that usury is unproductive and immoral, and it would not be until the 16th century and the Reformation that usury would be partially accepted by the Church and civil law. For the time being, usury remained forbidden—at least in theory.

Church officials, particularly from the 12th century on, frequently manipulated and selectively enforced the usury laws to bolster the financial power of the Church. When it wanted to keep its own borrowing cost low, the Church enforced the usury prohibition. At other times, the Church itself readily loaned money for interest. Monks were among the earliest moneylenders, offering carefully disguised interest-bearing loans throughout the Middle Ages.

The most common way to disguise loans—and the way in which banking began in Italy and grew to be a major business—was through money exchange. The wide variety of currencies made monetary exchange necessary but difficult, which led to certain merchants specializing in the field. With the rapid growth of international trade, these operations grew dramatically in scale, and merchants opened offices in cities all across Europe and the eastern Mediterranean. These merchants used the complexities associated with exchange of different currencies to hide loans and charge interest. For example, a loan might be made in one currency and returned in another months later in a different location—although the amount returned would be higher (i.e., would include an interest payment), this would be disguised by a new exchange rate. This is one of many mechanisms usurers and merchants invented to circumvent the restrictions. As one commentator notes, "the interest element in such dealings [was] normally . . . hidden by the nature of the transactions either in foreign exchange or as bills of exchange or, frequently, as both."[66] By such means, these merchants took deposits, loaned money, and made payments across borders, thus creating the beginnings of the modern banking system.

Although the merchant credit extended by these early banks was technically interest, and thus usury, both the papal and civic authorities

---

66. Davies, *A History of Money*, p. 154.

permitted the practice because the exchange service proved enormously valuable to both. In addition to financing all kinds of trade across vast distances for countless merchants, such lending also financed the Crusades for the Church and various wars for various kings.[67] Everyone wanted what usury had to offer, yet no one understood exactly what that was. So while the Church continued to forbid usury and punish transgressors, it also actively engaged in the practice. What was seen as moral by the Church apparently was not seen as wholly practical by the Church, and opportunity became the mother of evasion.

The Church also engaged in opportunistic behavior when it came to restitution. Where so-called victims of usury were known, the Church provided them with restitution from the usurer. But in cases where the "victims" were not known, the Church still collected restitution, which it supposedly directed to "the poor" or other "pious purposes." Clerics were sold licenses empowering them to procure such restitution, and, as a result, the number of usurers prosecuted where there was no identifiable "victim" was far greater than it otherwise would have been. The death of a wealthy merchant often provided the Church with windfall revenue. In the 13th century, the Pope laid claim to the assets of deceased usurers in England. He directed his agents to "inquire concerning living (and dead) usurers and the thing wrongfully acquired by this wicked usury . . . and . . . compel opponents by ecclesiastical censure."[68]

Also of note, Church officials regularly ignored the usury of their important friends—such as the Florentine bankers of the Medici family—while demonizing Jewish moneylenders and others. The result was that the image of the merchant usurer was dichotomized into "two disparate figures who stood at opposite poles: the degraded manifest usurer-pawnbroker, as often as not a Jew; and the city father, arbiter of elegance, patron of the arts, devout philanthropist, the merchant prince [yet no less a usurer!]."[69]

In theory, the Church was staunchly opposed to usury; in practice, however, it was violating its own moral law in myriad ways. The gap between the idea of usury as immoral and the idea of usury as impractical continued to widen as the evidence for its practicality continued to grow. The Church would not budge on the moral status, but it selectively practiced the vice nonetheless.

---

67. Ibid., pp. 146–74.

68. Robert Burton, *Sacred Trust* (Oxford: Oxford University Press, 1996), p. 118.

69. Ibid., pp. 118–20.

This selective approach often correlated with the economic times. When the economy was doing well, the Church, and the civil authorities, often looked the other way and let the usurers play. In bad times, however, moneylenders, particularly those who were Jewish, became the scapegoats. (This pattern continues today with anti-interest sentiment exploding whenever there is an economic downturn.)

To facilitate the Church's selective opposition to usury, and to avoid the stigma associated with the practice, religious and civil authorities created many loopholes in the prohibition. Sometime around 1220, a new term was coined to replace certain forms of usury: the concept of interest.[70] Under circumstances where usury was legal, it would now be called the collecting of interest. In cases where the practice was illegal, it would continue to be called usury.[71]

The modern word "interest" derives from the Latin verb *intereo*, which means "to be lost." Interest was considered compensation for a loss that a creditor had incurred through lending. Compensation for a loan was illegal if it was a gain or a profit, but if it was reimbursement for a loss or an expense it was permissible. Interest was, in a sense, "damages," not profit. Therefore, interest was sometimes allowed, but usury never.

So, increasingly, moneylenders were allowed to charge interest as a penalty for delayed repayment of a loan, provided that the lender preferred repayment to the delay plus interest (i.e., provided that it was seen as a sacrifice). Loans were often structured in advance so that such delays were anticipated and priced, and so the prohibition on usury was avoided. Many known moneylenders and bankers, such as the Belgian Lombards, derived their profits from such penalties—often 100 percent of the loan value.[72]

Over time, the view of costs or damages for the lender was expanded, and the lender's time and effort in making the loan were permitted as a reason for charging interest. It even became permissible on occasion for a lender to charge interest if he could show an obvious, profitable alternative use for the money. If, by lending money, the lender suffered from the inability to make a profit elsewhere, the interest was

---

70. Homer, *A History of Interest Rates*, p. 73.

71. As Blackstone's *Commentaries on the Laws of England* puts it: "When money is lent on a contract to receive not only the principal sum again, but also an increase by way of compensation for the use, the increase is called interest by those who think it lawful, and usury by those who do not," p. 1336.

72. Homer, *A History of Interest Rates*, pp. 72–74.

allowed as compensation for the potential loss. Indeed, according to some sources, even risk—economic risk—was viewed as worthy of compensation. Therefore, if there was risk that the debtor would not pay, interest charged in advance was permissible.[73]

These were major breakthroughs. Recognition of the economic need for advanced calculation of a venture's risk and for compensation in advance for that risk were giant steps in the understanding of and justification for moneylending.

But despite all these breakthroughs and the fact that economic activity continued to grow during the later Middle Ages, the prohibition on usury was still selectively enforced. Usurers were often forced to pay restitution; many were driven to poverty or excommunicated; and some, especially Jewish moneylenders, were violently attacked and murdered. It was still a very high-risk profession.

Not only were usurers in danger on Earth; they were also threatened with the "Divine justice" that awaited them after death.[74] They were considered the devil's henchmen and were sure to go to Hell. It was common to hear stories of usurers going mad in old age out of fear of what awaited them in the afterlife.

The Italian poet Dante (1265–1321) placed usurers in the seventh rung of Hell, incorporating the traditional medieval punishment for usury, which was eternity with a heavy bag of money around one's neck: "From each neck there hung an enormous purse, each marked with its own beast and its own colors like a coat of arms. On these their streaming eyes appeared to feast."[75] Usurers in Dante's Hell are forever weighed down by their greed. Profits, Dante believed, should be the fruits of labor—and usury entailed no actual work. He believed that the deliberate, intellectual choice to engage in such an unnatural action as usury was the worst kind of sin.[76]

It is a wonder that anyone—let alone so many—defied the law and their faith to practice moneylending. In this sense, the usurers were truly heroic. By defying religion and taking risks—both financial and existential—they made their material lives better. They made money.

---

73. Le Goff, *Your Money or Your Life*, p. 74.

74. Ibid., pp. 47–64.

75. Dante Alighieri, *The Inferno*, Canto XVII, lines 51–54.

76. Dorothy M. DiOrio, "Dante's Condemnation of Usury," in *Re: Artes Liberales* V, no. 1 (1978): pp. 17–25.

And by doing so, they made possible economic growth the likes of which had never been seen before. It was thanks to a series of loans from local moneylenders that Gutenberg, for example, was able to commercialize his printing press.[77] The early bankers enabled advances in commerce and industry throughout Europe, financing the Age of Exploration as well as the early seeds of technology that would ultimately lead to the Industrial Revolution.

By the end of the Middle Ages, although everyone still condemned usury, few could deny its practical value. Everyone "knew" that money-lending was ethically wrong, but everyone could also *see* that it was economically beneficial. Its moral status was divinely decreed and appeared to be supported by reason, yet merchants and businessmen *experienced* its practical benefits daily. The thinkers of the day could not explain this apparent dichotomy. And, in the centuries that followed, although man's understanding of the economic value of usury would advance, his moral attitude toward the practice would remain one of contempt.

Renaissance and Reformation

The start of the 16th century brought about a commercial boom in Europe. It was the Golden Age of Exploration. Trade routes opened to the New World and expanded to the East, bringing unprecedented trade and wealth to Europe. To fund this trade, to supply credit for commerce and the beginnings of industry, banks were established throughout Europe. Genoese and German bankers funded Spanish and Portuguese exploration and the importation of New World gold and silver. Part of what made this financial activity possible was the new tolerance, in some cities, of usury.

The Italian city of Genoa, for example, had a relatively relaxed attitude toward usury, and moneylenders created many ways to circumvent the existing prohibitions. It was clear to the city's leaders that the financial activities of its merchants were crucial to Genoa's prosperity, and the local courts regularly turned a blind eye to the usurious activities of its merchants and bankers. Although the Church often complained about these activities, Genoa's political importance prevented the Church from acting against the city.

The Catholic Church's official view toward usury remained

---

77. Davies, *A History of Money*, pp. 177–78.

unchanged until the 19th century, but the Reformation—which occurred principally in northern Europe—brought about a mild acceptance of usury. (This is likely one reason why southern Europe, which was heavily Catholic, lagged behind the rest of Europe economically from the 17th century onward.) Martin Luther (1483–1546), a leader of the Reformation, believed that usury was inevitable and should be permitted to some extent by civil law. Luther believed in the separation of civil law and Christian ethics. This view, however, resulted not from a belief in the separation of state and religion, but from his belief that the world and man were too corrupt to be guided by Christianity. Christian ethics and the Old Testament commandments, he argued, are utopian dreams, unconnected with political or economic reality. He deemed usury unpreventable and thus a matter for the secular authorities, who should permit the practice and control it.

However, Luther still considered usury a grave sin, and in his later years wrote:

> [T]here is on earth no greater enemy of man, after the Devil, than a gripe-money and usurer, for he wants to be God over all men. . . . And since we break on the wheel and behead highwaymen, murderers, and housebreakers, how much more ought we to break on the wheel and kill . . . hunt down, curse, and behead all usurers![78]

In other words, usury should be allowed by civil authorities (as in Genoa) because it is inevitable (men will be men), but it should be condemned in the harshest terms by the moral authority. This is the moral-practical dichotomy in action, sanctioned by an extremely malevolent view of man and the universe.

John Calvin, (1509–1564), another Reformation theologian, had a more lenient view than Luther. He rejected the notion that usury is actually banned in the Bible. Since Jews are allowed to charge interest from strangers, God cannot be against usury. It would be fantastic, Calvin thought, to imagine that by "strangers" God meant the enemies of the Jews; and it would be most unchristian to legalize discrimination. According to Calvin, usury does not always conflict with God's law, so not all usurers need to be damned. There is a difference, he believed, between taking usury in the course of business and setting up business as a

---

78. Paul M. Johnson, *A History of the Jews* (New York: HarperCollins, 1988), p. 242.

usurer. If a person collects interest on only one occasion, he is not a usurer. The crucial issue, Calvin thought, is the motive. If the motive is to help others, usury is good, but if the motive is personal profit, usury is evil.

Calvin claimed that the moral status of usury should be determined by the golden rule. It should be allowed only insofar as it does not run counter to Christian fairness and charity. Interest should never be charged to a man in urgent need, or to a poor man; the "welfare of the state" should always be considered. But it could be charged in cases where the borrower is wealthy and the interest will be used for Christian good. Thus he concluded that interest could neither be universally condemned nor universally permitted—but that, to protect the poor, a maximum rate should be set by law and never exceeded.[79]

Although the religious authorities did little to free usury from the taint of immorality, other thinkers were significantly furthering the economic understanding of the practice. In a book titled *Treatise on Contracts and Usury*, Molinaeus, a French jurist, made important contributions to liberate usury from Scholastic rationalism.[80] By this time, there was sufficient evidence for a logical thinker to see the merits of moneylending. Against the argument that money is barren, Molinaeus (1500–1566) observed that everyday experience of business life showed that the use of any considerable sum of money yields a service of importance. He argued, by reference to observation and logic, that money, assisted by human effort, does "bear fruit" in the form of new wealth; the money enables the borrower to create goods that he otherwise would not have been able to create. Just as Galileo would later apply Aristotle's method of observation and logic in refuting Aristotle's specific ideas in physics, so Molinaeus used Aristotle's method in refuting Aristotle's basic objection to usury. Unfortunately, like Galileo, Molinaeus was to suffer for his ideas: The Church forced him into exile and banned his book. Nevertheless, his ideas on usury spread throughout Europe and had a significant impact on future discussions of moneylending.[81]

The prevailing view that emerged in the late 16th century (and that, to a large extent, is still with us today) is that money is not barren and that usury plays a productive role in the economy. Usury, however, is unchristian; it is motivated by a desire for profit and can be used

---

79. Eugen von Böhm-Bawerk, *Capital and Interest: A Critical History of Economical Theory* (London: Macmillan and Co., 1890), trans. William A. Smart, bk 1, chap. 3.

80. Charles Dumoulin (Latinized as "Molinaeus"), *Treatise on Contracts and Usury* (1546).

81. Böhm-Bawerk, *Capital and Interest*, bk 1, chap. 3.

to exploit the poor. It can be practical, but it is not moral; therefore, it should be controlled by the state and subjected to regulation in order to restrain the rich and protect the poor.

This Christian view has influenced almost all attitudes about usury since. In a sense, Luther and Calvin *are* responsible for today's so-called capitalism. They are responsible for the guilt many people feel from making money and the guilt that causes people to eagerly regulate the functions of capitalists. Moreover, the Protestants were the first to explicitly assert and *sanction* the moral-practical dichotomy—the idea that the moral and the practical are necessarily at odds. Because of original sin, the Protestants argued, men are incapable of being good, and thus concessions must be made in accordance with their wicked nature. Men must be permitted to some extent to engage in practical matters such as usury, even though such practices are immoral.

In spite of its horrific view of man, life, and reality, Luther and Calvin's brand of Christianity allowed individuals who were not intimidated by Christian theology to practice moneylending to some extent without legal persecution. Although still limited by government constraints, the chains were loosened, and this enabled economic progress through the periodic establishment of legal rates of interest.

The first country to establish a legal rate of interest was England in 1545 during the reign of Henry VIII. The rate was set at 10 percent. However, seven years later it was repealed, and usury was again completely banned. In an argument in 1571 to reinstate the bill, Mr. Molley, a lawyer representing the business interests in London, said before the House of Commons:

> Since to take reasonably, or so that both parties might do good, was not hurtful; . . . God did not so hate it, that he did utterly forbid it, but to the Jews amongst themselves only, for that he willed they should lend as Brethren together; for unto all others they were at large; and therefore to this day they are the greatest Usurers in the World. But be it, as indeed it is, evil, and that men are men, no Saints, to do all these things perfectly, uprightly and Brotherly; . . . and better may it be born to permit a little, than utterly to take away and prohibit Traffick; which hardly may be maintained generally without this.
>
> But it may be said, it is contrary to the direct word of God, and therefore an ill Law; if it were to appoint men to take Usury, it were to be disliked; but the difference is great

between that and permitting or allowing, or suffering a matter to be unpunished.[82]

Observe that while pleading for a bill permitting usury—on the grounds that it is necessary ("Traffick . . . hardly may be maintained generally without [it]")—Molley concedes that it is evil. This is the moral-practical dichotomy stated openly and in black-and-white terms, and it illustrates the general attitude of the era. The practice was now widely accepted as practical but still regarded as immoral, and the thinkers of the day grappled with this new context.

One of England's most significant 17th-century intellectuals, Francis Bacon (1561-1626), realized the benefits that moneylending offered to merchants and traders by providing them with capital. He also recognized the usurer's value in providing liquidity to consumers and businesses. And, although Bacon believed that the moral ideal would be lending at 0 percent interest, as the Bible requires, he, like Luther, saw this as utopian and held that "it is better to mitigate usury by declaration than suffer it to rage by connivance." Bacon therefore proposed two rates of usury: one set at a maximum of 5 percent and allowable to everyone; and a second rate, higher than 5 percent, allowable only to certain licensed persons and lent only to known merchants. The license was to be sold by the state for a fee.[83]

Again, interest and usury were pitted against morality. But Bacon saw moneylending as so important to commerce that the legal rate of interest had to offer sufficient incentive to attract lenders. Bacon recognized that a higher rate of interest is economically justified by the nature of certain loans.[84]

The economic debate had shifted from whether usury should be legal to whether and at what level government should set the interest rate (a debate that, of course, continues to this day, with the Fed setting certain interest rates). As one scholar put it: "The legal toleration of interest marked a revolutionary change in public opinion and gave a clear indication of the *divorce of ethics from economics* under the pressure

---

82. Sir Simonds d'Ewes, "Journal of the House of Commons: April 1571" in *Journals of All the Parliaments During the Reign of Queen Elizabeth* (London: John Starkey, 1682), pp. 155–80, http://www.british-history.ac.uk/report.asp?compid=43684.

83. Francis Bacon, "Of Usury," in *Bacon's Essays* (London: Macmillan and Co., 1892), p. 109.

84. Davies, *A History of Money*, p. 222.

of an expanding economic system."[85]

In spite of this progress, artists continued to compare usurers to idle drones, spiders, and bloodsuckers, and playwrights personified the money-grubbing usurers in characters such as Sir Giles Overreach, Messrs. Mammon, Lucre, Hoard, Gripe, and Bloodhound. Probably the greatest work of art vilifying the usurer was written during this period—*The Merchant of Venice* by Shakespeare (1564–1616), which immortalized the character of the evil Jewish usurer, Shylock.

In *The Merchant of Venice*, Bassanio, a poor nobleman, needs cash in order to court the heiress, Portia. Bassanio goes to a Jewish moneylender, Shylock, for a loan, bringing his wealthy friend, Antonio, to stand as surety for it. Shylock, who has suffered great rudeness from Antonio in business, demands as security for the loan not Antonio's property, which he identifies as being at risk, but a pound of his flesh.[86]

The conflict between Shylock and Antonio incorporates all the elements of the arguments against usury. Antonio, the Christian, lends money and demands no interest. As Shylock describes him:

> SHYLOCK. [Aside.] How like a fawning publican he looks!
> I hate him for he is a Christian;
> But more for that in low simplicity
> He lends out money gratis, and brings down
> The rate of usance here with us in Venice.
> If I can catch him once upon the hip,
> I will feed fat the ancient grudge I bear him.
> He hates our sacred nation, and he rails,
> Even there where merchants most do congregate,
> On me, my bargains, and my well-won thrift,
> Which he calls interest. Cursed be my tribe,
> If I forgive him![87]

Shylock takes usury. He is portrayed as the lowly, angry, vengeful, and greedy Jew. When his daughter elopes and takes her father's money

---

85. Ibid., p. 222, emphasis added.

86. James Buchan, *Frozen Desire* (New York: Farrar, Strauss & Giroux, 1997), p. 87 (synopsis of the play).

87. William Shakespeare, *The Merchant of Venice*, Act 1, Scene 2.

with her, he cries, "My daughter! O my ducats! Oh my daughter!"[88]—not sure for which he cares more.

It is clear that Shakespeare understood the issues involved in usury. Note Shylock's (legitimate) hostility toward Antonio because Antonio loaned money without charging interest and thus brought down the market rate of interest in Venice. Even Aristotle's "barren money" argument is present. Antonio, provoking Shylock, says:

> If thou wilt lend this money, lend it not
> As to thy friends,—for when did friendship take
> A breed for barren metal of his friend?—
> But lend it rather to thine enemy:
> Who if he break, thou mayst with better face
> Exact the penalty.[89]

Friends do not take "breed for barren metal" from friends; usury is something one takes only from an enemy.

Great art plays a crucial role in shaping popular attitudes, and Shakespeare's depiction of Shylock, like Dante's depiction of usurers, concretized for generations the dichotomous view of moneylending and thus helped entrench the alleged link between usury and evil. As late as 1600, medieval moral and economic theories were alive and well, even if they were increasingly out of step with the economic practice of the time.

The Enlightenment

During the Enlightenment, the European economy continued to grow, culminating with the Industrial Revolution. This growth involved increased activity in every sector of the economy. Banking houses were established to provide credit to a wide array of economic endeavors. The Baring Brothers and the House of Rothschild were just the largest of the many banks that would ultimately help fuel the Industrial Revolution, funding railroads, factories, ports, and industry in general.

Economic understanding of the important productive role of usury continued to improve over the next four hundred years. Yet, the moral

---

88. Ibid., Act 3, Scene 2.

89. Ibid., Act 1, Scene 3.

evaluation of usury would change very little. The morality of altruism—the notion that self-sacrifice is moral and that self-interest is evil—was embraced and defended by many Enlightenment intellectuals and continued to hamper the acceptability of usury. After all, usury is a naked example of the pursuit of profit—which is patently self-interested. Further, it still seemed to the thinkers of the time that usury could be a zero-sum transaction—that a rich lender might profit at the expense of a poor borrower. Even a better conception of usury—let alone the misconception of it being a zero-sum transaction—is anathema to altruism, which demands the opposite of personal profit: self-sacrifice for the sake of others.

In the mid-17th century, northern Europe was home to a new generation of scholars who recognized that usury served an essential economic purpose, and that it should be allowed freely. Three men made significant contributions in this regard.

Claudius Salmasius (1588–1653), a French scholar teaching in Holland, thoroughly refuted the claims about the "barrenness" of moneylending; he showed the important productive function of usury and even suggested that there should be more usurers, since competition between them would reduce the rate of interest. Other Dutch scholars agreed with him, and, partially as a result of this, Holland became especially tolerant of usury, making it legal at times. Consequently, the leading banks of the era were found in Holland, and it became the world's commercial and financial center, the wealthiest state in Europe, and the envy of the world.[90]

Robert Jacques Turgot (1727–1781), a French economist, was the first to identify usury's connection to property rights. He argued that a creditor has the right to dispose of his money in any way he wishes and at whatever rate the market will bear, because it is *his* property. Turgot was also the first economist to fully understand that the passing of time changes the value of money. He saw the difference between the present value and the future value of money—concepts that are at the heart of any modern financial analysis. According to Turgot: "If . . . two gentlemen suppose that a sum of 1000 Francs and a promise of 1000 Francs possess exactly the same value, they put forward a still more absurd supposition; for if these two things were of equal value, why should any one borrow at all?"[91] Turgot even repudiated the medieval notion that time belonged to God. Time, he argued, belongs to the

---

90. Böhm-Bawerk, *Capital and Interest*, bk 1, chap. 3.

91. Ibid., bk 1, p. 56.

individual who uses it and therefore time could be sold.[92]

During the same period, the British philosopher Jeremy Bentham (1748–1832) wrote a treatise entitled *A Defense of Usury*. Bentham argued that any restrictions on interest rates were economically harmful because they restricted an innovator's ability to raise capital. Since innovative trades inherently involved high risk, they could only be funded at high interest rates. Limits on permissible interest rates, he argued, would kill innovation—the engine of growth. Correcting another medieval error, Bentham also showed that restrictive usury laws actually harmed the borrowers. Such restrictions cause the credit markets to shrink while demand for credit remains the same or goes up; thus, potential borrowers have to seek loans in an illegal market where they would have to pay a premium for the additional risk of illegal trading.

Bentham's most important contribution was his advocacy of contractual freedom:

> My neighbours, being at liberty, have happened to concur among themselves in dealing at a certain rate of interest. I, who have money to lend, and Titus, who wants to borrow it of me, would be glad, the one of us to accept, the other to give, an interest somewhat higher than theirs: Why is the liberty they exercise to be made a pretence for depriving me and Titus of ours.[93]

This was perhaps the first attempt at a moral defense of usury.

Unfortunately, Bentham and his followers undercut this effort with their philosophy of utilitarianism, according to which rights, liberty, and therefore moneylending, were valuable only insofar as they increased "social utility": "the greatest good for the greatest number." Bentham famously dismissed individual rights—the idea that each person should be free to act on his own judgment—as "nonsense upon stilts."[94] He embraced the idea that the individual has a "duty" to serve the well-being of the collective, or, as he put it, the "general mass of felicity."[95] Thus, in addition to undercutting Turgot's major achievement,

---

92. Ibid., bk 1, chap. 4.

93. Jeremy Bentham, *A Defence of Usury* (Philadelphia: Mathew Carey, 1787), p. 10.

94. Jeremy Bentham, *The Works of Jeremy Bentham*, ed. John Bowring (Edinburgh: W. Tait; London: Simpkin, Marshall, & Co., 1843), p. 501.

95. Ibid., p. 493.

Bentham also doomed the first effort at a moral defense of usury—which he himself had proposed.

An explicitly utilitarian attempt at a moral defense of usury was launched in 1774 in the anonymously published *Letters on Usury and Interest*. The goal of the book was to explain why usury should be accepted in England of the 18th century, and why this acceptance did not contradict the Church's teachings. The ultimate reason, the author argued, is one of utility:

> Here, then, is a sure and infallible rule to judge of the lawfulness of a practice. Is it useful to the State? Is it beneficial to the individuals that compose it? Either of these is sufficient to obtain a tolerance; but both together vest it with a character of justice and equity.... In fact, if we look into the laws of different nations concerning usury, we shall find that they are all formed on the principle of public utility. In those states where usury was found hurtful to society, it was prohibited. In those where it was neither hurtful nor very beneficial, it was tolerated. In those where it was useful, it was authorized. In ours, it is absolutely necessary.[96]

And:

> [T]he practice of lending money to interest is in this nation, and under this constitution, beneficial to all degrees; therefore it is beneficial to society. I say in this nation; which, as long as it continues to be a commercial one, must be chiefly supported by interest; for interest is the soul of credit and credit is the soul of commerce.[97]

Although the utilitarian argument in defense of usury contains some economic truth, it is morally bankrupt. Utilitarian moral reasoning for the propriety of usury depends on the perceived benefits of the practice to the collective or the nation. But what happens, for example, when usury in the form of subprime mortgage loans creates distress for a significant number of people and financial turmoil in some markets? How can it be justified? Indeed, it cannot. The utilitarian argument collapses in the face of any such economic problem,

---

96. Anonymous, *Letters on Usury and Interest* (London: J. P. Coghlan, 1774).

97. Ibid.

leaving moneylenders exposed to the wrath of the public and to the whips and chains of politicians seeking a scapegoat for the crisis.

Although Salmasius, Turgot, and Bentham made significant progress in understanding the economic and political value of usury, not all their fellow intellectuals followed suit. The father of economics, Adam Smith (1723–1790), wrote: "As something can everywhere be made by the use of money, something ought everywhere to be paid for the use of it." Simple and elegant. Yet, Smith also believed that the government must control the rate of interest. He believed that unfettered markets would create excessively high interest rates, which would hurt the economy—which, in turn, would harm society.[98] Because Smith thought that society's welfare was the only justification for usury, he held that the government must intervene to correct the errors of the "invisible hand."

Although Smith was a great innovator in economics, philosophically, he was a follower. He accepted the common philosophical ideas of his time, including altruism, of which utilitarianism is a form. Like Bentham, he justified capitalism only through its social benefits. If his projections of what would come to pass in a fully free market amounted to a less-than-optimal solution for society, he advocated government intervention. Government intervention is the logical outcome of any utilitarian defense of usury.

(Smith's idea that there need be a "perfect" legal interest rate remains with us to this day. His notion of such a rate was that it should be slightly higher than the market rate—what he called the "golden mean." The chairman of the Federal Reserve is today's very *visible* hand, constantly searching for the "perfect" rate or "golden mean" by alternately establishing artificially low and artificially high rates.)

Following Bentham and Smith, all significant 19th-century economists—such as David Ricardo, Jean Baptiste Say, and John Stuart Mill—considered the economic importance of usury to be obvious and argued that interest rates should be determined by freely contracting individuals. These economists, followed later by the Austrians—especially Carl Menger, Eugen von Böhm-Bawerk, and Ludwig von Mises—developed sound theories of the productivity of interest and gained a significant economic understanding of its practical role. But the moral-practical dichotomy inherent in their altruistic, utilitarian, social justification for usury remained in play, and the practice continued to be morally condemned and thus heavily regulated if not outlawed.

---

98. Ibid.

The 19th and 20th Centuries

Despite their flaws, the thinkers of the Enlightenment had created sufficient economic understanding to fuel the Industrial Revolution throughout the 19th century. Economically and politically, facts and reason had triumphed over faith; a sense of individualism had taken hold; the practicality of the profit motive had become clear; and, relative to eras past, the West was thriving.

Morally and philosophically, however, big trouble was brewing. As capitalism neared a glorious maturity, a new, more consistent brand of altruism, created by Kant, Hegel, and their followers, was sweeping Europe. At the political-economic level, this movement manifested itself in the ideas of Karl Marx (1818–1883).

Marx, exploiting the errors of the Classical economists, professed the medieval notion that all production is a result of manual labor; but he also elaborated, claiming that laborers do not retain the wealth they create. The capitalists, he said, take advantage of their control over the means of production—secured to them by private property—and "loot" the laborers' work. According to Marx, moneylending and other financial activities are not productive, but exploitative; moneylenders exert no effort, do no productive work, and yet reap the rewards of production through usury.[99] As one 20th-century Marxist put it: "The major argument against usury is that labor constitutes the true source of wealth."[100] Marx adopted all the medieval clichés, including the notion that Jews are devious, conniving money-grubbers.

What is the profane basis of Judaism? *Practical* need, *self-interest*. What is the worldly cult of the Jew? *Huckstering*. What is his worldly god? *Money*.

> Money is the jealous god of Israel, beside which no other god may exist. Money abases all the gods of mankind and changes them into commodities.[101]

Marx believed that the Jews were evil—not because of their religion,

---

99. For a thorough rebuttal of Marx's view, see Böhm-Bawerk, *Capital and Interest*, bk 1, chap. 12.

100. Gabriel Le Bras, quoted in Le Goff, *Your Money or Your Life*, p. 43.

101. Johnson, *A History of the Jews*, p. 351.

as others were clamoring at the time—but because they pursued their own selfish interests and sought to make money. And Marxists were not alone in their contempt for these qualities.

Artists who, like Marx, resented capitalists in general and money-lenders in particular, dominated Western culture in the 19th century. In Dickens's *A Christmas Carol*, we see the money-grubbing Ebenezer Scrooge. In Dostoyevsky's *Crime and Punishment*, the disgusting old lady whom Raskolnikov murders is a usurer. And in *The Brothers Karamazov*, Dostoyevsky writes:

> It was known too that the young person had . . . been giv-
> en to what is called "speculation," and that she had shown
> marked abilities in the direction, so that many people be-
> gan to say that she was no better than a Jew. It was not that
> she lent money on interest, but it was known, for instance,
> that she had for some time past, in partnership with old
> Karamazov, actually invested in the purchase of bad debts
> for a trifle, a tenth of their nominal value, and afterwards
> had made out of them ten times their value.[102]

In other words, she was what in the 1980s became known as a "vulture" capitalist buying up distressed debt.

Under Marx's influential ideas, and given the culture-wide contempt for moneylenders, the great era of capitalism—of thriving banks and general financial success—was petering out. Popular sentiment concerning usury was reverting to a dark-ages type of hatred. Marx and company put the moneylenders back into Dante's *Inferno*, and to this day they have not been able to escape.

The need for capital, however, would not be suppressed by the label "immoral." People still sought to start businesses and purchase homes; thus usury was still seen as practical. Like the Church of the Middle Ages, people found themselves simultaneously condemning the practice and engaging in it.

Consequently, just as the term "interest" had been coined in the Middle Ages to facilitate the Church's selective opposition to usury and to avoid the stigma associated with the practice, so modern man employed the term for the same purpose. The concept of moneylending was again split into two allegedly different concepts: the charging

---

102. Fyodor M. Dostoyevsky, *The Brothers Karamazov*, trans. Constance Garnett (Spark Publishing, 2004), p. 316.

of "interest" and the practice of "usury." Lending at "interest" came to designate lower-premium, lower-risk, less-greedy lending, while "usury" came to mean specifically higher-premium, higher-risk, more-greedy lending. This artificial division enabled the wealthier, more powerful, more influential people to freely engage in moneylending with the one hand, while continuing to condemn the practice with the other. Loans made to lower-risk, higher-income borrowers would be treated as morally acceptable, while those made to higher-risk, lower-income borrowers would remain morally contemptible. (The term "usury" is now almost universally taken to mean "excessive" or illegal premium on loans, while the term "interest" designates tolerable or legal premium.)

From the 19th century onward, in the United States and in most other countries, usury laws would restrict the rates of interest that could be charged on loans, and there would be an ongoing battle between businessmen and legislators over what those rates should be. These laws, too, are still with us.

As Bentham predicted, such laws harm not only lenders but also borrowers, who are driven into the shadows where they procure shady and often illegal loans in order to acquire the capital they need for their endeavors. And given the extra risk posed by potential legal complications for the lenders, these loans are sold at substantially higher interest rates than they would be if moneylending were fully legal and unregulated.

In the United States, demand for high-risk loans has always existed, and entrepreneurs have always arisen to service the demand for funds. They have been scorned, condemned to Hell, assaulted, jailed, and generally treated like the usurers of the Middle Ages—but they have relentlessly supplied the capital that has enabled Americans to achieve unprecedented levels of productiveness and prosperity.

The earliest known advertisement for a small-loan service in an American newspaper appeared in the *Chicago Tribune* in November 1869. By 1872, the industry was prospering. Loans collateralized by furniture, diamonds, warehouse receipts, houses, and pianos were available (called chattel loans). The first salary loan office (offering loans made in advance of a paycheck) was opened by John Mulholland in Kansas City in 1893. Within fifteen years he had offices all across the country. The going rate on a chattel loan was 10 percent a month for loans under $50, and 5–7 percent a month for larger loans. Some loans were made at very high rates, occasionally over 100 percent a month.[103]

---

103. James Grant, *Money of the Mind* (New York: Noonday Press, 1994), p. 79.

The reason rates were so high is because of the number of defaults. With high rates in play, the losses on loans in default could ordinarily be absorbed as a cost of doing business. In this respect, the 19th-century small-loan business was a precursor of the 20th-century "junk" bond business or the 21st-century subprime mortgage lender. However, unlike the "junk" bond salesman, who had recourse to the law in cases of default or bankruptcy, these small-loan men operated on the fringes of society—and often outside the law. Because of the social stigmatization and legal isolation of the creditors, legal recourse against a defaulting borrower was generally unavailable to a usurer. Yet these back-alley loans provided a valuable service—one for which there was great demand—and they enabled many people to start their own businesses or improve their lives in other ways.

Of course, whereas most of these borrowers paid off their loans and succeeded in their endeavors, many of them got into financial trouble—and the latter cases, not the former, were widely publicized. The moneylenders were blamed, and restrictions were multiplied and tightened.

In spite of all the restrictions, laws, and persecutions, the market found ways to continue. In 1910, Arthur Morris set up the first bank in America with the express purpose of providing small loans to individuals at interest rates based on the borrower's "character and earning power." In spite of the usury limit of 6 percent that existed in Virginia at the time, Morris's bank found ways, as did usurers in the Middle Ages, to make loans at what appeared to be a 6 percent interest rate while the actual rates were much higher and more appropriate. For instance, a loan for $100 might be made as follows: A commission of 2 percent plus the 6 percent legal rate would be taken off the top in advance; thus the borrower would receive $92. Then he would repay the loan at $2 a week over fifty weeks. The effective compound annual interest rate on such a loan was in excess of 18 percent. And penalties would be assessed for any delinquent payments.[104] Such camouflaged interest rates were a throwback to the Middle Ages, when bankers developed innovative ways to circumvent the restrictions on usury established by the Church. And, as in the Middle Ages, such lending became common as the demand for capital was widespread. Consequently, these banks multiplied and thrived—for a while.

(Today's credit card industry is the successor to such institutions. Credit card lenders charge high interest rates to high-risk customers,

---

104. Ibid., pp. 91–95.

and penalties for delinquency. And borrowers use these loans for consumption as well as to start or fund small businesses. And, of course, the credit card industry is regularly attacked for its high rates of interest and its "exploitation" of customers. To this day, credit card interest rates are restricted by usury laws, and legislation attempting to further restrict these rates is periodically introduced.)

In 1913, in New York, a moneylender who issued loans to people who could not get them at conventional banks appeared before a court on the charge of usury. In the decision, the judge wrote:

> You are one of the most contemptible usurers in your unspeakable business. The poor people must be protected from such sharks as you, and we must trust that your conviction and sentence will be a notice to you and all your kind that the courts have found a way to put a stop to usury. Men of your type are a curse to the community, and the money they gain is blood money.[105]

This ruling is indicative of the general attitude toward usurers at the time. The moral-practical dichotomy was alive and kicking, and the moneylenders were taking the blows. Although their practical value to the economy was now clear, their moral status as evil was still common "sense." And the intellectuals of the day would only exacerbate the problem.

The most influential economist of the 20th century was John Maynard Keynes (1883-1946), whose ideas not only shaped the theoretical field of modern economics but also played a major role in shaping government policies in the United States and around the world. Although Keynes allegedly rejected Marx's ideas, he shared Marx's hatred of the profit motive and usury. He also agreed with Adam Smith that government must control interest rates; otherwise investment and thus society would suffer. And he revived the old Reformation idea that usury is a necessary evil:

> When the accumulation of wealth is no longer of high social importance, there will be great changes in the code of morals. We shall be able to rid ourselves of many of the pseudo-moral principles which have hag-ridden us for two hundred years, by which we have exalted some of the most distasteful of human qualities into the position of the high-

---

105. Ibid., p. 83.

est virtues. . . . But beware! The time for all this is not yet. For at least another hundred years we must pretend to ourselves and to everyone that fair is foul and foul is fair; for foul is useful and fair is not. Avarice and usury and precaution must be our gods for a little longer still. For only they can lead us out of the tunnel of economic necessity into daylight.[106]

Although Keynes and other economists and intellectuals of the day recognized the need of usury, they universally condemned the practice and its practitioners as "foul" and "unfair." Thus, regardless of widespread recognition of the fact that usury is a boon to the economy, when the Great Depression occurred in the United States, the moneylenders on Wall Street were blamed. As Franklin Delano Roosevelt put it:

> The rulers of the exchange of mankind's goods have failed, through their own stubbornness and their own incompetence, have admitted failure, and have abdicated. Practices of the unscrupulous money changers stand indicted in the court of public opinion, rejected by the hearts and minds of men . . . [We must] apply social values more noble than mere monetary profit.[107]

And so the "solution" to the problems of the Great Depression was greater government intervention throughout the economy—especially in the regulation of interest and the institutions that deal in it. After 1933, banks were restricted in all aspects of their activity: the interest rates they could pay their clients, the rates they could charge, and to whom they could lend. In 1934, the greatest bank in American history, J. P. Morgan, was broken up by the government into several companies. The massive regulations and coercive restructurings of the 1930s illustrate the continuing contempt for the practice of taking interest on loans and the continuing distrust of those—now mainly bankers—who engage in this activity. (We paid a dear price for those regulations with the savings and loan crisis of the 1970s and 1980s, which cost

---

106. John Maynard Keynes, "Economic Possibilities for Our Grandchildren," in *Essays in Persuasion* (New York: W. W. Norton & Company, 1963), pp. 359, 362, http://www.econ.yale.edu/smith/econ116a/keynes1.pdf.

107. Franklin D. Roosevelt, First Inaugural Address, March 4, 1933, http://avalon.law.yale.edu/20th_century/froos1.asp.

American taxpayers hundreds of billions of dollars.[108] And we continue to pay the price of these regulations in higher taxes, greater financial costs, lost innovation, and stifled economic growth.)

The 21st Century

From ancient Greece and Rome, to the Dark and Middle Ages, to the Renaissance and Reformation, to the 19th and 20th centuries, moneylending has been morally condemned and legally restrained. Today, at the dawn of the 21st century, moneylending remains a pariah.

One of the latest victims of this moral antagonism is the business of providing payday loans. This highly popular and beneficial service has been branded with the scarlet letter "U"; consequently, despite the great demand for these loans, the practice has been relegated to the fringes of society and the edge of the law. These loans carry annualized interest rates as high as 1000 percent because they are typically very short term (i.e., to be paid back on payday). By some estimates there are 25,000 payday stores across America, and it is "a $6 billion dollar industry serving 15 million people every month."[109] The institutions issuing these loans have found ways, just as banks always have, to circumvent state usury laws. Bank regulators have severely restricted the ability of community banks to offer payday loans or even to work with payday loan offices, more than thirteen states have banned them altogether, and Congress is currently looking at ways to ban all payday loans.[110] This is in spite of the fact that demand for these loans is soaring, that they serve a genuine economic need, and that they are a real value for low-income households. As the *Wall Street Journal* reports, "Georgia outlawed payday loans in 2004, and thousands of workers have since taken to traveling over the border to find payday stores in Tennessee, Florida and South Carolina. So the effect

---

108. To understand the link between 1930s regulations and the savings and loan crisis, see Edward J. Kane, *The S&L Insurance Mess: How Did It Happen?* (Washington, D.C.: The Urban Institute Press, 1989); and Richard M. Salsman, *The Collapse of Deposit Insurance—and the Case for Abolition* (Great Barrington, MA: American Institute for Economic Research, 1993).

109. "Mayday for Payday Loans," *Wall Street Journal*, April 2, 2007, http://online.wsj.com/article/SB117546964173756271.html.

110. "U.S. Moves Against Payday Loans, Which Critics Charge Are Usurious," *Wall Street Journal*, January 4, 2002, http://online.wsj.com/article/SB1010098721429807840.html.

of the ban has been to increase consumer credit costs and inconvenience for Georgia consumers."[111]

A story in *LA Weekly*, titled "Shylock 2000"—ignoring the great demand for payday loans, ignoring the economic value they provide to countless borrowers, and ignoring the fact that the loans are made by mutual consent to mutual advantage—proceeded to describe horrific stories of borrowers who have gone bankrupt. The article concluded: "What's astonishing about this story is that, 400 years after Shakespeare created the avaricious lender Shylock, such usury may be perfectly legal."[112]

What is truly astonishing is that after centuries of moneylenders providing capital and opportunities to billions of willing people on mutually agreed-upon terms, the image of these persistent businessmen has not advanced beyond that of Shylock.

The "Shylocks" du jour, of course, are the subprime mortgage lenders, with whom this article began. These lenders provided mortgages designed to enable low-income borrowers to buy homes. Because the default rate among these borrowers is relatively high, the loans are recognized as high-risk transactions and are sold at correspondingly high rates of interest. Although it is common knowledge that many of these loans are now in default, and although it is widely believed that the lenders are to blame for the situation, what is not well known is, as Paul Harvey would say, "the rest of the story."

The tremendous growth in this industry is a direct consequence of government policy. Since the 1930s, the U.S. government has encouraged home ownership among all Americans—but especially among those in lower income brackets. To this end, the government created the Federal Home Loan Banks (which are exempt from state and local income taxes) to provide incentives for smaller banks to make mortgage loans to low-income Americans. Congress passed the Community Reinvestment Act, which requires banks to invest in their local communities, including by providing mortgage loans to people in low-income brackets. The government created Fannie Mae and Freddie Mac, both of which have a mandate to issue and guarantee mortgage loans to low-income borrowers.

In recent years, all these government schemes and more (e.g., artificially low-interest rates orchestrated by the Fed) led to a frenzy of borrowing and lending. The bottom line is that the government has artificially

---

111. "Mayday for Payday Loans," *Wall Street Journal*.

112. Christine Pelisek, "Shylock 2000," *LA Weekly*, February 16, 2000, http://www .laweekly.com/news/offbeat/shylock-2000/11565/.

mitigated lenders' risk, and it has done so on the perverse, altruistic premise that "society" has a moral duty to increase home ownership among low-income Americans. The consequence of this folly has been a significant increase in delinquent loans and foreclosures, which has led to wider financial problems at banks and at other institutions that purchased the mortgages in the secondary markets.

Any objective evaluation of the facts would place the blame for this disaster on the government policies that caused it. But no—just as in the past, the lenders are being blamed and scapegoated.

Although some of these lenders clearly did take irrational risks on many of these loans, that should be their own problem, and they should have to suffer the consequences of their irrational actions—whether significant financial loss or bankruptcy. (The government most certainly should not bail them out.) However, without the perception of reduced risk provided by government meddling in the economy, far fewer lenders would have been so frivolous.

Further, the number of people benefiting from subprime mortgage loans, which make it possible for many people to purchase a home for the first time, is in the millions—and the vast majority of these borrowers are *not* delinquent or in default; rather, they are paying off their loans and enjoying their homes, a fact never mentioned by the media.

It should also be noted that whereas the mortgage companies are blamed for all the defaulting loans, no blame is placed on the irresponsible borrowers who took upon themselves debt that they knew—or should have known—they could not handle.

After four hundred years of markets proving the incredible benefits generated by moneylending, intellectuals, journalists, and politicians still rail against lenders and their institutions. And, in spite of all the damage done by legal restrictions on interest, regulation of moneylenders, and government interference in financial markets, whenever there is an economic "crisis," there is invariably a wave of demand for *more* of these controls, not fewer.

Moneylenders are still blamed for recessions; they are still accused of being greedy and of taking advantage of the poor; they are still portrayed on TV and in movies as slick, murderous villains; and they are still distrusted by almost everyone. (According to a recent poll, only 16 percent of Americans have substantial confidence in the American financial industry.)[113] Thus, it should come as no surprise that the financial sector is the

---

113. *Wall Street Journal*, August 2, 2007, p. A4.

most regulated, most controlled industry in America today.

But what explains the ongoing antipathy toward, distrust of, and co-ercion against these bearers of capital and opportunity? What explains the modern anti-moneylending mentality? Why are moneylenders today held in essentially the same ill repute as they were in the Middle Ages?

The explanation for this lies in the fact that, fundamentally, 21st-century ethics is no different from the ethics of the Middle Ages.

All parties in the assault on usury share a common ethical root: al-truism—belief in the notion that self-sacrifice is moral and self-interest is evil. This is the source of the problem. So long as self-interest is con-demned, neither usury in particular, nor profit in general, can be seen as good—both will be seen as evil.

Moneylending cannot be defended by reference to its economic prac-ticality alone. If moneylending is to be recognized as a fully legitimate practice and defended accordingly, then its defenders must discover and embrace a new code of ethics, one that upholds self-interest—and thus personal profit—as moral.

Conclusion

Although serious economists today uniformly recognize the econom-ic benefits of charging interest or usury on loans, they rarely, if ever, at-tempt a philosophical or moral defense of this position. Today's econ-omists either reject philosophy completely or adopt the moral-practi-cal split, accepting the notion that although usury is practical, it is ei-ther immoral or, at best, amoral.

Modern philosophers, for the most part, have no interest in the top-ic at all, partly because it requires them to deal with reality, and partly be-cause they believe self-interest, capitalism, and everything they entail, to be evil. Today's philosophers, almost to a man, accept self-sacrifice as the standard of morality and physical labor as the source of wealth. Thus, to the extent that they refer to moneylending at all, they consider *it* unques-tionably unjust, and positions to the contrary unworthy of debate.

It is time to set the record straight.

Whereas Aristotle *united* productiveness with morality and there-by condemned usury as immoral based on his mistaken belief that the practice is unproductive—and whereas everyone since Aristotle (in-cluding contemporary economists and philosophers) has *severed* pro-ductiveness from morality and condemned usury on biblical or altru-istic grounds as immoral (or at best amoral)—what is needed is a view that again *unifies* productiveness and morality, but that also sees usury as productive, and morality as the means to practical success on earth. What is needed is the economic knowledge of the last millennium *combined with* a new moral theory—one that upholds the morality of self-interest and thus the virtue of personal profit.

Let us first condense the key economic points; then we will turn to a brief indication of the morality of self-interest.

The crucial economic knowledge necessary to a proper defense of usury includes an understanding of why lenders charge interest on money—and why they would do so even in a risk-free, noninflationary environment. Lenders charge interest because their money has alternative uses—uses they temporarily forego by lending the money to borrowers. When a lender lends money, he is thereby unable to use that money toward some benefit or profit for himself. Had he not lent it, he could have spent it on consumer goods that he would have enjoyed, or he could have invested it in alternative moneymaking ventures. And the longer the term of the loan, the longer the lender must postpone his alternative use of the money. Thus interest is charged because the lender views the loan as a better, more profitable use of his money over the period of the loan than any of his alternative uses of the same funds over the same time; he estimates that, given the interest charged, the benefit to him is greater from making the loan than from any other use of his capital.[114]

A lender tries to calculate in advance the likelihood or unlikelihood that he will be repaid all his capital plus the interest. The less convinced he is that a loan will be repaid, the higher the interest rate he will charge. Higher rates enable lenders to profit for their willingness to take greater risks. The practice of charging interest is therefore an expression of the human ability to project the future, to plan, to analyze, to calculate risk, and to act in the face of uncertainty. In a word, it is an expression of man's ability to *reason*. The better a lender's thinking, the more money he will make.

Another economic principle that is essential to a proper defense of usury is recognition of the fact that moneylending is *productive*. This fact was made increasingly clear over the centuries, and today it is incontrovertible. By choosing to whom he will lend money, the moneylender determines which projects he will help bring into existence and which individuals he will provide with opportunities to improve the

---

114. For an excellent presentation of this theory of interest, see Böhm-Bawerk, *Capital and Interest*, bk 2.

quality of their lives and his. Thus, lenders make themselves money by rewarding people for the virtues of innovation, productiveness, personal responsibility, and entrepreneurial talent; and they withhold their sanction, thus minimizing their losses, from people who exhibit signs of stagnation, laziness, irresponsibility, and inefficiency. The lender, in seeking profit, does not consider the well-being of society or of the borrower. Rather, he assesses his alternatives, evaluates the risk, and seeks the greatest return on his investment.

And, of course, lent money is not "barren"; it is fruitful: It enables borrowers to improve their lives or produce new goods or services. Nor is moneylending a zero-sum game: Both the borrower and the lender benefit from the exchange (as ultimately does everyone involved in the economy). The lender makes a profit, and the borrower gets to use capital—whether for consumption or investment purposes—that he otherwise would not be able to use.[115]

An understanding of these and other economic principles is necessary to defend the practice of usury. But such an understanding is *not* sufficient to defend the practice. From the brief history we have recounted, it is evident that all commentators on usury from the beginning of time have known that those who charge interest are self-interested, that the very nature of their activity is motivated by personal profit. Thus, in order to defend moneylenders, their institutions, and the kind of world they make possible, one must be armed with a moral code that recognizes rational self-interest and therefore the pursuit of profit as moral, and that consequently regards productivity as a virtue and upholds man's right to his property and to his time.

There is such a morality: It is Ayn Rand's Objectivist ethics, or rational egoism, and it is the missing link in the defense of usury (and capitalism in general).

According to rational egoism, man's life—the life of each individual man—is the standard of moral value, and his reasoning mind is his basic means of living. Being moral, on this view, consists in thinking and producing the values on which one's life and happiness depend—while leaving others free to think and act on their own judgment for their own sake. The Objectivist ethics holds that people should act rationally, in their own long-term best interest; that each person is the

---

115. For a discussion of the productive nature of financial activity, see my taped course "In Defense of Financial Markets," http://www.aynrandbookstore2.com/prodinfo.asp?number=DB46D.

proper beneficiary of his own actions; that each person has a moral right to keep, use, and dispose of the product of his efforts; and that each individual is capable of thinking for himself, of producing values, and of deciding whether, with whom, and on what terms he will trade. It is a morality of self-interest, individual rights, and personal responsibility. And it is grounded in the fundamental fact of human nature: the fact that man's basic means of living is his ability to reason.

Ayn Rand identified the principle that the greatest productive, life-serving power on earth is not human muscle but the human mind. Consequently, she regarded profit-seeking—the use of the mind to identify, produce, and trade life-serving values—as the essence of being moral.[116]

Ayn Rand's Objectivist ethics is essential to the defense of moneylending. It provides the moral foundation without which economic arguments in defense of usury cannot prevail. It demonstrates why moneylending is supremely *moral*.

The Objectivist ethics frees moneylenders from the shackles of Dante's inferno, enables them to brush off Shakespeare's ridicule, and empowers them to take an irrefutable moral stand against persecution and regulation by the state. The day that this moral code becomes widely embraced will be the day that moneylenders—and every other producer of value—will be completely free to charge whatever rates their customers will pay and to reap the rewards righteously and proudly.

If this moral ideal were made a political reality, then, for the first time in history, moneylenders, bankers, and their institutions would be legally permitted and morally encouraged to work to their fullest potential, making profits by providing the lifeblood of capital to our economy. Given what these heroes have achieved while scorned and shackled, it is hard to imagine what their productive achievements would be if they were revered and freed.

---

116. For more on Objectivism, see Leonard Peikoff, *Objectivism: The Philosophy of Ayn Rand* (New York: Dutton, 1991); and Ayn Rand, *Atlas Shrugged* (New York: Random House, 1957) and *Capitalism: The Unknown Ideal* (New York: New American Library 1966).

Finance Isn't Free and Never Really Was

By Don Watkins

Now that Trump is in office there is talk that his administration will support repealing or revising Dodd-Frank[117]—the government's regulatory response to the financial crisis of 2008. The bill was sold as a way to protect ourselves from future crises by making the financial system more stable.

One of the most striking things about financial crises is how sudden and unexpected they are. Nearly everyone, including America's top bankers and financial regulators, were unprepared for September 2008. Few foresaw the collapse of many of the nation's leading financial institutions, government bailouts putting taxpayers on the hook for hundreds of billions of dollars—not to mention the sheer fear of the unknown this calamity produced. We wondered: How many businesses would fail? How many jobs would be lost? How far would the stock market (and our retirement savings) fall?

The Great Recession made viscerally real for people the dangers of financial instability. We want the benefits of a healthy financial system—thriving businesses, available credit, low unemployment, stable prices—but we want to make sure the system doesn't collapse and leave us struggling to pick up the pieces.

What creates financial instability? The most popular narrative says that banking and finance are inherently unstable unless overseen and controlled by the government. Absent massive government intervention, greedy financiers will engage in reckless and sometimes predatory practices in order to line their own pockets, and then leave us with the tab once the system implodes.

That narrative shaped our response to the Panic of 1907, which led to the creation of America's central bank, the Federal Reserve, in 1913. It shaped our response to the Great Depression, which led to a massive new regulatory infrastructure, including the creation of the SEC (Securities and Exchange Commission), which regulates stocks and other securities, the FDIC (Federal Deposit Insurance Commission),

---

117. Ryan Tracy, "Dodd-Frank in Crosshairs as Law's Opponents Take Power," *Wall Street Journal*, January 18, 2017, http://www.wsj.com/articles/dodd-frank-in-crosshairs-as-laws-opponents-take-power-1484758800.

which insures bank deposits, and Glass-Steagall's separation of commercial and investment banking. And it shaped our response to 2008's financial crisis, which led to Dodd-Frank, the most sweeping set of financial controls since the New Deal.

Part of what has made this narrative plausible is the belief that financial markets and institutions were free in the lead up to the crisis—if not totally then at least in important respects. During the 2008 financial crisis, for instance, it was not uncommon to hear blame cast on "deregulation," "cowboy capitalism," and "laissez-faire banking."

That's a recipe for government intervention. If people think the unrestrained pursuit of self-interest by bankers, traders, speculators, and other financiers leads to crises, and they believe that financial markets lacked government control prior to crises, then why *wouldn't* the answer be greater government control going forward?

The truth is that finance has *never* been free in the United States—not even close. And the system that nearly collapsed in 2008 was in most ways *more* controlled by government than at any time in U.S. history.

Even more important, it is government interference that *makes* financial systems fragile. If we look at the most stable financial systems in history—the 19th-century Scottish system or the Canadian system, for instance—they are inevitably the *freest* systems. If we look at financial systems prone to panics and crises, what we inevitably find are price distortions, twisted incentives and regulatory straitjackets created by government intrusion.

It isn't the unrestrained pursuit of self-interest by financiers that makes financial markets fragile—it is the distortions and restraints governments put on the pursuit of self-interest. If we value a stable financial system, then government intervention is not the answer to our problem, it *is* the problem.

Financial freedom has two components: freedom from regulation and freedom from government *support*.

Financial regulations generally fall into two categories—I call them "fairness" regulations and "fragility" regulations. Fairness regulations include everything from proscriptions on fraud (which are proper) to rules governing conflicts of interest to undefined "crimes" like "stock manipulation"—all aimed at allegedly making sure financial dealings are, in the government's eyes at least, fair. Fragility regulation aims to promote prudence—to minimize risks that can potentially threaten a financial institution and the entire financial system. This can mean anything from bank capital requirements to regulators dictating which loans a bank can make. (In this essay, I'm going to focus on fragility regulation, although the two categories sometimes overlap.)

"Financial support" refers to the ways in which the government intervenes in the economy to *protect* financial institutions, including subsidies, bailouts, restrictions on competition—typically under the guise of benefiting the public (bank customers, mortgage borrowers, etc.).

Such "protections" are no less destructive than regulations: they reduce market discipline, distort banking incentives, and supply the justification for many financial regulations, making our financial system incredibly fragile.

In this essay I'll cover:

1. How government intervention, not free banking or the gold standard, led to the bank panics of the late 19th and early 20th centuries

2. How government intervention, not the gold standard or Wall Street speculators, made possible the Great Depression.

3. How the New Deal's response to the Great Depression did not address its root causes and laid the groundwork for future crises

4. How, despite the so-called deregulation of the late 20th century, the financial system was more controlled than ever on the eve of 2008's financial crisis

5. How the Great Recession was made possible by government intervention in the financial system— notably including the Federal Reserve's control of money and the moral hazard created by federal deposit insurance and its progeny, the "too big to fail" doctrine

Defining what a fully free financial system would look like and why it would be resilient rather than unstable is a complex undertaking, and beyond my scope. (If you're interested, start with the work of free-banking scholars such as George Selgin, Lawrence H. White, and Kevin Dowd.)

What we will see is how deeply wrong the conventional narrative blaming crises on "unregulated free markets" is—and why anyone concerned with a healthy financial system should take the time to look for solutions that don't involve handing the government enormous new powers.

Banking Panics and the Creation of the Federal Reserve

The Myth: *We tried free banking and the result was constant bank runs and panics. The Federal Reserve was created to make the system stable and it succeeded.*

The Reality: *America's recurrent panics were the product of financial control, and there is no evidence the Federal Reserve has made things better.*

No one disputes that America's banking system prior to the Federal Reserve's (the Fed's) creation in 1914 was unstable, prone to money shortages and recurrent panics. But what was the cause of that instability?

The conventional wisdom says that it was the inherent weakness of a free-banking system—in particular, not having a central bank that could act as a "lender of last resort" to banks in need of cash during times of stress and panic.

One major reason to doubt that story, however, is that the phenomenon of recurrent banking panics was unique to the U.S. during the late 19th century, even though the U.S. was far from the only country without a central bank. Canada, for example, lacked a central bank and was far less regulated than the U.S., yet its financial system was notoriously stable.[118]

In the U.S., government control over the banking system goes back to the earliest days of the republic. But when people speak about pre-Fed panics, what they usually have in mind is the period that runs from the Civil War to the creation of the Federal Reserve in 1913 (when the U.S. was on what was known as the National Currency System). During that era, there were two regulations that explain why the U.S. system was so volatile, while freer systems in Canada, Scotland, and elsewhere were remarkably stable:

1. Collateral banking
2. Restrictions on branch banking

How Bond-Collateral Banking and Branch Banking Restrictions Fostered Crises

To understand bond-collateral banking, we need to take a step back and look at the monetary system at the time. Today we think of money as

---

118. George Selgin, "There Was No Place like Canada," *Alt-M*, July 29, 2015, http://www.alt-m.org/2015/07/29/there-was-no-place-like-canada/.

green pieces of paper issued by the government. But during the 19th and early 20th centuries, money meant specie: gold (or sometimes gold and silver). Paper money existed, but it was an IOU issued by a bank, which you could redeem in specie.[119] A $10 bank note meant that if you brought the note to the bank, the bank had to give you $10 worth of gold.

In a fully free system, banks issue their own notes, and although those are redeemable in specie, banks don't keep 100 percent of the gold necessary to redeem their notes on hand. Instead, they hold some gold as well as a variety of other assets, including government bonds, commercial paper (basically a short-term bond issued by businesses), and the various loans on their books.

This is what's known as fractional reserve banking.[120] The basic idea is that not every depositor will seek to redeem his notes for gold at the same time, and so some of the funds deposited at the bank can be invested by the bank and earn a return (which gold sitting in the vault does not). This was an important innovation in banking, which among other benefits meant that banks could *pay* depositors interest on their deposits rather than *charge* depositors for holding their gold in the vault.

But fractional reserve banking also carries with it what's called *liquidity risk*. Even a solvent bank can be illiquid under a fractional reserve system. Although its assets (what it owns) are worth more than its liabilities (what it owes), the bank may not be able to quickly turn assets like long-term loans into cash. As a result, if too many depositors want to redeem their bank notes at once, the bank won't be able to meet its obligations, which can lead it to suspend redemptions or even go out of business.

In the banking systems that most closely approximated free banking, such as Scotland's system up to 1845, this was rarely a problem.[121] Even highly illiquid banks were able to operate without facing bank runs so long as they remained solvent (i.e., so long as their assets were worth more than their liabilities, meaning they could pay their debts).

But in the post–Civil War era, solvent banks frequently experienced liquidity crises. Why? Because of banking regulations.

We're taught to think of regulations as efforts to prevent "greedy"

---

119. George Selgin, "Private Money, Theoretically," *Alt-M*, March 7, 2016, https://www.alt-m.org/2016/03/07/private-money-theoretically/

120. George Selgin, "Should We Let Banks Create Money?" *Independent Review* V, no. 1 (2000): pp. 93–100, http://www.independent.org/pdf/tir/tir_05_1_selgin.pdf.

121. Lawrence H. White, "Free Banking in Britain," Institute of Economic Affairs, 1995, http://iea.org.uk/sites/default/files/publications/files/upldbook115pdf.pdf.

businesses from harming people. But historically banking regulations have often been designed to *exploit the banking system* in order to finance government spending. The typical pattern is to make the freedom of individuals to start banks or to engage in some banking activity, like issuing notes, contingent upon filling the government's coffers. That's what happened with the bond-collateral system imposed by the National Bank Act during the Civil War.

At the time, the federal government was in desperate need of funds to support the war effort, and so among other provisions it created an artificial market for its bonds by essentially forcing banks to buy them. Under the bond-collateral system, U.S. banks could only issue notes if those notes were backed by government bonds. For every $100 of government bonds a bank purchased, it was allowed to issue up to $90 in notes.

How did this make U.S. banking unstable? Imagine a bank that carries two liabilities on its books: the bank notes it has issued and checking account deposits. Now imagine that a customer with a checking account worth $200 wants to withdraw $90 worth of bank notes. In a free system, that's no problem: the bank simply debits his account and issues him $90 in notes. There is no effect on the asset side of the bank's balance sheet.

But consider what happens under the bond-collateral system. In order to issue the bank customer $90 in notes, the bank has to sell some of its assets and buy $100 of government bonds. At minimum that takes time and imposes a cost on the bank. But those problems were exacerbated because the U.S. government began retiring its debt in the 1880s, making its remaining bonds harder and more expensive to buy. The result was that, at a time when the economy was growing quickly, the available supply of paper money was *shrinking*.

This led to the problem of an *inelastic currency*. The demand for paper currency isn't constant—it rises and falls. This was especially true in 19th-century America, which was still a heavily agricultural society. During harvest season, farmers needed extra currency, say, to pay migrant workers to help them bring their crops to market. After the harvest season, demand for currency would shrink, as farmers deposited their notes back at the banks.

This left banks with a lousy set of options. They could either keep a bunch of expensive government bonds on their books (assuming they could get them), so that they could meet a temporary increase in demand for notes—or they could try to meet the temporary demand for cash by drawing down their gold reserves. Typically, they did the latter.

That would be bad enough if it simply meant that a small country bank would find its gold reserves dwindling. But making matters worse was the impact of branch banking restrictions.

Throughout America's history, banks were legally prevented from branching—that is, the same bank was barred from operating in multiple locations spread around the country, the way you can find a Chase bank whether you're in Virginia or California today. Instead Americans were left with what was known as a unit banking system. For the most part, every bank was a stand-alone operation: one office building serving the surrounding community.

One result was a banking system that was highly undiversified. A bank's fortunes were tied to its community. In an oil town, for instance, a downturn in the petroleum market could put the local bank out of business.

But the bigger problem was that unit banking made it harder for banks to deal with liquidity crises. A branched bank always had the option of calling on the cash reserves of its sister branches. This option was off limits to American banks. What developed instead was a system of correspondent banking and the so-called pyramiding of reserves, which concentrated problems in the heart of America's financial center: New York. As economist George Selgin explains, unit banking

> forced banks to rely heavily on correspondent banks for out-of-town collections, and to maintain balances with them for that purpose. Correspondent banking, in turn, contributed to the "pyramiding" of bank reserves: country banks kept interest-bearing accounts with Midwestern city correspondents, sending their surplus funds there during the off season. Midwestern city correspondents, in turn, kept funds with New York correspondents, and especially with the handful of banks that dominated New York's money market. Those banks, finally, lent the money they received from interior banks to stockbrokers at call.
>
> The pyramiding of reserves was further encouraged by the National Bank Act, which allowed national banks to use correspondent balances to meet a portion of their legal reserve requirements. Until 1887, the law allowed "country" national banks—those located in rural areas and in towns and smaller cities—to keep three-fifths of their 15 percent reserve requirement in the form of balances with correspondents or "agents" in any of fifteen designated "reserve

cities," while allowing banks in those cities to keep half of their 25 percent requirement in banks at the "central reserve city" of New York. In 1887 St. Louis and Chicago were also classified as central reserve cities. Thanks to this arrangement, a single dollar of legal tender held by a New York bank might be reckoned as legal reserves, not just by that bank, but by several; and a spike in the rural demand for currency might find all banks scrambling at once, like players in a game of musical chairs, for legal tender that wasn't there to be had, playing havoc in the process with the New York stock market, as banks serving that market attempted to call in their loans....

Nationwide branch banking, by permitting one and the same bank to operate both in the countryside and in New York, would have avoided this dependence of the entire system on a handful of New York banks, as well as the periodic scramble for legal tender and ensuing market turmoil.[122]

It sounds complex, but in the final analysis it's all pretty straightforward. Bankers were not free to run their businesses in a way that would maximize their profits and minimize their risks. The government forced them to adopt an undiversified, inflexible business model they would have never chosen on their own. America's banking system was unstable because government regulations made it unstable, and the solution would have been to liberate the system from government control.

That's not what happened.

The Creation of the Federal Reserve and Its Unimpressive Record

There was widespread recognition at the time that branching restrictions and bond-collateral banking were responsible for the turmoil in the American system. Neither of these regulations existed in Canada, and Canada's stability was anything but a secret. As Americans debated what to do about the financial system during the early 20th century, many pointed to Canada's success and urged repealing these restrictions in the U.S. As economist Kurt Schuler observes:

---

122. George Selgin, "New York's Bank: The National Monetary Commission and the Founding of the Fed," Cato Institute, June 21, 2016, http://www.cato.org/publications/policy-analysis/new-yorks-bank-national-monetary-commission-founding-fed.

Many American economists and bankers admired Canada's relatively unregulated banking system. The American Bankers' Association's "Baltimore plan" of 1894 and a national business convention's "Indianapolis plan" of 1897 referred to Canada's happy experience without American-style bond collateral requirements.[123]

And Selgin also notes:

> Proposals to eliminate or relax regulatory restrictions on banks' ability to issue notes had as their counterpart provisions that would allow banks to branch freely. The Canadian system supplied inspiration here as well. Canadian banks enjoyed, and generally took full advantage of, nationwide branching privileges.[124]

Of course, the push for deregulation of banking did not carry the day, thanks to various pressure groups and the general ideological climate of the country, which had shifted away from the pro-capitalist ideas that had characterized the 19th century. Instead, following the Panic of 1907, America got the Federal Reserve.

The Federal Reserve is America's central bank, which today exercises enormous control over the money supply and the entire financial system. At the time of its creation, however, the Fed was seen as having a more limited function: to protect the safety and soundness of the banking system primarily by furnishing an elastic currency and acting as a "lender of last resort," providing liquidity to banks in times of crises.

So what was the Fed's track record? Did it put an end to the instability of the not-so-free banking period? Most people think so. But most people are wrong.

Bank runs and panics did not decrease in the first decades after the Fed was established. As economist Richard Salsman observes, "Bank failures reached record proportions even before the Great Depression of 1929–1933 and the collapse of the banking system in 1930. From 1913–1922, bank failures averaged 166 per year and the

---

123. Kevin Dowd, *The Experience of Free Banking* (Routledge, 1992), chap. 4.

124. Selgin, "New York's Bank," http://www.cato.org/publications/policy-analysis/new-yorks-bank-national-monetary-commission-founding-fed.

failure rate increased to 692 per year from 1923–1929 despite that period's economic boom."[125]

True, bank panics do decline following the Great Depression, but
that's not thanks to the Fed—the credit for that goes to deposit insurance. (And, as we'll see, deposit insurance laid the groundwork for severe troubles down the road.)

But even if we ignore the period from 1914, when the Fed was established, to the end of World War II...even *then* it is not clear that the
Federal Reserve has been a stabilizing force in the financial system. In
their study "Has the Fed Been a Failure?," economists George Selgin,
William D. Lastrapes, and Lawrence H. White find that:

> (1) The Fed's full history (1914 to present) has been char-
> acterized by more rather than fewer symptoms of mone-
> tary and macroeconomic instability than the decades lead-
> ing to the Fed's establishment. (2) While the Fed's perfor-
> mance has undoubtedly improved since World War II, even
> its postwar performance has not clearly surpassed that of
> its undoubtedly flawed predecessor, the National Banking
> system, before World War I. (3) Some proposed alternative
> arrangements might plausibly do better than the Fed as
> presently constituted.[126]

Those may be controversial claims—although the evidence the authors marshal is impressive—but the key point is this: the conventional wisdom that America's history shows that an unregulated financial system leads to disaster and only a government controlled one can
save the day is without merit. On the contrary, there is far more reason
to suspect that the story runs the other way: that it's government control that takes a naturally stable financial system and makes it fragile.

---

125. Richard Salsman, *Breaking the Banks: Central Banking Problems and Free Banking
Solutions*, American Institute for Economic Research, January 1990, https://
www.researchgate.net/publication/283077988_Breaking_the_Banks_Central_
Banking_Problems_and_Free_Banking_Solutions.

126. George Selgin, William D. Lastrapes, and Lawrence H. White, "Has the Fed
Been a Failure?," Cato Working Papers, December 2010, http://object.cato.org/
sites/cato.org/files/pubs/pdf/WorkingPaper-2.pdf.

The Great Depression and the Role of Government Intervention

The Myth: *An unregulated free market and unrestricted Wall Street greed caused the Great Depression and only the interventionist policies of Franklin D. Roosevelt got us out.*

The Reality: *The Great Depression was caused by government intervention, above all a financial system controlled by America's central bank, the Federal Reserve—and the interventionist policies of Hoover and FDR only made things worse.*

The precise causes of the Great Depression remain a subject of debate, although, as economist Richard Timberlake observed in 2005, "Virtually all present-day economists . . . deny that a capitalist free-market economy in any way caused" it.[127]

At the time, however, the free market was blamed, with much of the ire directed at bankers and speculators. Financiers were seen as having wrecked the economy through reckless speculation. President Hoover came to be viewed as a laissez-faire ideologue who did nothing while the economy fell deeper and deeper into depression, and Franklin D. Roosevelt's interventionist policies under the New Deal were credited with rescuing us from disaster.

Americans came to conclude that the basic problem was the free market and the solution was government oversight and restraint of financiers and financial markets. It's a view that the public, unaware of the consensus of modern economists, continues to embrace.

But the conventional story ignores the elephant in the room: the Federal Reserve. To place the blame for the Great Depression on a free financial system is like placing the blame for the fall of Rome on credit default swaps: you can't fault something that didn't exist. And by the time of the Great Depression, America's financial system was controlled by the Fed.

It's hard to overstate the importance of this fact. The Federal Reserve isn't just any old government agency controlling any old industry. It controls the supply of money, and money plays a role in every economic transaction in the economy. If the government takes over the shoe industry, we might end up with nothing but Uggs and Crocs. But when the government messes with money, it can mess up the entire economy.

The two deadly monetary foes are inflation and deflation. We tend

---

127. Richard H. Timberlake, "Gold Standards and the Real Bills Doctrine in U.S. Monetary Policy," *Econ Journal Watch* 2, no. 2 (August 2005): pp.196–233, https://econjwatch.org/articles/gold-standards-and-the-real-bills-doctrine-in-us-monetary-policy.

to think of inflation as generally rising prices and deflation as generally falling prices. But not all price inflation or price deflation is malignant—and not all price stability is benign. What matters is the relationship between the supply of money and the demand for money—between people's desire to hold cash balances and the availability of cash.

Economic problems emerge when the supply of money does not match the demand for money, i.e., when there is what economists call monetary disequilibrium.[128] Inflation, on this approach, refers to a situation where the supply of money is greater than the public's demand to hold money balances at the current price level. Deflation refers to a situation where the supply of money is less than necessary to meet the public's demand to hold money balances at the current price level.

In a free banking system, as George Selgin has argued, market forces work to keep inflation and deflation in check, i.e., there is a tendency toward monetary equilibrium.[129] Not so when the government controls the money supply. Like all attempts at central planning, centrally planning an economy's monetary system has to fail: a central bank has neither the knowledge nor the incentive to match the supply and demand for money. And so what we find when the government meddles in money are periods where the government creates far too much money (leading to price inflation or artificial booms and busts) or far too little money (leading to deflationary contractions).

And it turns out there are strong reasons to think that the Great Depression was mainly the result of the Federal Reserve making *both* mistakes.

The goal here is not to give a definitive, blow-by-blow account of the Depression. It's to see in broad strokes the way in which government regulation was the *sine qua non* of the Depression. The free market didn't fail: government intervention failed. The Great Depression doesn't prove that the financial system needs regulation to ensure its stability—instead it reveals just how unstable the financial system can become when the government intervenes.

---

128. Steven Horwitz, "Capital Theory, Inflation and Deflation: The Austrians and Monetary Disequilibrium Theory Compared," *Journal of the History of Economic Thought* 18 (Fall 1996): pp. 287-318, http://myslu.stlawu.edu/~shorwitz/Papers/Monetary_JHET_1996.pdf.

129. George Selgin, *The Theory of Free Banking: Money Supply under Competitive Note Issue* (Lanham, MD: Rowman & Littlefield, 1988), http://oll.libertyfund.org/titles/selgin-the-theory-of-free-banking-money-supply-under-competitive-note-issue.

Creating the Boom

Was the stock market crash of 1929 rooted in stock market speculation fueled by people borrowing money to buy stock "on margin," as those who blamed the bankers for the Great Depression claimed? Few economists today think so. As economist Gene Smiley observes:

> There was already a long history of margin lending on stock exchanges, and margin requirements—the share of the purchase price paid in cash—were no lower in the late twenties than in the early twenties or in previous decades. In fact, in the fall of 1928 margin requirements began to rise, and borrowers were required to pay a larger share of the purchase price of the stocks.[130]

For my money, the most persuasive account of the initial boom/bust that set off the crisis places the blame, not on speculators, but on central bankers.

Prior to the publication of John Maynard Keynes's *General Theory* in 1936, the most influential account of the cause of the Great Depression was the Austrian business cycle theory pioneered by Ludwig von Mises and further developed by Friedrich Hayek.[131] The Austrians, in fact, were among the few who predicted the crisis (though not its depth).

What follows is a highly simplified account of the Austrian theory. For a more in-depth treatment, see Lawrence H. White's uniformly excellent book *The Clash of Economic Ideas*, which summarizes the Austrian theory and its account of the Great Depression.[132] For a detailed theoretical explanation of the Austrian theory of the business cycle see Roger W. Garrison's *Time and Money: The Macroeconomics of Capital Structure*.[133]

---

130. Lawrence W. Reed, "Great Myths of the Great Depression," Foundation for Economic Education, November 18, 2012, https://fee.org/resources/great-myths-of-the-great-depression-pdf-and-audio/.

131. Lawrence H. White, *The Clash of Economic Ideas* (2009), chapter 3, http://econfaculty.gmu.edu/pboettke/workshop/Fall2009/White.pdf.

132. Lawrence H. White, *The Clash of Economic Ideas: The Great Policy Debates and Experiments of the Last Hundred Years* (Cambridge University Press, 2012).

133. Roger W. Garrison, *Time and Money: The Macroeconomics of Capital Structure* (Routledge, 2000).

The Austrian theory, in the briefest terms, says that when a central bank creates too much money and expands the supply of credit in the economy, it can spark an artificial boom that ultimately has to lead to a bust.

It's a pretty technical story, so let's start with a simple analogy. Imagine you are planning a dinner party, and you're an organized person, so you keep an inventory of all the items in your kitchen. But the night before your party, some prankster decides to sneak in and rewrite the list so that it shows you have double the ingredients you actually have.

The next morning you wake up and check your inventory list. With so many ingredients available, you decide to invite a few more friends to the dinner. Meanwhile, your kid unexpectedly comes home from college and decides to make herself a large breakfast—but it's no big deal. According to your inventory, you have more than enough eggs and butter to finish your recipe. Of course, your inventory is wrong, and half an hour before your guests arrive, you realize you're short what you need to finish the meal. The dinner is a bust.

Well, something like that happens when the government artificially expands the supply of credit in the economy. It causes everyone to think they're richer than they are and, just like someone planning a meal with an inaccurate inventory list, they end up making decisions—about what to produce and how much to consume—that wouldn't have made sense had they known how many resources were actually available to carry out their plans.

Under the Austrian theory, the key mistake is for the central bank to inject new money into the economic system, typically by creating additional bank reserves.[134] Bank reserves are a bank's cash balance. Just as your cash balance consists of the money you have in your wallet and in your checking account, so a bank's cash balance consists of the cash it has

---

134. How central banks go about conducting monetary policy has varied throughout history. Richard Timberlake explains the process as it took place during the 1920s and 1930s in Richard Timberlake, "Money in the 1920s and 1930s," Foundation for Economic Education, n.d., https://fee.org/articles/money-in-the-1920s-and-1930s/. George Selgin describes the process in more recent times, both prior to the 2008 financial crisis and since in George Selgin, "A Monetary Policy Primer, Part 7: Monetary Control, Then," *Alt-M*, September 20, 2016, https://www.alt-m.org/2016/09/20/monetary-policy-primer-part-7-monetary-control/ and George Selgin, "A Monetary Policy Primer, Part 9: Monetary Control, Now," *Alt-M*, January 10, 2016, https://www.alt-m.org/2017/01/10/monetary-policy-primer-part-9-monetary-control-now/.

in its vault and in the deposit account it maintains with the central bank.

When a central bank creates additional bank reserves, it encourages the banks to lend out the new money at interest, rather than sit on a pile of cash that isn't earning a return. To attract borrowers for this additional money, the banks will lower the interest rate they charge on loans, leading entrepreneurs to invest in plans that would not have been profitable at the previous, higher interest rate.

This is a big problem. In a free market, interest rates coordinate the plans of savers and investors. Investment in productive enterprises requires that real resources be set aside rather than consumed immediately. If people decide to spend less today and save more for the future, there are more resources available to fund things like new businesses or construction projects, and that will be reflected in a lower rate of interest.

But when the central bank pushes down interest rates by creating new money, the lower interest rate does *not* reflect an increase in genuine savings by the public. It is *artificially* low—the prankster has falsified the inventory list. The result is unsustainable boom. The increased business activity is using up resources while at the same time people start consuming more thanks to cheaper consumer credit and a lower return on savings. There is what economist Lawrence H. White calls "a tug-of-war for resources between longer processes of production (investment for consumption in the relatively distant future) and shorter processes (consumption today and in the near future)."[135]

Eventually prices and interest rates start to rise, and entrepreneurs find that they cannot profitably complete the projects they started. The unsustainable boom leads inevitably to a bust. As Mises writes in his 1936 article "The 'Austrian' Theory of the Trade Cycle," once

> a brake is thus put on the boom, it will quickly be seen that the false impression of "profitability" created by the credit expansion has led to unjustified investments. Many enterprises or business endeavors which had been launched thanks to the artificial lowering of the interest rate, and which had been sustained thanks to the equally artificial increase of prices, no longer appear profitable. Some enterprises cut back their scale of operation, others close down or fail. Prices collapse; crisis and depression follow the boom. The crisis and the ensuing period of depression are the culmination of the peri-

---

135. White, *The Clash of Economic Ideas* (2009), chap. 3, http://econfaculty.gmu.edu/pboettke/workshop/Fall2009/White.pdf.

od of unjustified investment brought about by the extension of credit. The projects which owe their existence to the
fact that they once appeared "profitable" in the artificial conditions created on the market by the extension of credit and
the increase in prices which resulted from it, have ceased to be
"profitable." The capital invested in these enterprises is lost to
the extent that it is locked in. The economy must adapt itself
to these losses and to the situation that they bring about.[136]

This, the Austrians argued, was precisely what happened in the
lead up to the 1929 crash. (Two economists, Barry Eichengreen and Kris
Mitchener, who are not part of the Austrian school and who by their own
admission "have vested interests . . . emphasizing other factors in the
Depression," nevertheless found that the empirical record is consistent
with the Austrian story.)[137]

The Federal Reserve during the late 1920s held interest rates artificially low, helping spark a boom—notably in the stock market, which saw
prices rise by 50 percent in 1928 and 27 percent in the first 10 months of
1929. Starting in August of 1929, the Fed tried to cool what it saw as an
overheated stock market by tightening credit. The boom came to an end
on October 29.

Magnifying the Bust

When the government sparks an inflationary boom, the boom has to
end eventually. One way it can end is that the government can try to
keep it going, ever-more rapidly expanding the money supply until price
inflation wipes out the value of the currency, as happened in Germany
during the 1920s.

The other way is for the central bank to stop expanding credit and
allow the boom to turn into a bust. Some businesses go out of business,
some people lose their jobs, investments lose their value: the market
purges itself of the mistakes that were made during the boom period.

That adjustment process is painful but necessary. But what isn't

---

136. Ludwig von Mises, Murray N. Rothbard, F. A. Hayek, and Richard M. Ebeling,
    Austrian Theory of the Trade Cycle and Other Essays (Ludwig von Mises Institute, 2009).

137. Barry Eichengreen and Kris Mitchener, "The Great Depression as a Credit Boom
    Gone Wrong," Bank for International Settlements Working Papers, September
    2003, http://www.bis.org/publ/work137.pdf.

necessaryis for there to be an economy-wide contraction in spend-ing—a deflationary contraction.[138] A deflationary contraction occurs when the central bank allows the money supply to artificially contract, thus not allowing the demand for money to be met. As people scramble to build up their cash balances, they cut back on their spending, which sends ripple waves through the economy. In economist Steven Horwitz's words:

> As everyone reduces spending, firms see sales fall. This reduction in their income means that they and their employees may have less to spend, which in turn leads them to reduce their expenditures, which leads to another set of sellers seeing lower income, and so on. All these spending reductions leave firms with unsold inventories because they expected more sales than they made. Until firms recognize that this reduction in expenditures is going to be economy-wide and ongoing, they may be reluctant to lower their prices, both because they don't realize what is going on and because they fear they will not see a reduction in their costs, which would mean losses. In general, it may take time until the downward pressure on prices caused by slackening demand is strong enough to force prices down. During the period in which prices remain too high, we will see the continuation of unsold inventories as well as rising unemployment, since wages also remain too high and declining sales reduce the demand for labor. Thus monetary deflations will produce a period, perhaps of several months or more, in which business declines and unemployment rises. Unemployment may linger longer as firms will try to sell off their accumulated inventories before they rehire labor to produce new goods. If such a deflation is also a period of recovery from an inflation-generated boom, these problems are magnified as the normal adjustments in labor and capital that are required to eliminate the errors of the boom get added on top of the deflation-generated idling of resources.[139]

---

138. Lawrence H. White, "Did Hayek and Robbins Deepen the Great Depression?," *Journal of Money Credit and Banking* 40, no. 4 (June 2008): pp. 751–68, https://www.researchgate.net/publication/5168713_Did_Hayek_and_Robbins_Deepen_the_Great_Depression.

139. Steven Horwitz, "Deflation: The Good, the Bad, and the Ugly," Foundation for Economic Education, January 5, 2010, https://fee.org/articles/deflation-the-good-the-bad-and-the-ugly/.

In short, a deflationary contraction can unleash a much more severe and widespread drop in prices, wages, and output and a much more severe and widespread rise in unemployment than is necessary to correct the mistakes of an artificial boom.

Unfortunately, that's exactly what happened during the Great Depression. Three factors were particularly important in explaining the extreme deflationary contraction that occurred during the 1930s.

1. Bank failures

Earlier, I discussed how government regulation of banking made banks more fragile. In particular, I noted that government regulations prevented banks from branching, making them far less robust in the face of economic downturns.

That remained true throughout the 1920s and '30s, leaving U.S. banks vulnerable in a way that Canadian banks, which could and did branch, were not. Not a single Canadian bank failed during the Depression. In the United States, 9,000 banks failed between 1930 and 1933 (roughly 40 percent of all U.S. banks), destroying the credit these banks supplied and so further contracting the money supply.

A report from the Federal Reserve Bank of St. Louis describes it this way:

> Starting in 1930, a series of banking panics rocked the U.S. financial system. As depositors pulled funds out of banks, banks lost reserves and had to contract their loans and deposits, which reduced the nation's money stock. The monetary contraction, as well as the financial chaos associated with the failure of large numbers of banks, caused the economy to collapse.
>
> Less money and increased borrowing costs reduced spending on goods and services, which caused firms to cut back on production, cut prices and lay off workers. Falling prices and incomes, in turn, led to even more economic distress. Deflation increased the real burden of debt and left many firms and households with too little income to repay their loans. Bankruptcies and defaults increased, which caused thousands of banks to fail.[140]

---

140. David C. Wheelock, "The Great Depression, an Overview," *The Great Depression*,

(The banking panics of 1932, it should be noted, were at least in part the result of fears that incoming president FDR would seize Americans' gold and take the nation off the gold standard—which he ultimately did. Another contributing factor was the protectionist Smoot-Hawley tariff passed in 1930, which, among many other negative impacts on the economy, devastated the agricultural sector and many of the unit banks dependent on it.[141])

Thanks to these massive bank failures, the U.S. was being crippled by a severe deflation, and yet the Federal Reserve—which, despite being on a pseudo-gold standard, could have stepped in[142]—did nothing.

2. The check tax

Also contributing to the collapse of the money supply was the check tax, part of the Revenue Act of 1932, signed into law by Hoover. The Act raised taxes in an effort to balance the budget, which was bad enough in the midst of a deflationary crisis. But the worst damage was done by the check tax. This measure placed a 2-cent tax (40 cents today) on bank checks, prompting Americans to flee from checks to cash, thereby removing badly needed cash from the banks. The result, economists William Lastrapes and George Selgin argue, was to reduce the money supply by an additional 12 percent.[143]

3. Hoover's high-wage policy

The net result of the bank failures and the check tax was a credit-driven

n.d., https://www.stlouisfed.org/~/media/Files/PDFs/Great-Depression/the-great-depression-wheelock-overview.pdf.

141. Theodore Phalan, "The Smoot-Hawley Tariff and the Great Depression," Foundation for Economic Education, February 29, 2012, https://fee.org/articles/the-smoot-hawley-tariff-and-the-great-depression/.

142. George Selgin, "The Rise and Fall of the Gold Standard in the United States," *Policy Analysis*, no. 729 (June 20, 2013), http://object.cato.org/sites/cato.org/files/pubs/pdf/pa729_web.pdf; and Timberlake, "Gold Standard and the Real Bills Doctrine," https://econjwatch.org/articles/gold-standards-and-the-real-bills-doctrine-in-us-monetary-policy.

143. William D. Lastrapes and George Selgin, "The Check Tax: Fiscal Folly and the Great Monetary Contraction," *Journal of Economic History* 57, no. 4 (December 1997): pp. 859–78), http://www.jstor.org/stable/2951163.

deflation the likes of which the U.S. had never seen. As Milton Friedman and Anna Schwartz explain in their landmark *Monetary History of the United States*:

> The contraction from 1929 to 1933 was by far the most severe business-cycle contraction during the near-century of U.S. history we cover, and it may well have been the most severe in the whole of U.S. history. . . . U.S. net national product in constant prices fell by more than one-third. . . . From the cyclical peak in August 1929 to the cyclical trough in March 1933, the stock of money fell by over a third.[144]

Why is a deflationary contraction so devastating? A major reason is because prices don't adjust uniformly and automatically, which can lead to what scholars call economic dis-coordination. In particular, if wages don't fall in line with other prices, this effectively raises the cost of labor, leading to—among other damaging consequences—unemployment. And during the Great Depression, although most prices fell sharply, wage rates did not.

One explanation is that wages are what economists call "sticky downward": people don't like seeing the number on their paychecks go down, regardless of whether economists are assuring them that their purchasing power won't change. The idea of sticky prices is somewhat controversial, however—in earlier downturns, after all, wages fell substantially, limiting unemployment.

What is certainly true is that *government intervention* kept wages from falling—particularly the actions of President Hoover and, later, President Roosevelt.

Hoover believed in what was called the "high-wage doctrine," a popular notion in the early part of the 20th century. The high-wage doctrine said that keeping wages high helped cure economic downturns by putting money into the pockets of workers who would spend that money, thereby stimulating the economy.

When the Depression hit and prices began falling, Hoover urged business leaders not to cut wages. And the evidence suggests that they listened (whether at Hoover's urging or simply because they too accepted the high-wage doctrine). According to economists John Taylor and George Selgin:

---

144. Milton Friedman and Anna Jacobson Schwartz, *A Monetary History of the United States 1867–1960* (Princeton University Press, 1971), http://press.princeton.edu/titles/746.html.

> Average hourly nominal wage rates paid to 25 manufac-
> turing industries were 59.3 cents in October 1929, and
> 59.5 cents by April 1930. Wage rates had fallen only to 59.1
> cents by September 1930, despite substantially reduced
> output prices and profits. Compare this to the 20 percent
> decline in nominal wage rates during the 1920–21 depres-
> sion. During the first year of the Great Depression the av-
> erage wage rate fell less than four-tenths of one percent.[145]

Hoover would go on to put teeth into his request for high wages, signing into law the Davis-Bacon Act in 1931 and the Norris-
LaGuardia Act of 1932, both of which used government power to prop
up wages.[146] FDR would later go on to implement policies motivated by the high-wage doctrine, including the 1933 National Industrial
Recovery Act, the 1935 National Labor Relations Act, and the 1938
Fair Labor Standards Act.

The problem is that the high-wage doctrine was false—propping
up wages only meant that labor became increasingly expensive at the
same time that demand for labor was falling. The result was mass
unemployment.

The Aftermath

It's worth repeating: this is far from a full account of the Great Depression. It's not even a full account of the ways the *Federal Reserve* contributed to the Great Depression (many scholars fault it for the so-called
Roosevelt Recession of 1937–38).[147] What we have seen is that there are
strong reasons to doubt the high school textbook story of the Great Depression that indicts free markets and Wall Street.

---

145. Jason Taylor and George Selgin, "By Our Bootstraps: Origins and Effects of the
     High-Wage Doctrine and the Minimum Wage," *Journal of Labor Research* XX, no.
     4 (Fall 1999), http://people.terry.uga.edu/selgin/files/Bootstraps.pdf.

146. Steven Horwitz, "Herbert Hoover: Father of the New Deal," Cato Institute,
     September 29, 2011, http://www.cato.org/publications/briefing-paper/herbert-
     hoover-father-new-deal.

147. Douglas A. Irwin, "Gold Sterilization and the Recession of 1937–1938,"
     Financial History Review 19, no. 3 (December 2012): pp. 249–67, http://www
     .dartmouth.edu/~dirwin/1937.pdf.

We've also started to see a pattern that recurs throughout history: government controls create problems, but the response is almost never to get rid of the problematic controls. Instead, it's to pile new controls on top of old ones, which inevitably creates even more problems.

And that's what happened with the Great Depression.

Did we abolish the Fed? No.

Did we return to the pre–World War I classical gold standard? No.

Did we abolish branch banking restrictions? No.

Instead, we created a vast new army of regulatory bodies and regulatory acts, which would spawn future problems and crises: above all, the Glass-Steagall Act of 1933, which separated investment and commercial banking and inaugurated federal deposit insurance. I'll turn to that next.

How the New Deal Made the Financial System Less Safe

The Myth: *New Deal regulation of the financial system made the system safer.*

The Reality: *New Deal regulation of the financial system failed to address the real source of the problems that led to the Great Depression and laid the foundation for future crises.*

Although there is widespread agreement among economists that the Great Depression was not caused by the free market, there is also widespread, if not universal, agreement that the government's regulatory *response* to the Great Depression made the system safer. Many commentators on the 2008 financial crisis argue that it was the abandonment of the post–New Deal regulatory regime during the 1980s and 1990s that set the stage for our current troubles.

There are three major parts of the government's regulatory response to the Great Depression:

1. Banking regulation
2. Housing regulation
3. Securities regulation

The government's top priority on housing was to bail out mortgage borrowers and lenders, spawning the creation of the Federal Housing Administration and Fannie Mae. The Securities Act of 1933 and the Securities Exchange Act of 1934, which established the Securities and Exchange Commission, were passed to control the trading of securities in the name of protecting investors and making securities markets more orderly and fair.

Here I'm going to focus on banking regulation, specifically the Banking Act of 1933, often referred to as Glass-Steagall. Among other provisions, Glass-Steagall created a separation between commercial and investment banking activities, and established the Federal Deposit Insurance Corporation (FDIC), which insures banking deposits.

Conventional wisdom says Glass-Steagall made the system safer. The truth is that it failed to address the causes of the Great Depression, and instead contributed to future crises.

The Senseless Separation of Commercial and Investment Banking

During the 1920s, commercial banks (i.e., those that accepted deposits and made loans) started expanding into lines of business traditionally dominated by investment banks, such as underwriting and trading securities. The development of universal banking allowed commercial banks to become, in effect, one-stop shops for their customers, and they grew quickly by taking advantage of economies of scope and offering customers major discounts on brokerage services. (Technically, commercial banks did not usually engage in investment banking activities, but instead operated through closely allied security affiliates.)

In 1932, the government launched an investigation of the crash of '29, which became known as the Pecora hearings. The hearings regaled Americans with claims of banking abuses arising from banks' involvement in securities, although the evidence for these claims was, to be generous, scant.[148]

---

148. See, for instance, Norbert Michel, "The Glass-Steagall Act: Unraveling the Myth," Heritage Foundation, April 28, 2016, http://www.heritage.org/research/reports/2016/04/the-glasssteagall-act-unraveling-the-myth; Anthony Saunders, "Securities Activities of Commercial Banks: The Problem of Conflicts of Interest," *Federal Reserve Bank of Philadelphia Business Review* (July/August 1985): pp. 17–27, https://www.fedinprint.org/items/fedpbr/y1985ijul-augp17-27.html; Randall S. Kroszner and Raghuram G. Rajan, "Is the Glass-Steagall Act Justified? A Study of the U.S. Experience with Universal Banking Before 1933," *American Economic Review* 84, no. 4 (September 1994): pp. 810–32, http://www.jstor.org/stable/2118032; and James S. Ang and Terry Richardson, "The Underwriting Experience of Commercial Bank Affiliates Prior to the Glass–Steagall Act: A Reexamination of Evidence for Passage of the Act," *Journal of Banking and Finance* 18, no. 2 (January 1994): pp. 351-95.

Whatever the truth, the Pecora hearings enraged the public and bolstered a number of pressure groups and politicians who argued that universal banking made banks and the financial system more fragile and demanded the separation of commercial and investment banking activities.

The opponents of universal banking made several arguments to support their agenda, but the central claim was that securities were inherently more risky than the traditional banking activities of taking deposits and making loans, and so allowing banks to have securities affiliates made them less sound.

But the starting premise—that securities activities were riskier than commercial banking activities—was not obviously true. As economist Robert Litan writes, "the underwriting of corporate securities probably involves less risk than extending and holding loans."[149] That's because underwriting risk typically only lasts a few days and involves assets that are more liquid than a standard loan, which can stay on a bank's books for years and be difficult to sell.

Certainly *some* activities of securities affiliates were riskier than some activities of traditional commercial banks. But it doesn't follow that a commercial bank that engages in securities activities via its affiliate is taking on more risk overall. That's because it is also gaining the benefits of diversification.

Diversification reduces risk. A single bond may be less risky than any given stock, yet a diversified portfolio of stocks can be less risky than the single bond. Similarly, even if a commercial bank that accepts deposits and makes loans enjoys less risk than an investment bank, that doesn't imply that the commercial bank increases its overall risk by taking on investment banking activities. On the contrary, it is entirely possible for the risk-reducing features of diversification to outweigh the additional risk.

Apparently, this was true of most banks with securities affiliates in the lead up to the Great Depression. The best analysis of the pre-1933 period, by economist Eugene White, finds that banks with securities affiliates were *more* stable than those without them:

> One of the most convincing pieces of evidence that the union
> of commercial and investment banking posed no threat to

149. Robert E. Litan, "Reuniting Investment and Commercial Banking," *Cato Journal* 7, no. 3 (Winter 1988): pp. 803–21), https://object.cato.org/sites/cato.org/files/serials/files/cato-journal/1988/1/cj7n3-12.pdf.

parent banks is the significantly higher survival rate of banks with securities operations during the massive bank failures of 1930–1933. While 26.3% of all national banks failed during this period, only 6.5% of the 62 banks which had affiliates in 1929 and 7.6% of the 145 banks which conducted large operations through their bond departments closed their doors.[150]

This suggests that, by limiting banks' ability to diversify their activities, Glass-Steagall *made banks more risky*. This risk would become manifest later in the century when commercial banks increasingly found themselves unable to compete with foreign universal banks. (As for the claim that the repeal of Glass-Steagall in 1999 contributed to the 2008 financial crisis, I'll address that later.)

Deposit Insurance and the Problem of Moral Hazard

The proximate cause of the Great Depression was the wave of bank failures that took place in the early 1930s. Federal deposit insurance was touted as a way to stop bank runs, protecting depositors and shielding sound but illiquid banks from the so-called contagion effects of bank failures.

But why was deposit insurance seen as the solution? Canada, as I've noted, did not experience a single bank failure during the Depression, even though it lacked deposit insurance. U.S. banks were unstable because, unlike Canadian banks, they could not branch, a fact that was widely recognized at the time.

And deposit insurance did not exactly have a great record. It had been tried at the state level for more than a hundred years, and every deposit insurance scheme that looked anything like the system eventually adopted under Glass-Steagall ended in failure.[151]

The obvious solution to banking instability would have been to eliminate branch banking restrictions, allowing banks to consolidate and diversify geographically. But there were pressure groups who wanted to

---

150. Eugene N. White, "Before the Glass-Steagall Act: An Analysis of the Investment Banking Activities of National Banks," *Explorations in Economic History* 23, no. 1 (January 1986): pp. 33–55, https://ideas.repec.org/a/eee/exehis/v23y1986i1p33-55.html.

151. Charles W. Calomiris, "Is Deposit Insurance Necessary? A Historical Perspective," *Journal of Economic History* 50, no. 2 (June 1990): pp. 283–95, http://web.mit.edu/14.71/www/Calomiris%20deposit%20insurance.pdf.

protect unit banking and who thereby benefited from deposit insurance.[152] As Representative Henry Steagall, the politician who was the driving force behind deposit insurance, admitted, "This bill will preserve independent dual banking [i.e., unit banking] in the United States . . . that is what the bill is intended to do."[153]

What were the effects? As is so often the case in the history of finance, government support for the industry creates problems that are used to justify government control of the industry.

Deposit insurance encourages risk-taking.[154] Given the nature of the doctrine of limited liability, bank owners are always incentivized to take risks, since they enjoy unlimited upside gains and are insulated from the downside: their stock can become worthless, but they aren't personally liable for the business's debts. (Although, it's worth mentioning that prior to 1933, U.S. bankers faced double liability: if their bank went out of business, they could be required to pay up to two times their initial investment to reimburse depositors.) Depositors act as a counterweight: they are risk averse and will flee imprudent banks.

Deposit insurance reduces that counterweight by introducing moral hazard into the banking system. "Moral hazard" refers to the fact that when risks are insured against, people take more risks because they bear a smaller cost if things go wrong. In the case of deposit insurance, depositors are incentivized to patronize the bank that offers the highest interest rate, regardless of how much risk it is taking. As economist Richard Salsman puts it: "Deposit insurance was established in order to avert future bank runs. But its history has demonstrated a singular inducement to bankers to become reckless and pay excess yields, while encouraging depositors to run *to* bad banks instead of *away* from them."[155] If things

---

152. Carter H. Golembe, "The Deposit Insurance Legislation of 1933: An Examination of Its Antecedents and Its Purposes," *Political Science Quarterly* LXXVI, n.d., https://fraser.stlouisfed.org/docs/meltzer/goldep60.pdf.

153. Eugene N. White, *The Regulation and Reform of the American Banking System, 1900–1929* (Princeton University Press, 2014).

154. Matthew Jaremski and Charles Calomiris, "Stealing Deposits: Deposit Insurance, Risk-Taking, and the Removal of Market Discipline in Early 20th-Century Banks," Heritage Foundation, January 27, 2017, http://www.heritage.org/research/reports/2017/01/stealing-deposits-deposit-insurance-risk-taking-and-the-removal-of-market-discipline-in-early-20th-century-banks.

155. Richard Salsman, "The Collapse of Deposit Insurance—and the Case for Abolition," American Institute for Economic Research, 1993, https://www.researchgate.net/publication/266485826_THE_COLLAPSE_OF_DEPOSIT_

go bad, after all, the depositors will be bailed out—at least up to the cap set by the FDIC, a cap that has ballooned over time from $2,500 in 1934 (more than $40,000 in 2008 dollars) to $250,000 in 2008.

The moral hazard introduced by deposit insurance was particularly intense given the scheme adopted by the FDIC. In normal insurance plans, such as car insurance or life insurance, if you are riskier you pay more for your insurance.[156] But until a 1991 rule change, the FDIC charged banks a flat rate based on the size of their deposits. This meant that riskier banks were effectively being subsidized by prudent banks.

The government was not blind to this moral hazard problem. FDR had initially opposed deposit insurance on the grounds that, as he put it in a letter to the *New York Sun* in 1932:

> It would lead to laxity in bank management and careless-
> ness on the part of both banker and depositor. I believe that
> it would be an impossible drain on the Federal Treasury to
> make good any such guarantee. For a number of reasons of
> sound government finance, such plan would be quite dan-
> gerous.[157]

(There's no evidence FDR ever changed his mind on this point: deposit insurance made it into law because the president saw no other way to get his banking bill passed.[158])

In order to deal with the moral hazard problem created by deposit insurance, the government sought to limit risk-taking through command-and-control regulation. Discussing Glass-Steagall, economist Gerald O'Driscoll writes:

> Among other things, the act prevented banks from being af-
> filiated with any firm engaged in the securities business; es-

INSURANCE_-_AND_THE_CASE_FOR_ABOLITION.

156. Robert L. Hetzel, "Too Big to Fail: Origins, Consequences, and Outlook," *FRB Richmond Economic Review* 77, no. 6 (November/December 1991): (pp. 3–15), http://papers.ssrn.com/sol3/papers.cfm?abstract_id=2126164.

157. Norbert J. Michel, "The Other Glass-Steagall: The FOMC and the FDIC," Heritage Foundation, January 13, 2016, http://www.heritage.org/research/commentary/2016/1/the-other-glass-steagall-the-fomc-and-the-fdic.

158. Michael Perino, "What FDR Hated About Glass-Steagall," *Bloomberg*, June 14, 2013, https://www.bloomberg.com/view/articles/2013-06-14/what-fdr-hated-about-glass-steagall.

tablished limits on loans made by banks to affiliates, including holding company affiliates; prohibited the payment of interest on demand accounts; and empowered the Federal Reserve Board to regulate interest rates paid on savings and time deposits. These regulations were intended to provide for the safety and soundness of the banking system.[159]

However, these and other regulations meant to address the risks created by deposit insurance would fail to restrain government-encouraged risk-taking by banks and actually create even greater problems in the future. I'll be discussing those problems far below. But it's worth noting here that it was deposit insurance that set the stage for the doctrine that would eventually become known as "too big to fail."[160]

The Origins of "Too Big to Fail"

Businesses fail all the time and life goes on. What's so different about financial institutions? It goes back to the peculiar nature of their business model; namely, even healthy financial institutions are typically illiquid. In industry parlance, banks borrow short and lend long. That is, they take in money from depositors who can draw down their accounts at any time and they lend those funds to business and consumer borrowers who repay their loans over a longer time horizon.

It's a brilliant system in that it dramatically increases the financial capital available in the economy without forcing depositors to tie up their money in long-term investments. But it also carries with it a vulnerability: a healthy bank can fail if too many of its depositors demand their money back at once.

Most people—today and in the past—have believed that banking failures are "contagious": a run on an insolvent bank can lead depositors at healthy banks to fear their money isn't safe, setting off a cascade of bank failures and the collapse of the financial system.

Historically,[161] this was seldom a genuine problem in systems that

---

159. Gerald P. O'Driscoll, Jr., "Deposit Insurance in Theory and Practice," *Cato Journal* 7, no. 3 (Winter 1988): pp. 661–81, http://object.cato.org/sites/cato.org/files/serials/files/cato-journal/1988/1/cj7n3-6.pdf.

160. Hetzel, "Too Big to Fail," pp. 3–15, http://papers.ssrn.com/sol3/papers.cfm?abstract_id=2126164.

161. Lawrence H. White, "Free Banking in History and Theory," GMU Working

approximated free banking: solvent banks rarely suffered bank runs as the result of runs on insolvent banks. And financiers had developed effective private mechanisms,[162] such as last-resort lending by clearinghouses, for dealing with widespread panics when they did occur. Nevertheless, concern over the contagion effects of bank failures has played an important role in justifying the expansion of government control over banking.

One solution to the problem of contagion was for the government to institute central banks, which would act as a lender of last resort. The idea, as formulated by Walter Bagehot in his famous 1873 work *Lombard Street*, was that a central bank's role in a crisis should be to lend to *solvent* banks on good collateral at high interest rates.[163]

But during the 1930s, the Federal Reserve didn't perform this function. As Norbert Michel points out, "In 1929, the Federal Reserve Board prohibited the extension of credit to any member bank that it suspected of stock market lending, a decision that ultimately led to a 33 percent decline in the economy's stock of money."[164] But instead of insisting that the central bank do better, politicians decided that additional regulations were needed to address the problem.

This led to the creation of deposit insurance. Now, instead of propping up solvent but illiquid institutions, the FDIC would try to prevent runs by promising to bail out depositors (up to a legally defined limit) even of insolvent banks.

But now regulators started to see contagion lurking around every corner, and came to believe that large financial institutions could not be allowed to fail lest that lead to the failure of other banking institutions tied to them in some way, thus setting off a chain of failures that could bring down the system. Thus was born the doctrine of "too big to fail."

Paper in Economics, no. 14-07, May 10, 2014, https://papers.ssrn.com/sol3/papers.cfm?abstract_id=2435536.

162. Norbert Michel, "The Fed's Failure as a Lender of Last Resort: What to Do About It," Heritage Foundation, August 20, 2014, http://www.heritage.org/research/reports/2014/08/the-feds-failure-as-a-lender-of-last-resort-what-to-do-about-it.

163. George Selgin, "The Courage to Refuse," Alt-M, October 31, 2015, http://www.alt-m.org/2015/10/31/courage-to-refuse/.

164. Michel, "The Fed's Failure as a Lender of Last Resort," http://www.heritage.org/research/reports/2014/08/the-feds-failure-as-a-lender-of-last-resort-what-to-do-about-it.

Actually, that name is misleading. A "too big to fail" institution can be allowed to fail in the sense that the company's shareholders can be wiped out. What the government doesn't let happen to such companies is for their debt holders (including depositors) to lose money: they are made whole.

Under Section 13(c) of the Federal Deposit Insurance Act of 1950, the FDIC was empowered to bail out a bank "when in the opinion of the Board of Directors the continued operation of such bank is essential to provide adequate banking service in the community."[165] It would first use that authority in 1971 to save Boston's Unity Bank, but such bailouts would quickly become the norm, with the major turning point being the bailout of Continental Illinois in 1984.[166]

As a result of "too big to fail," much of the remaining debt holder-driven discipline was eliminated from the system. Thanks to the moral hazard created by the government's deposit insurance and "too big to fail" subsidies, financial institutions were able to grow larger, more leveraged, and more reckless than ever before, creating just the sort of systemic risk that deposit insurance was supposed to prevent.

The bottom line is that Glass-Steagall failed on two counts: it did not fix the problems that had led to the Great Depression and it created new problems that would in time contribute to further crises.

The Myth of Banking Deregulation

Myth: *Finance was deregulated during the 1980s and 1990s, laying the groundwork for the 2008 financial crisis.*

Reality: *Although some financial regulations were rolled back during the late 20th century, the overall trend was toward increased government control.*

According to many commentators, the New Deal regulatory regime led to the longest period of banking stability in U.S. history, but that regime was destroyed by free market ideologues who, during the late

---

165. United States Congress, "Federal Deposit Insurance Corporation Act (FDIC Act)," Public Law 81-797, 81st Congress, S. 2822, September 21, 1950, https://fraser.stlouisfed.org/scribd/?title_id=1101&filepath=/docs/historical/congressional/federal-deposit-insurance-act.pdf.

166. Russel Roberts, "Gambling with Other People's Money: How Perverted Incentives Caused the Financial Crisis," Mercatus Center, George Mason University, May 2010, https://www.mercatus.org/system/files/RUSS-final.pdf.

20th century, oversaw a radical deregulation of the financial industry. This, they conclude, laid the groundwork for the 2008 financial crisis.

But while some restrictions on finance were lifted during this period, other controls were added—and the *subsidization* of finance that drained the system of market discipline only increased. As we entered the 21st century, our financial system was not a free market but a Frankenstein monster: large and imposing but inflexible and unstable.

The Collapse of the New Deal Regulatory Regime and the Re-Regulatory Response

The banking system was in many respects fairly stable in the decades following the New Deal, with far fewer bank failures than in the past.

By far the most important factor in postwar stability was not New Deal financial regulations, however, but the strength of the overall economy from the late 1940s into the 1960s, a period when interest rates were relatively stable, recessions were mild, and growth and employment were high.

Part of the credit for this stability goes to monetary policy. Although the classical gold standard[167] that had achieved unrivaled monetary stability during the late 19th century had fallen apart during World War I, the Bretton Woods Agreement struck in the aftermath of World War II retained some link between national currencies and gold, limiting the government's power to meddle with money. According to economist Judy Shelton:

> [T]here can be little question that the sound money environment that reigned in the postwar years contributed to the impressive economic performance of both the victors and the vanquished and enabled the world to begin reconstructing an industrial base that would raise living standards to new heights for the generations that followed.[168]

This would change as an increasingly expansive and expensive

---

167. George Selgin, "Ten Things Every Economist Should Know About the Gold Standard," *Alt-M*, June 4, 2015, https://www.alt-m.org/2015/06/04/ten-things-every-economist-should-know-about-the-gold-standard-2/.

168. Judy Shelton, *Money Meltdown* (Free Press, 1998), https://www.amazon.com/Money-Meltdown-Judy-Shelton/dp/0684863944.

U.S. government cut its remaining ties to gold in 1971. The volatile in-flation and interest rates that followed would throw the financial sys-tem into disarray, revealing the hidden weaknesses created by the New Deal regulatory regime.[169] The failure of the New Deal regime would become most clear during the Savings & Loan crisis.[170]

The New Deal had divided up the financial industry into high-ly regimented, tightly controlled silos. Insurance companies, invest-ment banks, commercial banks, and Savings & Loans (or thrifts, as they were often called) all operated in their own universes, free from outside competition. The players in each sub-industry faced their own unique set of restrictions as well as their own government subsidies and privileges.

Thrifts were limited by the government almost exclusively to ac-cepting deposits and making loans to homebuyers. In exchange for promoting home ownership, they were given special privileges by the government, including protection from competition and the ability to pay a slightly higher interest rate on their deposits than traditional banks. It was a simple business model best summed up by the famous 3-6-3 rule: borrow at 3 percent, lend at 6 percent, and be on the golf course by 3.

But this setup made thrifts enormously vulnerable to interest rate risk. They were making long-term loans—often thirty years—at fixed interest rates, yet were borrowing short-term via savings ac-counts. What would happen if depositors could suddenly get a high-er return on their savings elsewhere, say by parking their savings in one of the new money market accounts? What would happen if infla-tion rose and their savings actually began losing its purchasing power? Depositors might flee, depriving the thrifts of capital. Thrifts, mean-while, would have their hands tied: Regulation Q set a cap on the in-terest rate they could pay on deposits.[171] And even if their hands weren't tied by Regulation Q, paying higher interest rates would cause thrifts to lose money on their existing loans: they could end up paying out

---

169. https://www.researchgate.net/publication/283077988_Breaking_the_Banks_
    Central_Banking_Problems_and_Free_Banking_Solutions.

170. Salsman, *Breaking the Banks*, http://www.econlib.org/library/Enc/Savingsand
    LoanCrisis.html.

171. R. Alton Gilbert, "Requiem for Regulation Q: What It Did and Why It Passed
    Away," Federal Reserve Bank of St. Louis, February 1986, https://research.stlouisfed
    .org/publications/review/86/02/Requiem_Feb1986.pdf.

10 percent or more in interest to their depositors while receiving only 6 percent in interest payments from the loans already on their books.

All of this is exactly what happened when, starting in the late 1960s, the Federal Reserve began expanding the money supply to help the government finance a burgeoning welfare state and the Vietnam War. By the late 1970s, inflation had reached double digits.

As interest rates rose, thrifts began to fail in large numbers, but rather than unwind them, the government tried to save them. It did so in part through a program of partial deregulation. For example, the government allowed thrifts to diversify their assets, e.g., by moving into commercial real estate or through purchasing high yield bonds, and eliminated Regulation Q's cap on deposit interest rates. Meanwhile, the government also dramatically expanded its deposit insurance subsidy for banks, including thrifts, increasing coverage in 1980 from $40,000 to $100,000.[172]

The government's program was disastrous—but not because of any problem inherent in deregulation. Had the government pursued a genuine free-market policy by allowing failed institutions to go out of business, ending the moral hazard created by deposit insurance, and *then* allowing the remaining thrifts to enter new lines of business and pay market interest rates, there still would have been pain and the process would have been messy, but the financial system would have moved in a more sound, more stable direction. Instead, the government created one of the greatest catastrophes in U.S. banking history by propping up and subsidizing insolvent "zombie banks," giving them the power and incentive to gamble with taxpayers' money.

To say a thrift is insolvent is to say that its capital has been wiped out. The bank no longer has any skin in the game. That creates a perverse set of incentives. It pays the thrift's owners to make huge gambles, which, if they pay off, will make them rich, and if they don't, will leave them no worse off. Deposit insurance, meanwhile, gives them virtually unlimited access to capital, since they can promise to pay high interest rates on deposits to depositors who don't have to worry about the risks the bank is taking.

Well, the thrifts that took huge gambles generally ended up taking huge losses, destroying far more wealth than if they had simply been wound down when they reached insolvency. This was not an indictment

172. Christine M. Bradley, "A Historical Perspective on Deposit Insurance Coverage," *FDIC Banking Review*, n.d., https://www.fdic.gov/bank/analytical/banking/2000dec/brv13n2_1.pdf.

of deregulation. It was an indictment of *re-regulation*—of regulatory reform that removed or changed *some* controls while retaining and expanding other controls and subsidies.

There are two lessons here. The first is that the New Deal regulatory regime could not last. It was (partially) dismantled because it collapsed under the pressure of bad monetary policy from the Federal Reserve and the perverse constraints and incentives imposed by regulators. (Technological innovations in the financial industry and other economic forces, such as increased global competition, also played a role.)

The second lesson is that if we want to evaluate the conventional narrative about financial deregulation, we have to investigate more carefully which regulations and subsidies were repealed, which regulations and subsidies were changed (and in what way), which regulations and subsidies *weren't* changed or repealed, and what the consequences were. To speak simply of "deregulation" blinds us to the fact that in many respects financial intervention was increasing during this period, and that even when some regulations were altered or rescinded, the system itself was dominated by government distortions and controls.

The Big Picture

At the time of the 2008 financial crisis, there were—in addition to hundreds of state-level regulators—seven federal regulators overseeing the financial industry:[173]

- Federal Reserve
- Office of the Comptroller of the Currency
- Office of Thrift Supervision
- Securities and Exchange Commission
- Federal Deposit Insurance Corporation
- Commodities Futures Trading Commission
- National Credit Union Administration

No matter what metric you look at, it's hard to find any evidence

---

173. Lee Hudson Teslik, "The U.S. Financial Regulatory System," *Global Economy in Crisis*, October 1, 2008, http://www.cfr.org/financial-regulation/us-financial-regulatory-system/p17417.

that financial regulation by these bodies was decreasing overall.[174] According to a study from the Mercatus Center, outlays for banking and financial regulation grew from $190 million in 1960 to $1.9 billion in 2000.[175] By 2008 that number had reached $2.3 billion. (All in constant 2000 dollars.) In the years leading up to the financial crisis, regulatory staff levels mostly rose, budgets increased, and the annual number of proposed new rules went up. There were also major expansions of government regulation of the financial industry, including Sarbanes-Oxley, the Privacy Act, and the Patriot Act.

None of this comes close to conveying the scale of industry regulation, however. The simple fact is that there was virtually nothing a financial firm could do that wasn't overseen and controlled by government regulators.

There were, to be sure, some cases of genuine deregulation, but on the whole, these were policies that were undeniably positive, such as the elimination of Regulation Q and other price controls, and the removal of branch banking restrictions. And typically the bills that instituted these policies expanded regulation in others ways.[176]

But consider what didn't change. As we've seen, the major sources of instability in the U.S. financial system were branch banking restrictions, the creation of the Federal Reserve with its power to control the monetary system, and the creation of deposit insurance and the "too big to fail" doctrine, which encouraged risky behavior by banks.

Yet it was only the first of those problems that was addressed during the era of deregulation, when the Riegle-Neal Interstate Banking and Branching Efficiency Act eliminated restrictions on branching in 1994. The Federal Reserve was left untouched, and the scope of deposit insurance expanded: the government raised the cap on uninsured deposits to $100,000, though in reality it effectively insured most deposits

---

174. Mark A. Calabria, "Did Deregulation Cause the Financial Crisis?," Cato Institute, July/August 2009, http://www.cato.org/policy-report/julyaugust-2009/did-deregulation-cause-financial-crisis.

175. Veronique de Rugy and Melinda Warren, "Regulatory Agency Spending Reaches New Height: An Analysis of the U.S. Budget for Fiscal Years 2008 and 2009," Mercatus Center at George Mason University and Murray Weidenbaum Center on the Economy, Government, and Public Policy, August 2008, https://wc.wustl.edu/files/wc/imce/2009regreport.pdf.

176. Norbert Michel, "The Myth of Financial Market Deregulation," Heritage Foundation, April 28 2016, http://www.heritage.org/research/reports/2016/04/the-myth-of-financial-market-deregulation.

through its policy of bailing out the creditors of institutions seen as "too big to fail."

What, then, do people have in mind when they say that deregulation led to the Great Recession? Advocates of this view generally point to two examples: the "repeal" of Glass-Steagall, and the failure of the government to regulate derivatives.

Did the "Repeal" of Glass-Steagall Make the Banking System More Fragile?

When people say that Glass-Steagall was repealed, they're referring to the Gramm-Leach-Bliley Act of 1999 (GLBA). The GLBA did not actually repeal Glass-Steagall.[177] Instead, it repealed Section 20 and Section 32 of the Glass-Steagall Act. There was nothing banks could do after the repeal that they couldn't do before the repeal, save for one thing: they could be affiliated with securities firms. Under the new law, a single holding company could provide banking, securities, and insurance services, increasing competition and allowing financial institutions to diversify.

Why this change? There were numerous factors. First of all, the barriers between commercial and investment banks had been eroding, due in part to innovations in the financial industry, such as money market mutual funds, which allowed investment banks to provide checking deposit-like services. Glass-Steagall didn't change what was going on in financial markets so much as recognize that a distinction between commercial and investment banking was no longer tenable.

At a theoretical level, the case *for* Glass-Steagall had always been tenuous, and this had been reinforced by more recent scholarship that argued that the Great Depression was not in any significant way the result of banks dealing in securities.

Even more compelling, virtually no other country separated commercial and investment banking activities. In fact, as the authors of a 2000 report on the GLBA noted, "compared with other countries, U.S. law still grants fewer powers to banks and their subsidiaries than to financial holding companies, and still largely prohibits the mixing of

---

177. Oonagh McDonald, "The Repeal of the Glass-Steagall Act: Myth and Reality," Cato Institute, November 16, 2016, https://www.cato.org/publications/policy-analysis/repeal-glass-steagall-act-myth-reality.

banking and commerce."[178] The authors go on to observe that less restrictive banking laws were associated with greater banking stability, not less. The question, then, is whether the GLBA's marginal increase in banking freedom played a significant role in the financial crisis.[179] Advocates of this thesis claim that it allowed the risk-taking ethos of investment banks to pollute the culture of commercial banking. But here are the facts:

- The two major firms that failed during the crisis, Bear Stearns and Lehman Brothers, were pure investment banks, unaffiliated with depository institutions. Merrill-Lynch, which came close to failing, wasn't affiliated with a commercial bank either.[180] Their problems were not caused by any affiliation with commercial banking, but by their traditional trading activities.
- On the whole, institutions that combined investment banking and commercial banking did better during the crisis than banks that didn't.[181]
- Glass-Steagall had stopped commercial banks from underwriting and dealing securities, but it hadn't barred them from investing in things like mortgage-backed securities or collateralized debt obligations: to the extent banks suffered losses on those instruments during the crisis, Glass-Steagall wouldn't have prevented it.[182]

---

178. James R. Barth, R. Dan Brumbaugh Jr., and James A. Wilcox, "Policy Watch: The Repeal of Glass-Steagall and the Advent of Broad Banking," *Journal of Economic Perspectives* 14, no. 2 (Spring 2000): pp. 191–204, http://pubs.aeaweb.org/doi/pdfplus/10.1257/jep.14.2.191.

179. Yaron Brook and Don Watkins, "Why the Glass-Steagall Myth Persists," *Forbes*, November 12, 2012, http://www.forbes.com/sites/objectivist/2012/11/12/why-the-glass-steagall-myth-persists/.

180. Mark A. Calabria, "Did Deregulation Cause the Financial Crisis?," Cato Institute, July/August 2009, http://www.cato.org/policy-report/julyaugust-2009/did-deregulation-cause-financial-crisis.

181. Calabria, "Did Deregulation Cause the Financial Crisis?," http://www.cato.org/policy-report/julyaugust-2009/did-deregulation-cause-financial-crisis.

182. Peter J. Wallison, "Did the 'Repeal' of Glass-Steagall Have Any Role in the Financial Crisis? Not Guilty. Not Even Close," *Financial Market Regulation*, 2011, http://faculty.msmc.edu/hossain/grad_bank_and_money_policy/did%20the%20repeal%20of%20glass%20steagall_wallison.pdf.

In light of such facts, even Barack Obama acknowledged that "there is not evidence that having Glass-Steagall in place would somehow change the dynamic."[183]

Finally, it is important to emphasize that the GLBA was not a deregulatory act, strictly speaking. As with much else that went on during the era, it was an instance of *re*-regulation. The government still dictated what financial institutions could and couldn't do down to the smallest detail. Indeed, aside from repealing two sections from Glass-Steagall, the GLBA expanding banking subsidies and regulations, including regulations on thrifts, new privacy and disclosure rules, as well as new Community Reinvestment requirements for banks.

Were Derivatives Unregulated?

The role of derivatives in fostering the financial crisis has been wildly overstated. Take the credit default swaps (CDSs) that contributed to the downfall of insurance giant AIG.[184] In the simplest terms, a CDS is a form of insurance. If I make a loan to Acme Corp., I can buy a CDS from a CDS seller that pays me if Acme defaults on its obligations. All I've done is transfer an existing risk—Acme's default on a debt—from me to the CDS seller.

On the whole, CDSs and other derivatives didn't create new risks: they mainly transferred risks among financial players, from those who didn't want to bear them to those who did. True, these instruments were used by some firms, not just to hedge existing risks, but to take on new risks in the belief their bets would pay off—and the firms that made bad bets should have suffered the consequences. But focusing on derivatives detracts from the real story of the financial crisis.

At the most basic level, the financial crisis resulted from financial institutions using enormous leverage to buy mortgage-backed securities that turned out to be far riskier than most people assumed. Take CDSs out of the equation, and the crisis still would have happened. The details

183. Matt Taibbi, "Obama Defends His Finance Reform to *Rolling Stone*: A Response," *Rolling Stone*, October 26, 2012, http://www.rollingstone.com/politics/news/obama-defends-his-finance-reform-record-to-rolling-stone-a-brief-response-20121026.

184. Peter J. Wallison, "Credit-Default Swaps Are Not to Blame," American Enterprise Institute, June 1, 2009, https://www.aei.org/publication/credit-default-swaps-are-not-to-blame/.

would have played out differently, but the bottom line would have been the same.

That said, it simply wasn't true that derivatives were "unregulated." As Heritage's Norbert Michel points out, "Federal banking regulators, including the Federal Reserve and the OCC [Options Clearing Corporation], constantly monitor banks' financial condition, including the banks' swaps exposure."[185] In particular, banking capital requirements explicitly took into account swaps. (To the extent CDSs were a problem they were a problem *encouraged* by regulation, since, under Basel I capital regulations, CDSs allowed banks to hold less capital.[186])

When people say that derivatives were unregulated, they are typically referring to the 2000 Commodity Futures Modernization Act (CFMA). But the CFMA didn't prevent regulation of CDSs. It merely prevented the Commodities Futures Trading Commission from regulating them, and (likely) treating them as futures contracts that had to be traded on an exchange. (For various technical reasons, CDSs don't generally make sense to trade on an exchange rather than "over-the-counter.")

It is possible that *different* regulations or behavior by regulators might have prevented the financial crisis. Certainly it is easy to concoct such scenarios after the fact. But the "deregulation" story pretends that regulators were eager to step in and prevent a crisis and simply lacked the power. That view is completely without merit. The government had all the power it needed to control the financial industry, and such deregulation as did take place was largely (though not universally) *good*.

The real problem, as we'll see, was that *government intervention* had created an unstable system that encouraged the bad decisions that led to the crisis.

Free Markets Didn't Create the Great Recession

Myth: *The Great Recession was caused by free-market policies that led to irrational risk taking on Wall Street.*

---

185. Norbert Michel, "The Myth of Financial Market Deregulation," Heritage Foundation, April 28, 2016, http://www.heritage.org/research/reports/2016/04/the-myth-of-financial-market-deregulation.

186. Arnold Kling, "Not What They Had in Mind: A History of Policies that Produced the Financial Crisis of 2008," Mercatus Center, September 2009, https://www.mercatus.org/publication/not-what-they-had-mind-history-policies-produced-financial-crisis-2008.

Reality: *The Great Recession could not have happened without the vast web of government subsidies and controls that distorted financial markets.*

As with the Great Depression, the causes of the Great Recession remain controversial, even among free-market-leaning economists. What we know for sure is that the free market can't be blamed, because there was no free market in finance: finance (including the financial side of the housing industry) was one of the most regulated industries in the economy. And we also know that, absent some of those regulations, the crisis could *not* have occurred.

What Everyone Agrees On

The basic facts aren't in dispute. During the early to mid-2000s, housing prices soared. At the same time, lending standards started to decline as the government encouraged subprime lending (i.e., lending to borrowers who had a spotty credit history and found it difficult to get conventional mortgages), and as businesses saw profit opportunities in extending loans to riskier borrowers and in offering riskier kinds of loans.

Increasingly, mortgage originators did not keep the loans they made on their own books, but sold them off to Fannie Mae, Freddie Mac, investment banks, or other financial firms, which bundled these loans into mortgage-backed securities (MBSs) and other financial instruments—instruments often rated super-safe by the three government-approved credit ratings agencies—and sold them to investors.

Financial institutions of all kinds invested heavily in housing, often financing these investments with enormous leverage (i.e., far more debt than equity). These investments went bad when housing prices began to decline and the underlying loans began to default at higher rates than expected.

As the value of MBSs and other mortgage-related instruments fell, the financial institutions that held them started to suffer losses, setting off a chain of failures and bailouts by the federal government, and ultimately causing credit markets to freeze up, threatening the entire financial system.

On these points, there is agreement. But why did this happen? What led so many institutions to invest so heavily in housing? Why did they make these investments using extreme amounts of leverage—and why were they able to take on so much debt in the first place? What led credit markets to break down in 2008? And what led the problems in housing and finance to spill over into the rest of the economy, turning a financial crisis into the Great Recession?

As with our discussion of the Great Depression, this is not intended to be a definitive, blow-by-blow account of the crisis. The goal is to lay to rest the myth that our financial system was anything close to free, and to see some of the ways in which government intervention played a role in creating the Great Recession.

The Federal Reserve Makes the Housing Boom Possible

We typically speak of central bankers controlling interest rates. More precisely, they influence interest rates by expanding or contracting the money supply. Recall from our discussion of the Great Depression that central bankers can make two crucial mistakes when it comes to monetary policy: they can be too loose (leading to price inflation or credit booms) or they can be too tight (leading to deflationary contractions).

The best explanation of the root cause of the housing boom is that, during the early 2000s, the Federal Reserve's monetary policy was too loose, setting off—or at least dramatically magnifying—a boom in housing.

There are various metrics you can look at to assess whether monetary policy is too tight or too expansionary, but they all point in the same direction during this period. Take interest rates. As economist Lawrence H. White points out:

> The Fed repeatedly lowered its target for the federal funds interest rate until it reached a record low. The rate began 2001 at 6.25 percent and ended the year at 1.75 percent. It was reduced further in 2002 and 2003; in mid-2003, it reached a then-record low of 1 percent, where it stayed for one year. The real Fed funds rate was negative—meaning that nominal rates were lower than the contemporary rate of inflation—for more than three years. In purchasing power terms, during that period a borrower was not paying, but rather gaining, in proportion to what he borrowed.[187]

As White and others have argued, the Fed's easy credit found its way

---

187. David Beckworth, *Boom and Bust Banking: The Causes and Cures of the Great Recession* (Independent Institute, 2012).

(mostly) into the residential home market, where it had two major effects.[188]

First, it helped drive up housing prices, as lower interest rates made buying a home more attractive.[189] A $150,000 mortgage would have cost $2,400 a month at the 18 percent interest rates borrowers faced in 1980. But at the 6 percent rate they could often get during the 2000s that fell to a mere $1,050 a month. Low interest rates, then, made it possible for more people to buy homes, to buy bigger homes, and to speculate in housing, helping spark the boom in housing.

Second, the Fed's policies encouraged riskier lending practices. Partly this was a side-effect of the rising price of housing. As long as home prices are rising, the risk that a borrower will default on his mortgage is low, because he can always sell the house rather than quit paying down the debt. But if housing prices stop rising or even fall? Then the home might end up being worth less than what is owed on the mortgage and it can make economic sense for the underwater home buyer to walk away from the home.

Fed policy also encouraged more risky *kinds* of loans. One obvious example was the proliferation of adjustable-rate mortgages (ARMs), where borrowers took on the risk that interest rates would rise. ARMs dominated subprime and other non-prime lending by 2006 as borrowers sought to take advantage of the Fed's ultra-low short-term interest rates—a trend encouraged by Greenspan.[190] But the net result was that when interest rates *did* eventually rise, defaults went, well, through the roof.

And the riskiest kinds of loans—no-money down, interest-only adjustable-rate mortgages, low-doc and no-doc loans? All of them seemed to make sense only because of the boom in housing prices.

Absent cheap money from the Fed, there would have been no crisis. The groundwork for 2008 was laid in 1914.

What Role Did Government Housing Policy Play?

During the 1990s and 2000s, the government attempted to increase

---

188. David Beckworth, "Was Monetary Policy Loose During the Housing Boom?," *Alt-M*, April 25, 2015, http://www.alt-m.org/2015/04/25/was-monetary-policy-loose-during-the-housing-boom/.

189. Mark Zandi, *Financial Shock: A 360° Look at the Subprime Mortgage Implosion, and How to Avoid the Next Financial Crisis* (FT Press, 2008).

190. Sue Kirchhoff and Barbara Hagenbaugh, "Greenspan Says ARMs Might Be Better Deal," *USA Today*, February 23, 2004, http://usatoday30.usatoday.com/money/economy/fed/2004-02-23-greenspan-debt_x.htm.

home ownership, especially by subprime borrowers. Through the Community Reinvestment Act, tax incentives, Fannie Mae and Freddie Mac, and other channels, the government actively sought to put more Americans in homes.

But what role did the government's housing crusade play in creating the Great Recession? There seem to be at least two important roles.

First, it contributed to the Fed's easy money becoming concentrated in the housing market. In 1997, the government passed the Taxpayer Relief Act, which eliminated capital gains taxes on home sales (up to $500,000 for a family and $250,000 for an individual). According to economists Steven Gjerstad and Vernon Smith, "the 1997 law, which favored houses over all other investments, would have naturally led more capital to flow into the housing market, causing an increased demand—and a takeoff in expectations of further increases in housing prices."[191] By the time the Federal Reserve started easing credit in 2001, they argue, the housing market was the most rapidly expanding part of the economy and became a magnet attracting the Fed's new money.

Second, government housing policy encouraged the lowering of lending standards that further inflated the housing bubble.[192] Two key forces here were the Community Reinvestment Act (CRA) and especially the Government-Sponsored Enterprises (GSEs), Fannie Mae and Freddie Mac, which were the main conduits through which the government pursued its affordable housing agenda.[193]

Starting in 1992, Fannie and Freddie were required to help the government meet its affordable housing goals by repurchasing mortgages made to lower income borrowers. Over the next decade and a half, the Clinton and Bush administrations would increase the GSEs' affordable housing quotas, which over time forced them to lower their underwriting standards by buying riskier and riskier mortgages. American Enterprise Institute scholar Peter J. Wallison sums up the role this would ultimately play in the crisis:

191. Jeffrey Friedman and Richard A. Posner, *What Caused the Financial Crisis* (University of Pennsylvania Press, 2010).

192. Charles Calomiris and Stephen Haber, "Calomiris and Haber on Fragile by Design," *Library of Economics and Liberty*, podcast, February 17, 2014, http://www.econtalk.org/archives/2014/02/calomiris_and_h.html.

193. Richard M. Salsman, "Altruism: The Moral Root of the Financial Crisis," *Objective Standard* 4, no. 1, n.d., https://www.theobjectivestandard.com/issues/2009-spring/altruism-financial-crisis/.

By 2008, before the financial crisis, there were 55 million mortgages in the US. Of these, 31 million were subprime or otherwise risky. And of this 31 million, 76% were on the books of government agencies, primarily Fannie and Freddie. This shows where the demand for these mortgages actually came from, and it wasn't the private sector. When the great housing bubble (also created by the government policies) began to deflate in 2007 and 2008, these weak mortgages defaulted in unprecedented numbers, causing the insolvency of Fannie and Freddie, the weakening of banks and other financial institutions, and ultimately the financial crisis. [194]

To be sure, lending standards would decline industry-wide during the 2000s. In large part this was because other financial institutions could not compete with the GSEs without dropping their own lending standards. And although the government was not the sole force driving increased risk-taking in housing, it was the government that first insisted it was virtuous to exercise less caution if it meant getting more people into homes, and that continued to *approve* of declining lending standards throughout the housing boom. It started the trend of lower standards, which only later spread to the rest of the market.

Had the government not encouraged the imprudent lending that defined the crisis, it is unlikely the crisis would have occurred.

Government Policy and the Financial Sector

The Fed's monetary policy and the government's housing policy helped ensure that there would be a massive malinvestment in real estate. But why did those risks become concentrated and magnified in the financial sector?

The main transmission mechanism was MBSs and other derivatives, which moved mortgage risk from mortgage originators to large financial institutions such as Fannie Mae, Freddie Mac, and the big commercial and investment banks, as well as institutional investors. Not only did these players make big bets on housing, they did so using enormous

---

194. Natalie Goodnow, "'Hidden in Plain Sight': A Q&A with Peter Wallison on the 2008 Financial Crisis and Why It Might Happen Again," American Enterprise Institute, January 13, 2015, https://www.aei.org/publication/hidden-plain-sight-qa-peter-wallison-2008-financial-crisis-might-happen/.

leverage—often thirty or forty dollars of debt for every one dollar of equity by the end of the crisis. (Fannie and Freddie were levered even more.)

Why? Was it irrationality and greed run amok? Well, no. Although there was plenty of irrationality and greed, government interference in financial markets once again played a key role in what happened.

Specifically, there are at least three major forces at play here: (1) the credit ratings agencies, (2) bank capital regulation, and (3) government-created moral hazard.

1. The ratings agencies

The conventional view is that financiers loaded up on mortgage derivatives because they placed the desire for riches above fear of risk. The truth is more complex. In large part the reason mortgage products became so popular was because they seemed relatively *safe*.[195]

Why did they appear safe? One reason is that the credit ratings agencies tasked with evaluating credit instruments said they *were* safe.

The three credit ratings agencies in the lead up to the crisis—Moody's, Standard and Poor's, and Fitch—were not free-market institutions. By the time of the crisis, they were the only institutions the government permitted to supply official ratings on securities. As political scientist Jeffrey Friedman notes, "A growing number of institutional investors, such as pension funds, insurance companies, and banks, were prohibited from buying bonds that had not been rated 'investment grade' (BBB- or higher) by these firms, and many were legally restricted to buying only the highest-rated (AAA) securities."[196]

But no one could compete with the ratings agencies, and so they had virtually no incentive to assess risks accurately. Thanks to bad incentives, incompetence, and honest error, the ratings agencies stamped many mortgage derivatives AAA—as safe as ExxonMobil's and Berkshire Hathaway's debt. These products thereby seemed to be safe but relatively high-yielding assets.

---

195. Nicola Gennaioli, Andrei Shleifer, and Robert Vishny, "Neglected Risks, Financial Innovation, and Financial Fragility," *Journal of Financial Economics* 104 (2012): pp 452–68, http://www.econ.nyu.edu/user/galed/fewpapers/FEW%20 S13/Gennaioli-Shleifer-Vishny.pdf.

196. Jeffrey Friedman, "A Crisis of Politics, Not Economics: Complexity, Ignorance, and Policy Failure," *Critical Review* 21, no. 2–3 (2009): pp. 127–83, http:// criticalreview.com/crf/pdfs/Friedman_intro21_23.pdf.

Did the buyers of mortgage-backed securities put stock in the quality of the ratings agencies' assessments? Many did. Research from economist Manuel Adelino found that while investors did not rely on ratings agencies to assess the riskiness of most investments, they did take AAA ratings at face value.[197] Anecdotal evidence backs Adelino up. For example, a *New York Times* article from 2008 reported:

> When Moody's began lowering the ratings of a wave of debt in July 2007, many investors were incredulous.
>
> "If you can't figure out the loss ahead of the fact, what's the use of using your ratings?" asked an executive with Fortis Investments, a money management firm, in a July 2007 e-mail message to Moody's. "You have legitimized these things, leading people into dangerous risk."[198]

But from another perspective, it hardly mattered whether anyone *believed* the ratings were accurate. The sheer fact these instruments were rated AAA and AA gave financial institutions an incentive to load up on them thanks to government-imposed capital regulations.

2. Bank-capital regulations

As we saw when we looked at the New Deal's regulatory response to the Great Depression, at the same time that the government began subsidizing banks through federal deposit insurance it started regulating banks to limit the risk taking deposit insurance encouraged.[199] In particular, the government sought to limit how leveraged banks could be through bank-capital regulations.

---

197. Manuel Adelino, "Do Investors Rely Only on Ratings? The Case of Mortgage-Backed Securities," MIT Sloan School of Management and Federal Reserve Bank of Boston, November 24, 2009, https://fisher.osu.edu/supplements/10/9861/01132010-Manuel%20Adelino.pdf.

198. Gretchen Morgenson, "Debt Watchdogs: Tamed or Caught Napping?," *New York Times*, December 6, 2008, http://www.nytimes.com/2008/12/07/business/07rating.html.

199. Don Watkins, "How the New Deal Made the Financial System Less Safe," *Voices for Reason*, Ayn Rand Institute, blog, February 8, 2017, https://ari.aynrand.org/blog/2017/02/08/how-the-new-deal-made-the-financial-system-less-safe.

Bank capital is a bank's cushion against risk.[200] It's made up of the cash a bank holds and the equity it uses to finance its activities, which can act as a shock absorber if its assets decline in value. The greater a bank's capital, the more its assets can decline in value before the bank becomes insolvent. Prior to the FDIC, it wasn't unusual for banks' capital levels to hover around 25 percent. By the time of the 2008 financial crisis, bank capital levels were generally below 10 percent—sometimes well below 10 percent.

Bank-capital regulations forced banks to maintain a certain amount of capital. Until the 1980s, there were no worked-out standards governing capital regulation, but in 1988, the U.S. and other nations adopted the Basel Capital Accord, or what became known as Basel I.[201]

Basel is what's known as risk-based capital regulation. That means that the amount of capital a bank has to have is determined by the riskiness of its assets, so that the riskier an asset, the more a bank has to finance it with equity-capital rather than debt. Assets the Basel Committee on Banking Supervision regarded as riskless, such as cash and government bonds, required banks to use no capital. For assets judged most risky, such as commercial loans, banks had to use at least 8 percent of equity-capital to fund them. Other assets fell somewhere in between 0 and 8 percent.

What's important for our story is that securities issued by "public-sector entities," such as Fannie and Freddie, were considered half as risky as conventional home mortgages: a bank could dramatically reduce its capital requirements by buying mortgage-backed securities from Freddie Mac and Fannie Mae rather than making mortgage loans and holding them on its books. In 2001, the U.S. adopted the Recourse Rule, which meant that privately issued asset-backed securities rated AAA or AA were considered just as risky as securities issued by the GSEs.

The net result was that banks were encouraged by government regulators to make big bets on mortgage derivatives rated AAA or AA by the ratings agencies.

---

200. Russ Roberts and Charles Calomiris, "Calomiris on Capital Requirements, Leverage, and Financial Regulation," *EconTalk*, podcast, March 5, 2012, http://www.econtalk.org/archives/2012/03/calomiris_on_ca.html.

201. Susan Burhouse, John Feid, and Keith Ligon, "Basel and the Evolution of Capital Regulation: Moving Forward, Looking Back," *FDIC*, January 14, 2013, https://www.fdic.gov/bank/analytical/fyi/2003/011403fyi.html.

3. Moral hazard

As we've seen, many financial players really did believe that mortgage-related products were relatively safe. Government certainly encouraged that impression. The Federal Reserve was assuring markets that interest rates would remain low and that it would fight any significant declines in securities markets with expansionary monetary policy.[202] The credit ratings agencies were stamping many mortgage derivatives AAA. Congress and the president were touting the health of the mortgage market, which was putting ever more Americans into homes.

But it is mysterious why more people weren't worried. Contrary to the housing industry's bromide, there were examples of housing prices going down—even nationally, as in the Great Depression. There was also evidence that many of the loans underlying the mortgage instruments were of increasingly poor quality. And we can find plenty of examples of Cassandras who foresaw the problems that were to come.

Some market participants did understand how risky mortgage-related derivatives were, but were not overly concerned with those risks because they could pass them on to others. Mortgage originators, for instance, were incentivized to make bad loans because they could pawn off the loans to securitizers such as Fannie and Freddie.

But what about the people ultimately buying the mortgage securities? Why were they willing to knowingly take big risks? Part of the answer is that the moral hazard introduced through government policies including (but not limited to) "too big to fail" had convinced them that they would reap the rewards on the upside, yet would be protected on the downside thanks to government intervention. We've seen, after all, how the government had started bailing out financial institutions seen as "too big to fail" decades before the crisis.

Many people resist this hypothesis. It simply doesn't seem plausible that investors were thinking to themselves, "This could easily blow up, but it's okay, I'll get bailed out." But tweak that thought just a bit: "There's some risk this will blow up, as there is with every financial investment, but there's also a good probability the government will step in and shield me from most if not all of the losses." How could that *not* influence investor decision-making?

---

202. Greg Ip and John D. McKinnon, "Fed's Greenspan Pledges to Keep Rates Low, Roiling Bond Market," *Wall Street Journal,* July 16, 2003, https://www.wsj.com/articles/SB105827765311988700.

And there is also another, more subtle effect of moral hazard to consider. Over the course of decades, the government had increasingly insulated debt holders from downside risk. Thanks to deposit insurance, "too big to fail," and other government measures, debt holders simply weren't hit over the head by the message that they could get wiped out if they weren't careful.

More generally, the regulatory state had taught people that they need not exercise their own independent judgment about risk. Is your food safe? The FDA has seen to that. Is your airplane safe? The FAA has seen to that. Is your doctor competent? If he wasn't, the government wouldn't allow him to practice medicine. Is it surprising, then, that even many sophisticated investors thought they didn't need to check the work of the ratings agencies?

To be clear, I don't think government regulation fully explains the widespread failure to accurately assess the risks of mortgages. Part of it I chalk up to honest error. It's easy to see the folly of people's judgment with hindsight, but people aren't making decisions with hindsight. I also think there are psychological reasons why many people are vulnerable to speculative bubbles. But moral hazard almost certainly played a role in reducing investors' sensitivity to risk and in allowing many financial institutions to take on dangerous amounts of leverage.

The Federal Reserve Made Things Worse

Given the massive malinvestment in residential real estate, the declining lending standards, and the concentration of mortgage risks in the financial sector that took place during the 2000s, the bust was inevitable. But was the bust sufficient to explain the economy-wide recession that followed?

No doubt there was going to be a recession as the result of the crisis, but there is a compelling argument that the severity of the recession—the thing that made it the *Great* Recession—was causally tied to the government's response. In particular, what turned a crisis into a catastrophe was overly *tight* monetary policy from the Federal Reserve in response to the crisis.

Tight money, recall, can lead to deflationary spirals, where debtors have trouble repaying their debts, putting stress on financial institutions, and output and employment fall as people have trouble adjusting to declining prices. And the argument is that although the Federal Reserve started easing money in mid-2008, it did not do so nearly enough, leading to a monetary contraction and hence the deflation that turned a financial crisis into the Great Recession.

Judging whether monetary policy is too tight isn't straightforward. Typically people look to interest rates, but interest rates alone can be deceiving. Although the low interest rates of the early 2000s were associated with easy money, easy money can also lead to *high interest rates*, as it did in the late 1970s (or in Zimbabwe during its bout of hyperinflation).

But by looking at other, more revealing indicators, a number of economists have concluded that monetary policy tightened substantially during 2008–2009, leading to a decline in total spending in the economy and helping spread the pain in the housing and financial sectors to the rest of the economy.[203]

The Ultimate Lesson

Ayn Rand often stressed that the U.S. isn't and has never been a fully free, fully capitalist nation. Rather, it's been a mixed economy, with elements of freedom and elements of control. This means that we cannot, as is so often done, automatically blame bad things on the free element and credit good things to the controlled element. As Rand explained:

> When two opposite principles are operating in any issue, the scientific approach to their evaluation is to study their respective performances, trace their consequences in full, precise detail, and then pronounce judgment on their respective merits. In the case of a mixed economy, the first duty of any thinker or scholar is to study the historical record and to discover which developments were caused by the free enterprise of private individuals, by free production and trade in a free market—and which developments were caused by government intervention into the economy.[204]

---

203. Scott Summer, "The Real Problem Was Nominal," *Cato Unbound*, September 14, 2009, https://www.cato-unbound.org/2009/09/14/scott-sumner/real-problem-was-nominal.

204. Ayn Rand, "The Intellectual Bankruptcy of Our Age," Ayn Rand Institute Campus, 1962 recorded lecture, https://campus.aynrand.org/works/1962/01/01/the-intellectual-bankruptcy-of-our-age. See also Ayn Rand, Leonard Peikoff, and Peter Schwartz, *The Voice of Reason: Essays in Objectivist Thought* (New York: Meridian, 1990).

As we've seen, the field of finance has been dominated by government intervention since this country's founding. In this series, I've tried to highlight some of the most important government subsidies and controls affecting the industry, and indicate how *they* were often responsible for the very problems they were supposedly created to solve.

If you examine the historic and economic evidence carefully, the conclusion that follows is clear: if we value economic stability, our top priority should be to liberate the field of finance from government support and government control.

The Dubious Origins and Purpose of Central Banking

By Raymond C. Niles

For more than a century, economists, politicians, and bankers—from across the political spectrum—have seen central banking as a necessary and vital institution. It is seen as a vital stabilizer of the economy and a backstop and regulator to a financial system otherwise prone to crisis.

The last chapter has shown that our financial system never operated in a free, laissez-faire manner. Numerous problems that our banking system experienced—ranging from bank runs and periodic money stringencies in the 19th century, to massive lending failures such as the most recent housing crisis—are not the result of a freely operating system. Rather, they are the result of government interference in the banking system.

In the 19th century, unit banking laws that prohibited nation-wide banking networks and bond-collateral requirements that impeded the elastic issuance of money led to our banking system being fragile, unresponsive to the needs of the economy, and crisis-prone. This provided the impetus for the formation of America's central bank, the Federal Reserve System, in 1913.

However, the Federal Reserve System was not the first central bank in the Western capitalist economies. In form and purpose, it was modeled after the Bank of England. A look at the history of the Bank of England shows that all central banks, regardless of their putative reason for existing, end up having one primary function: to finance government spending.

The Bank of England: The First Modern Central Bank

The beginning of modern central banking can be traced to 1694, the year that the new King William III of England had to raise a lot of money and needed a new way to do it. Just six years before, the Dutch prince and princess William and Mary of Holland had assumed the throne of England in a bloodless coup that became known as the Glorious Revolution. The coup was instigated by members of England's Parliament, who became appalled at the financial and other excesses of King Charles II and his successor, King James II. Among these depredations were confiscations and taxations, all imposed without the consent of Parliament.

The new King William III, invited in by Parliament, would have to adhere to a new rule: no taxation without approval of Parliament.

This presented a dilemma to the new king, who brought to England the enmities of his native Holland. Within a year of assuming the throne, England was allied with Holland in the Nine Year's War against France, with fighting spanning from North America to Ireland and the European Continent. The challenge the new king faced was how to pay for it. Until this time, a nascent private banking industry had emerged in England, begun out of the practice of goldsmithing. Goldsmiths, who accepted gold for safekeeping by customers, issued receipts for this gold. Soon these receipts circulated as money, since they could be exchanged, on demand, for gold at the offices of the goldsmith. In the mid-1600s, the goldsmiths became bankers in the modern sense. They extended loans and began paying interest to depositors, in order to attract more gold deposits to facilitate the making of further loans (White 1999, 12).

The goldsmith banks made money by lending to importers and domestic manufacturers and, eventually, the government. King Charles II was an especially large borrower, and when he could not repay his debts, he simply reneged on them in 1672 (Smith 1990, 11).

Given this sorry history, the goldsmith bankers were reluctant to extend new loans to the English Crown, even several decades after the default.

To make it worthwhile for a nervous banker to extend a loan to the government, King William III had to sweeten the deal. He persuaded Parliament to charter a new bank, named the Bank of England, for the express purpose of providing a loan to the government of £1,200,000 ($225,000,000 in current U.S. dollars). The government authorized the Bank to issue banknotes for the full amount, even though the Bank was not yet fully capitalized, and then immediately loan that amount to the government. The note issue was so large that the English economy actually suffered from price inflation, which occurs when too many new banknotes (i.e., money) chase a given quantity of goods (Smith 1990, 12).

Over the years, the attractiveness of getting bank loans and avoiding the need to levy new taxes led to many more borrowings from the Bank of England. However, to overcome the riskiness of making further loans to the government, still more privileges had to be given to the bank to "sweeten the pot" and make it profitable for the bank. As these privileges were piled on by Acts of Parliament, the status of the Bank of England changed to one of privilege with respect to the goldsmith banks, which operated under ordinary commercial law and had no such advantages. In 1697, the government banned the formation of new banks without consent of Parliament, awarded the owners of the Bank of England limited liability (which the goldsmith bankers did not have), and mandated that all taxes and custom duties had to be paid through the Bank of England. As a quid pro quo for these valuable privileges, the Bank of England made a further large loan to the English Crown (Smith 1990, 12).

In 1709, Parliament forbade any other bank from operating as a joint stock company. All other banks had to operate as partnerships with six or fewer partners. This ensured that the banks competing with the Bank of England would be small and poorly capitalized compared to the Bank of England. In gratitude, the Bank of England made another large loan to the English government (Smith 1990, 13).

Further privileges were enacted to the Bank of England, in exchange for still more loans, in 1713, 1742, 1751, 1781, and 1800. The Bank of England had become the piggybank for the English government. With these special privileges and its exclusive banking relationship with the government, the Bank of England grew in size. Competing banks in London shrank in number and size and stopped issuing banknotes around 1780. The Bank of England had achieved a monopoly on the issuance of banknotes in London and the surrounding area. A monopoly on money issuance is a feature of modern central banking. In the United States, all money is issued by the Federal Reserve System, America's central bank, just as all banknotes in England are issued today by the Bank of England (Smith 1990, 13).

The reliance of the government on financing from the Bank of England accelerated with the onset of the Napoleonic War in 1803. The war in many respects was the first World War, spanning from the Americas to all parts of Europe, and involving land and sea forces. England had the largest navy in the world, an expensive undertaking, with which it blockaded the entire European continent to starve Napoleon of essential raw materials.

To pay for all this, the government extracted so much new money from the Bank of England that the bank was forced to dishonor its obligation to pay gold to its noteholders upon demand. Under ordinary commercial law, this would have meant the bankruptcy of the Bank, but Parliament needed the Bank's money and it authorized the suspension of gold payments. The pattern of authorizing suspensions of the obligation to pay gold would happen many times in subsequent years, both in England and later in the United States, usually during periods of war.

The obligation to convert its notes into gold upon demand would normally place a severe limit on how many banknotes the Bank of England could issue, just as it had placed a severe limit on how many banknotes the goldsmith banks could issue decades earlier when they were still in the business of providing banknotes. Without that convertibility requirement, the Bank of England could now effectively fire up the printing presses and print large numbers of new notes. Matching the volume of those notes, pound for pound, it provided new loans to the government, which the government used to finance its war with Napoleon.

All of this money-printing resulted in a large price inflation during the Napoleonic War and continued for some time thereafter, until the gold standard was restored in 1819 (see the section "Note Creation and Inflation," below).

As the purchasing power of Bank of England notes fell during the Napoleonic War inflation, why would people continue to hold them or use them in transactions? They always had the option to use gold or silver coins, whose purchasing power remained steady, or to use checks or other means of payment. One of the reasons was that competing banknotes had already disappeared by around 1780, due to the privileged position afforded the Bank of England. However, to ensure that the public would continue to use the depreciating Bank of England notes, Parliament enacted a further privilege to the Bank of England by declaring its notes "legal tender." Taxes had to be paid in these notes and all private individuals and businesses were compelled by law to accept them (Smith 1990).

Legal tender laws are a feature of modern central banking, where the central bank's monopoly on money creation is enhanced by the legal requirement that everyone must accept its notes in commerce and to pay taxes. Today, on a U.S. dollar bill—called a "Federal Reserve Note"—can be seen the words: "This note is legal tender for all debts public and private." The U.S. legal tender law was modeled after the first-ever legal tender law, which was enacted to privilege Bank of England notes, thereby making it easier for the bank to loan money to the government and pass off the newly created and depreciating banknotes to the public (Smith 1990).

How Banks Create Money by Lending

Now we'll take a moment to explain the connection between banknotes and lending. An older term for money is "banknote." Banknotes originated in the depository receipts that the goldsmith bankers issued for deposits of gold. The receipts, which began to circulate anonymously, enabled the holder to exchange the receipt for the stated quantity of gold. The gold was payable immediately when the holder presented it for payment at the bank. Thus, the note represented an obligation of the bank, an IOU, that it owed the stated amount of gold to the noteholder.

As long as banks readily honored their obligation to redeem notes for gold, the notes would circulate at "par value," i.e., at the purchasing power equivalent of the stated amount of gold. Thus, a $20 banknote in the United States in the 1800s was roughly equivalent to an ounce of gold.[205] Going to a merchant with either the $20 note or a one-ounce gold coin would buy the equivalent amount of goods because the merchant knew that the note was "good as gold"; he could redeem it at any time for gold at the bank. In practice, this meant that merchants rarely exchanged their notes for gold. It was simply easier for merchants and customers to carry and trade the notes, rather than bulky gold coins. When a gold standard worked well—i.e., when convertibility was standard banking practice and the public knew it could rely on it—very few gold coins actually circulated. Rather, circulation was predominantly in the form of trusted banknotes.[206]

A surprising fact about how banks operate is that a bank creates an equivalent amount of money (i.e., banknotes) whenever it makes a loan. When a banker makes a loan, he simultaneously creates a new deposit account for the borrower in the amount of the loan. The borrower can immediately spend the proceeds of the loan either by writing checks on it, or by withdrawing the amount in the form of banknotes. Money created in this way is often called "bank money." Most money, even today, is created in this way by private banks through the process of lending. Lending is matched by new money creation, dollar for dollar (White 1999).

Thus, a limiting factor for the volume of lending is the willingness of members of the public to accept the banknotes. If merchants or members

---

205. Until 1914, one ounce of gold = $20.67.

206. Scotland had a well-functioning system of private banks operating on the gold standard from 1725–1844. During that time, less than 3 percent of the circulating money was actually in the form of gold or silver coins. The other 97 percent were banknotes that circulated "at par" with gold (White 1995).

of the public do not trust the banknotes, either because they do not believe the bank will redeem them for gold or because the banknotes are depreciating in value, then the bank will be unable to make new loans.

The English government wanted ever larger loans from the Bank of England to finance the Napoleonic Wars. To do this, it needed to make sure that the public would accept the newly created banknotes that emerged from these loans. Thus, the English government made the notes "legal tender," forcing Englishmen to accept Bank of England banknotes for payment of "all debts public and private."

Note Creation and Inflation

When loans—and the resulting new banknotes—were made in excess, too many notes "chased" the existing supply of gold. In practice, this results in too many noteholders seeking to exchange their notes for gold, which forced the British government to allow the Bank of England to suspend the convertibility of its notes for gold. Coupled with the legal tender laws, the suspension of the requirement to convert notes into gold enabled many more new loans—and notes—to be created.

The result of this excess creation of notes was price inflation. Too many notes chasing a given quantity of goods meant that the purchasing power of each banknote declined. This deterioration of purchasing power always happens when too much money is created relative to the supply of goods. The economist Milton Friedman summarized this phenomenon by saying that "Inflation is always and everywhere a monetary phenomenon in the sense that it is and can be produced only by a more rapid increase in the quantity of money than in output." (Friedman 1970). Monetary inflation is a hallmark of central bank finance. When a central bank issues new loans to the government or buys Treasury bonds (which is the same thing), it creates new money, which ultimately results in price inflation.

The deterioration in purchasing power due to inflation effectively acts as a *tax* imposed on everyone who uses or holds money. Economists call this tax "seigniorage." The term "seigniorage" originates from the practice of royal mints that would debase the coinage by re-minting it with cheaper metal alloys. Modern-day seigniorage happens in the form of price inflation when the purchasing power of notes declines due to over-issuance (White 1999).

Inflation—or seigniorage—has been a concomitant of the rise of central banking. It is an insidious way for the government to raise money because it acts as a hidden tax. Voters are generally unaware that their money is depreciating in value or, if the inflation rate is high, they are slow to identify its cause in government borrowing that has been facilitated by the central bank. Because it is "hidden," the ability to raise money by seigniorage allows for a greater level of government spending than would occur if Parliament or Congress had to approve specific tax increases to pay for each spending increase. In this way, central bank finance is a sine qua non of "big government" (Salsman 2017).

Major suspensions of the convertibility of notes into gold, in order to finance wars and other measures, occurred under the Bank of England and later on in the United States. In the United States, inflation began to "take off" after the Federal Reserve Bank began operations in 1914. Initially, the U.S. Federal Reserve Bank, like the Bank of England, had an obligation to convert its notes into gold. This checked the issuance of notes. However, during World War I convertibility was suspended. During the Great Depression, convertibility for individuals was again suspended and private gold holdings were outlawed. During the next several decades only *governments* could still redeem their dollars for gold.

During the 1960s, the U.S. began to increase government spending dramatically to pay for the Vietnam War and the new "Great Society" welfare programs begun by President Johnson. To do this, the U.S. government increased its borrowing dramatically from the Federal Reserve System, which concurrently created an equivalent amount of money that entered the economy. Inflation increased as the purchasing power of the U.S. dollar declined. In response, foreign government institutions, in particular the Bank of France, began exchanging their depreciating U.S. dollars for gold bullion, which held steady value (De Vries 1987).

Gold bullion was leaving the U.S. in such large amounts that the U.S. was unable to maintain convertibility, and the last vestige of convertibility of the dollar into gold was suspended in 1971.

Just as during the Napoleonic War, without the requirement to convert notes into gold, many more notes could now be created. This meant that lending to the government could accelerate. Inflation took off. The chart below shows the Consumer Price Index, a measure of the purchasing power of the dollar over the past two hundred years. Inflation increased—i.e., purchasing power declined—whenever gold convertibility was suspended. This usually happened during wars— the War of 1812, the Civil War, and World War I. However, until the 20th century, gold convertibility and the purchasing power of the dollar were eventually restored after each war.

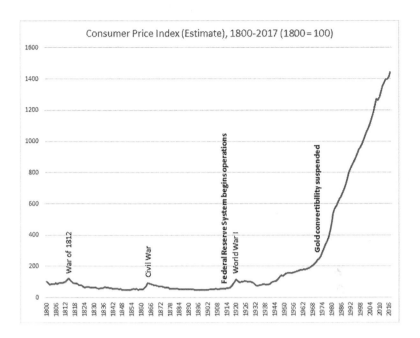

Source: Federal Reserve Bank of Minneapolis, "Consumer Price Index (Estimate), 1800–", Handbook of Labor Statistics, U.S. Department of Labor, Bureau of Labor Statistics, https://www.minneapolisfed.org/community/teaching-aids/cpi-calculator-information/consumer-price-index-1800.

That changed after the Federal Reserve System began operations in 1914, when a new, permanent trend toward higher inflation emerged. Gradually, in phases, the U.S. completely went off the gold standard. After the final break happened in 1971, the purchasing power of the dollar rapidly declined. During the entire century of the 1800s, the purchasing power of the dollar was roughly constant. One dollar in 1800 could buy about the same amount of goods as one dollar in 1900. However, a 2017 dollar can only buy the equivalent of 4 cents worth of goods in 1914, the year the Federal Reserve System began operating. During the years of central banking, and the gradual abandonment of gold convertibility, the purchasing power of the dollar declined 96 percent.

The Formation of the Federal Reserve System

The National Monetary Commission recommendation following the

Panic of 1907 was to form a U.S. central bank modeled after the Bank of England and the New York Clearing House Association (NYCHA). The NYCHA was a private organization formed in 1853 by the largest banks in the country, which were headquartered in New York, to facilitate inter-bank clearings of banknotes and checks. The NYCHA worked efficiently to clear banknotes and checks, monitor the financial health of its member banks, and aid them during crises (White 1999). The clearing function of the NYCHA would be taken over by the Federal Reserve System. The "lender of last resort" function that the Bank of England provided in the 1800s and the NYCHA provided to its member banks would also be taken over by the Federal Reserve System. Passed in December 1913, the purpose of the Federal Reserve Act was "To provide for the establishment of Federal reserve banks, to furnish an elastic currency, to afford means of rediscounting commercial paper, to establish a more effective supervision of banking in the United States, and for other purposes."[207]

The establishment of the Federal Reserve System was a "solution" to the problems of fragmented banking and an inflexible currency. Unlike other countries, since the nation's founding U.S. banks were generally prohibited from operating across state lines and, in many states (the so-called unit banking states) were restricted to a single office.[208] This made the banks highly vulnerable to local economic problems, and resulted in frequent failures and "runs on the bank."[209]

The Great Depression highlighted the problem of U.S. branch banking restrictions. In 1929, on the eve of the Great Depression, 25,568 banks operated in the United States, most of them unit banks.[210] In contrast, our northern neighbor Canada had only twelve banks, most of which

---

207. https://www.federalreserve.gov/aboutthefed/officialtitle-preamble.htm.

208. In 1929, on the eve of the Great Depression, there were eighteen "unit banking" states, concentrated mainly in the West and South (Nadler 2012). Bank failures were most frequent in these states.

209. A "run on the bank" was a frequent occurrence in the 19th and early 20th centuries. If a local problem developed, rumors may spread that a particular bank was likely to fail. Depositors would literally run to the bank to be first in line to withdraw their deposits before the bank ran out of money. These runs would often become self-fulfilling prophecies. Otherwise solvent banks may have to shut down because depositors panicked and hastily withdrew their funds.

210. Board of Governors, Table A-1: United States Summary, Appendix A: All Banks—Continental United States, p. 33.

operated extensive branch networks spanning the country.[211] During the first years of the Great Depression, from 1929 until 1933, 10,797 or 42 percent of all U.S. banks failed.[212] Although Canada's economy also suffered greatly in the Depression, *not a single bank failed* (White 1999).

Restrictions on branch banking remained a problem in the United States until very recently. Many of the banks that failed in the 1980s' savings and loan crisis were unit banks or banks operating in states that had prohibited inter-state branching. Nationwide banking was not fully legalized in the United States until 1994.[213]

U.S. banks in the 19th and early 20th centuries also suffered from a problem of an inflexible currency. As explained in the last chapter, this was caused by state charters that required banks to purchase state bonds (and later federal bonds) in order to issue currency. This made it prohibitively expensive for banks to issue more currency to accommodate seasonal cash withdrawals such as during the fall harvest season.

The Federal Reserve System "solved" these twin problems by becoming the "lender of last resort" to the banks. As had happened earlier with the Bank of England, the Federal Reserve System also became the monopoly issuer of all money. The monopoly on money would allow the Federal Reserve to respond to seasonal variations in demand. Unlike the state banks, the Federal Reserve was exempted from any requirement to hold bonds to match its monetary issuances, giving it a flexibility to create new money in response to seasonal changes in demand that the state banks were not permitted to have.

The twin problems of regional bank failures and an inflexible currency would have been easily solved simply by repealing branching restrictions and the rules requiring banks to buy state bonds in order to issue banknotes. A minority at the National Monetary Commission recognized this, but they were outvoted in the final recommendation, which Congress used to justify passing the Federal Reserve Act (Smith 1990).

---

211. Canada's population is 11 percent of the U.S. population. If Canada had a similarly fragmented banking system, proportionally it should have had 2,851 banks. Instead, because it permitted nationwide branching, it only had twelve banks, each with many branches.

212. Board of Governors, ibid.

213. Riegle-Neal Interstate Banking and Branching Efficiency Act of 1994.

Central Banking and Volatility of Economic Output

The first big test of the new Federal Reserve System came with the onset of the Great Depression. In previous panics/crises, shortages of money were ameliorated by the actions of the NYCHA, which provided emergency liquidity to its members and indirectly to correspondent banks throughout the country. In contrast, the Federal Reserve at that time operated under a principle called the "real bills doctrine," a rule it slavishly followed, which only permitted lending (or "discounting") to banks upon the presentation of good commercial paper as collateral (Smith 1990).[214]

As the recession worsened and became a depression, the quantity of good quality commercial paper declined as businesses shrank and failed. As a result, the Federal Reserve System, instead of providing emergency money to banks facing liquidity problems, *reduced* the quantity of money in the economy. This made the plight of the fragmented regional banks much worse, and accelerated the downturn into becoming the worst in American history. More than 42 percent of all U.S. banks failed (Friedman and Schwartz 1971).

Later, as the U.S. economy began to recover, officials at the Fed incongruously decided that credit conditions had become too easy and again tightened the quantity of money, creating a "depression within the depression" in 1937 (Friedman and Schwartz 1971).

The Fed was entrusted with ensuring the stability of the U.S. banking system and providing a flexible currency. Instead, poorly thought-out central management led it to worsen the condition of U.S. banks and help create the worst banking crisis in American history. As explained in the last chapter, the Federal Reserve System reprised its mismanagement of the money supply during the 2007–2009 housing finance crisis.

Economists, such as John Maynard Keynes, have noted this power of the central bank over the economy and hypothesized that it can be used to smooth out economic booms and busts (Keynes 1936). In practice, however, as economist Milton Friedman has noted, the central bank always seems to time its monetary injections and contractions badly, exacerbating instead of ameliorating business cycles (Friedman and Schwartz 1971). As we shall see in the next section, this persistent mis-timing is inherent in the practice of central banking because it is

---

214. Commercial paper are short-term loans to established businesses, usually backed by receivables or other high-quality, easily liquidated assets.

a form of central planning.

This ability of central banks to affect economic activity has even been used by politicians to try to temporarily stimulate economic growth ahead of elections. President Nixon famously "twisted the arm" of Federal Reserve chairman Arthur Burns ahead of the 1972 election to increase the money supply and stimulate the economy so that voters would re-elect him (Boettke and Smith 2014). However, the result of this monetary stimulation was an acceleration of inflation and recession.

The Austrian theory of the business cycle holds that the only result of attempts to artificially stimulate economic growth through central bank money creation is to create "mal-investment" and *greater* economic volatility. Artificial injections of money make it *too easy* for banks to lend and businesses to borrow. The result is that long-term projects are funded that are not really economically viable. However, the economic failure of these projects only shows up much later, creating an economic downturn when it does (Mises 1949).

A unique aspect of the Austrian theory of the business cycle is its identification that the new money created by the Fed enters the economy at specific points.[215] Usually, it is large, capital-intensive businesses that benefit first from the injections of new money since they are large borrowers. Since the money creation by the Fed reduces interest rates below normal levels, these businesses borrow too much to invest in long-lived assets. Ultimately, because they were bought with artificially cheap credit, these new assets prove to be unviable, and they are liquidated in a painful process of writedowns, defaults, and bankruptcies. The (artificially created) boom becomes a bust (Hayek 1932, Garrison 2000).

In the early 2000s, the existence of subsidies for mortgage borrowing created a different pathway for the flood of new money created by the Fed. The new money entered the housing market and pushed up home prices to unsustainably high levels. Again, boom becomes bust, but via a different monetary pathway (Niles 2010).

---

215. This stands in contrast to standard macroeconomic theories, such as Keynesianism or monetarism, which simply assumes that money enters the economy in an aggregate, non-specific way. Austrian theory holds that the key to explaining the business cycle is identifying that money enters the economy in a specific way that affects some sectors earlier and to a different degree than other sectors. In this manner, the injection of money results in mis-coordination of economic plans and price distortions that leads to destructive booms and busts.

Central Banking and Cronyism

Central banks hold a great degree of power over the rest of the financial system. The ability to create bank reserves, a monopoly on note issue, and privileges such as legal tender laws ensure that central banks hold a great degree of power over the profitability and success of other banks. The central bank's position as "lender of last resort" to the banks also gives it the ability, in a crisis, to decide which banks will be bailed out and survive, and which banks will face liquidation.

As the last essay, "Finance Isn't Free and Never Really Was," illustrates, this power is regularly exercised by the central bank. In the 1980s, the Federal Reserve bailed out Continental Illinois, one of the nation's largest banks. In doing so, it helped instigate the 1980s' savings and loan crisis when other banks began to believe that they, too, would be bailed out if they mismanaged their bank. Thus, the doctrine of "too big to fail" was born.[216]

As the emergency "lender of last resort" to the banks and implementer of the "too big to fail" doctrine, the central bank bails out poorly run banks, subsidizes irresponsible banking practices and, in effect, punishes successful banks. During the recent housing finance crisis, this cronyism showed itself when the Treasury Department and Federal Reserve decided to bail out Bear Stearns and Merrill Lynch, arguably intervened in markets to help Goldman Sachs, yet inexplicably decided to let Lehman Brothers fail. Commentators have speculated that the decisions reflected personal loyalties of Treasury Secretary Hank Paulson, who was a former partner and large shareholder of Goldman Sachs, and who also had personal loyalties to the executives at Bear Stearns, but held antipathy towards senior executives at Lehman Brothers (Allison 2013, pp. 128-29).

The central bank holds incredible power over bankers' careers and over the success and profitability of the banks they work at. This is augmented by the growing regulatory power the Federal Reserve has accumulated to supervise banks and banking practices.

Such power fosters cronyism as a defensive measure by bankers, and as a way of quashing competition. Thus, large banking institutions such as Citigroup or Goldman Sachs have developed a "revolving door" where their executives rotate between agencies such as the Federal Reserve and the Treasury Department and their firms. By

---

216. https://www.federalreservehistory.org/essays/failure_of_continental_illinois.

doing so, they can increase the odds that during a crisis or otherwise, the policies of these agencies will favor their banks. As a saying goes, "If you aren't seated at the dinner table, you are on the menu."

The Impossibility of Central Planning and Central Banking

In its essence, central banking is a form of central planning over the banking system. The central bank today has taken over many of the banking functions that banks used to take on individually themselves or through voluntary associations, such as clearinghouses.

Decisions that banks used to make themselves or via a clearinghouse, such as the level of reserves to maintain, are now made centrally by central bank regulators. The central bank can mandate the level and type of reserves that the banking system holds—and ultimately the volume of lending—through its money creation policies.

Before there were central banks, these decisions were made at the local level in the offices of individual bankers who made lending decisions based on the merits of the borrowers who came in to their offices. It was a *decentralized* process. It was decentralized because that is where the knowledge resided of who was an attractive or unattractive prospect. After judging the relative merits of different potential borrowers, the banker extended loans of varying size, which resulted in the creation of checks and banknotes, which other banks received and cleared through the clearinghouse.

Coordination of the activities of the banks happened at the level of the clearinghouse and in market data that resulted from the bankers' activities, such as the general level of interest rates. If demand for borrowing was strong, say because of a major technological innovation that fueled an entrepreneurial demand for funds (such as the invention of the railroad), interest rates may rise. This would also allow the banks to raise interest paid on deposits, thus bringing more reserves into the banks and facilitating the increase in borrowing.

Interest rates and interbank clearings at the clearinghouses fluctuate, reflecting the totality of the individual lending decisions of the individual bankers, each of whom responds to the changing lending opportunities that he is witnessing. In turn, those lending opportunities reflect changing demand factors such as innovation and the launch of entrepreneurial new firms.

Interest rates provide signals to all parties that allow them to alter their behavior to reflect the behavior of the other bankers and borrowers. For example, if interest rates rise, some borrowers will delay borrowing, thus reducing the pressure on interest rates. Bankers may also raise deposit interest rates to bring in more deposits and facilitate the granting of more loans.

Interest rates are the *price* of money and credit. Fluctuations in this price due to changes in market conditions *coordinate* the supplies of money and credit in the economy, keeping it in balance.

The economist Friedrich Hayek explains how a similar price mechanism governs the regular economic market for goods and services (Hayek 1948). Say a blight reduces the supply of wheat, so the price of wheat rises. A breadmaker may not even know about the blight, but he responds to the price increase by raising the price of bread. In turn, the consumer responds to the increase in the price of bread by reducing consumption. Thus, the quantity consumed of wheat is brought down naturally through the price signal to match the reduced supply.

In similar manner interest rates and clearing balances coordinate the actions of bankers and borrowers. Where it was permitted to operate most freely, as in Scotland in the period 1726–1844 and in Canada in the 19th century, it worked well. Bank failures and runs were rare. Banknotes circulated at par with gold. Gold itself did not have to circulate much because customers trusted the banknotes (White 1995, 1999).

In contrast, from its beginning the U.S. banking system suffered from government interventions that weakened it at the outset and prevented this natural regulating process from occurring. Unit banking and branching restrictions made the banking system weak and prone to failures and runs. State requirements to buy bonds made currencies inflexible and unresponsive to the changing seasonal demands.

The solution ultimately imposed for these problems—a U.S. central bank, the Federal Reserve System—was a blunt instrument. It confiscated and centralized bank reserves to be held at the Federal Reserve. It outlawed gold and tried to micromanage economic ups and downs through "monetary policy."

The track record of central banking is poor (Selgin, LaStrapes, and White 2012). It significantly deepened and worsened the Great Depression, and it has resulted in a continuous inflation that has enabled our government to spend money without having to get the permission of the electorate to raise taxes. In this sense, it has helped fund a bigger, more intrusive state (Salsman 2017).

However, economic theory shows that central banking had to fail because it is a form of central planning. Central planning, as economist Friedrich Hayek has shown, cannot work because of what he called the "knowledge problem" (Hayek 1948). The requisite knowledge to make effective economic decisions is dispersed and exists in the minds of myriad individual participants. Their actions are coordinated naturally, "as if by an invisible hand" (Smith 1776), by the price mechanism that signals to all participants when supply and demand conditions have changed.

A central bank is a top-down institution that interferes with the price mechanism that banks as well as borrowers and lenders rely on to coordinate their actions. The most important of those prices is interest rates. The central bank, by artificially adding or subtracting money in the economy as it finances government spending, moves these interest rates higher or lower than their natural economic rate. The result is economic instability, malinvestment and price inflation.

The Unsolvable Task of the Central Planner-Banker: Finding the Right Interest Rate

Some economists hold that the central bank can effectively manage money and credit by applying a rule to target a certain monetary variable. Milton Friedman, for example, proposed the "k-percent rule," which holds that the money supply should simply be grown by a fixed, predetermined percentage each year. Friedman's rule was shown to fail (after Friedman had written about it), when other factors not easily controlled, such as "monetary velocity," had changed (Salter 2014).

More recent proposed rules are the "Taylor Rule" and "nominal income" targeting (Salter 2014, Selgin 2017). Like the "k-percent" rule, all such rules must fail. Human behavior—the demand and supply for loans—cannot follow an unchanging mathematical function. Any attempt to automate the growth of the money supply according to a fixed rule is simply another form of central planning.

The only place one can find knowledge of the right interest rate is inside the heads of thousands of bankers and borrowers and savers. The right interest rate is the result of their voluntary interactions in a system of free banking. The right interest rate is the market-determined one that results from their individual actions. No central planner can find it.

Free Banking Is the Solution

The solution to our problem of central banking is to eliminate the central bank and provide a framework that allows robust, secure and opportunistic private banking institutions to emerge.[217] Government can help this process by limiting its borrowing from the banking system. More importantly, government should simply perform its basic function of enforcing contracts and ensuring the rule of law. Only banks themselves should decide to whom to lend, in what quantities, and how much monetary reserves they need to hold. No government planner or regulator should interfere with this process. The only role for government is to hold the bank to its promises. If a banker promises that a banknote is convertible into gold on demand, the bank will be held to that promise, or face liquidation/bankruptcy if it doesn't.

Based on the experience with relatively (but not completely) free banking systems in Canada and Scotland, the result will be few banks with many branches, stability, and no bank runs (White 1999, 79). And a high rate of economic growth as profit-motivated bankers match their loans with the most compelling, creditworthy borrowers. Evidence of its success will be when paper—i.e., private banknotes—become the predominant circulating money. Ironically, because customers will trust the redeemability of the banknotes into gold, they will generally not need to do so.

At the "top" of this structure will be one or more private bank clearinghouses, such as the 19th-century New York Clearing House Association, that will effectively monitor the banks by setting financial requirements for bank membership in the clearinghouse and providing an effective method for banks to clear each other's' notes and checks and to monitor their financial condition.

Central banks are not just unnecessary. By distorting the value of money and creating malinvestment and other problems, they retard economic growth and distort production in the economy. True free, gold-based banking has only partially been tried. It is time for *laissez-faire* in banking.

---

217. For a practical proposal to end central banking and establish free banking, see Salsman 2013.

Bibliography

Allison, John A. (2013). *The Financial Crisis and the Free Market Cure: Why Pure Capitalism Is the World Economy's Only Hope*. New York: McGraw-Hill.

Board of Governors of the Federal Reserve System (U.S.), 1935-. *All-Bank Statistics, United States, 1896–1955*, https://fraser.stlouisfed. org/scribd/?title_id=39&filepath=/files/docs/publications/ allbkstat/1896-1955/allbankstats_complete.pdf, accessed on June 6, 2017.

Boettke, Peter J., and Daniel J. Smith. (2014). "Federal Reserve Independence: A Centennial Review." *Journal of Prices & Markets* 1(1): 31–48.

Calomiris, Charles W., and Stephen H. Haber. (2014). *Fragile by Design: The Political Origins of Banking Crises and Scarce Credit*. Princeton University Press.

De Vries, Margaret Garritsen. (1987). *The International Monetary Fund, 1966–71: The System Under Stress*. International Monetary Fund.

Friedman, Milton M. (1970). *The Counter-Revolution in Monetary Theory*. Transatlantic Arts.

Friedman, Milton, and Anna Jacobson Schwartz. (1971). *A Monetary History of the United States, 1867–1960*. New ed. Princeton University Press.

Garrison, Roger W. (2000). *Time and Money: The Macroeconomics of Capital Structure*. Routledge.

Hayek, Friedrich A. (1948). "The Use of Knowledge in Society," *Individualism and the Monetary Order*. University of Chicago Press.

Hayek, Friedrich A. (1932). *Prices and Production*, 2d ed. London: George Routledge.

Keynes, John Maynard. ([1936] 1965). *The General Theory of Employment, Interest, and Money*. Harcourt, Brace & World.

Mises, Ludwig von. (1966). *Human Action: A Treatise on Economics*, 4th edition. Irvington-on-Hudson, NY: The Foundation for Economic Education.

Mises, Ludwig von. (2011). *On the Manipulation of Money and Credit.* Indianapolis, IN: Liberty Fund.

Nadler, Marcus, and Jules Bogen. (2012). *The Banking Crisis: The End of an Epoch.* Volume 24 of Routledge Library Editions: Banking & Finance. Routledge.

Niles, Raymond C. (2010). "Eighty Years in the Making: How Housing Subsidies Caused the Financial Meltdown," *Journal of Law, Economics and Policy, George Mason University School of Law,* Spring 2010.

Nadler, Marcus, and Jules Bogen. (2012). *The Banking Crisis: The End of an Epoch.* Volume 24 of Routledge Library Editions: Banking & Finance. Routledge.

Salsman, Richard M. (1990). *Breaking the Banks: Central Banking Problems and Free Banking Solutions.* American Institute for Economic Research.

Salsman, Richard M. (2013). "The End of Central Banking, Part II." *Objective Standard.* Summer 2013. Vol. 8, No. 2.

Salsman, Richard M. (2017). *The Political Economy of Public Debt.* Northampton, MA: Edward Elgar.

Salter, Alexander W. (2014). "An Introduction to Monetary Policy Rules," Mercatus Working Paper, Mercatus Institute, George Mason University. Available at: https://www.mercatus.org/system/files/Salter-Monetary-PolicyRules.pdf.

Selgin, George. (2017). *Money Free and Unfree.* Washington, DC: Cato Institute.

Selgin, George, William D. LaStrapes, and Lawrence H. White. (2012). "Has the Fed Been a Failure?" *Journal of Macroeconomics.* 34 (3). September 2012. 569–96.

Smith, Adam. (1776). *The Wealth of Nations.*

Smith, Vera. (1990). *The Rationale of Central Banking: And the Free Banking Alternative.* Indianapolis, IN: Liberty Fund.

White, Lawrence. (1999). *The Theory of Monetary Institutions.* Malden, MA: Blackwell.

White, Lawrence H. (1995). *Free Banking in Britain: Theory, Experience and Debate, 1800–1845*, 2d ed. London: The Institute for Economic Affairs.

Steve Jobs, Bernie Madoff, and Wall Street Greed

By Don Watkins

This essay was first published in *The American* (American Enterprise Institute), September 26, 2013, http://www.aei.org/publication/bernie-madoff-steve-jobs-and-wall-street-greed/.

Who commits the most murders, according to Hollywood? Serial killers? Gangsters? Terrorists? High school science teachers turned drug kingpins?

It turns out the answer is businessmen.

In 2006, the Business and Media Institute published a study[218] in which it concluded that "According to primetime TV, you are 21 times more likely to be kidnapped or murdered at the hands of a businessman than the mob. Businessmen also committed crimes five times more often than terrorists and four times more often than gangs."

A different study[219] by the Business and Media Institute found that by age eighteen, "the average TV viewer has seen businessmen attempt more than ten thousand murders and countless lesser offenses, all in the name of greed."

It's more than a Hollywood convention: it's a cultural stereotype. Businessmen are seen as greedy, selfish SOBs who care about nothing save for their bank accounts. And like all stereotypes, this one has consequences.

Look at how the press covers any economic problem or crisis. No one waits for actual evidence or peer-reviewed studies. Hardly anyone examines how government might have messed things up by distorting market forces. They just look for evidence of greed and connect it to the problem at hand.

When fraud was exposed in a handful of companies in the early 2000s, for example, the explanation was "corporate greed." The

---

218. Matthew Balan, "Bad Company: Executive Summary," Media Research Center, 2006, http://www.mrc.org/special-reports/bad-company-executive-summary.

219. Michael Fumento, "Why Hollywood Hates Business," *Michael Fumento*, blog, January 3, 1992, http://www.fumento.com/crime/hollywood.html.

solution? Sarbanes-Oxley, which treated all businessmen as guilty of accounting fraud until proven innocent. When the financial crisis hit, the explanation was "Wall Street greed." The solution? Congress passed Dodd-Frank, generating nearly 14,000 pages—and counting—of complex regulations all aimed to stop greedy businessmen from being so greedy.

What's striking is that it is virtually impossible to find a successful businessman who has not been criticized for his greed or selfishness. Even the late Steve Jobs, one of the most popular businessmen of his or any era, was routinely derided as selfish. Whatever his virtues, people said, Jobs was primarily concerned with his vision and his company's success, not with the welfare of others. In the wake of his resignation from Apple, shortly before his death, some even rushed to condemn Jobs for focusing his efforts on profit seeking rather than philanthropy. Journalist Andrew Sorkin, for example, penned a missive[220] in the New York Times in which he acknowledged that Jobs was a "visionary" and an "innovator" who "clearly never craved money for money's sake and has never been ostentatious with his wealth." Nevertheless, Sorkin complained, "there is no public record of Mr. Jobs giving money to charity." A 2006 column in Wired put it more bluntly: Jobs was "nothing more than a greedy capitalist who's amassed an obscene fortune. It's shameful."[221]

In some ways, though, Jobs is the exception that proves the rule. Unique among businessmen, he was admired by many for his unrivaled creativity and passion for making "insanely great" products. If even he could not escape charges of selfishness and greed, then what chance have other producers had? History speaks: from Morgan to Rockefeller to Ford to Walton to Gates, hardly any successful businessmen have been immune from the accusation that they are selfish.

The Madoff Comparison

And what is even more striking is that the charges of greed and the image of the greedy profit-seeker have led us to put the pantheon of

---

220. Andrew Ross Sorkin, "The Mystery of Steve Jobs's Public Giving," *New York Times*, August 29, 2011, https://dealbook.nytimes.com/2011/08/29/the-mystery-of-steve-jobss-public-giving/?_r=3.

221. *Wired* staff, "Jobs vs. Gates: Who's the Star?" *Wired*, January 25, 2006, https://www.wired.com/2006/01/jobs-vs-gates-whos-the-star.

business greats into the same moral category as some of the worst predators in history—predators such as Bernie Madoff, the Wall Street elder statesman who in 2008 was exposed as having orchestrated the largest Ponzi scheme in history.

From the start, Madoff was treated not as a criminal who pretended to be a businessman but as the symbol of business greed. He was, in the words of Diana Henriques, author of The Wizard of Lies: Bernie Madoff and the Death of Trust, "a creature of the world he helped create, a world that was greedy for riskless gain . . . arrogantly certain of success, woefully deluded about what could go wrong, and selfishly indifferent to the damage done to others."[222]

The world around us has been shaped by a theory that says the Madoffs and Jobses of the world are brothers in spirit—or, rather, brothers in spiritual impoverishment.

But what if actual profit-seekers have nothing important in common with monsters such as Madoff? What if the profit motive is radically different from some unhinged "greed" capable of turning producers into predators? Then perhaps we owe businessmen an apology—and maybe, just maybe, a significant part of the justification for today's regulatory state should be relegated to history's ash heap.

Early in his business career, Madoff encountered his first major setback. The young investor had about twenty investment advisory clients—friends and family, mostly—whose money he had put into highly speculative stocks. "I realized I never should have sold them those shares," Madoff later admitted.[223] For two years the stocks soared, but in May of 1962, the market collapsed, and with it their value.

Madoff's reaction was revealing. He used all the profits his firm had made up to that point to buy back the stocks from his clients' accounts at their original offer price, leaving his investors with the illusion he had avoided any losses. In Henriques's words, "rather than admit the truth that he had failed, he covered up those losses and lied about it." The move wiped out Madoff's capital, but he was able to dupe his investors into believing he was a genius; the market had tanked but he hadn't lost a cent. It was a litmus test, Henriques says.[224]

---

222. Diana B. Henriques, *The Wizard of Lies: Bernie Madoff and the Death of Trust* (New York: Times Books, 2011), p. xxiv.

223. Ibid., p. 28.

224. "Diana Henriques on Early Bernie Madoff—Bad from the Start," *YouTube*, June 8, 2011, http://www.youtube.com/watch?v=I3kMq2GRe2E.

"Faced with admitting failure or cheating, Madoff would cheat."

The incident helps pull back the curtain on the motives that would later lead Madoff to con thousands of people out of billions of dollars. From the start, he seemed to be out to prove something. "He had an inferiority complex," Marcia Mendelsohn, a childhood acquaintance, told Madoff biographer Andrew Kirtzman. "He never felt he was good enough."[225]

Kirtzman elaborates: "Time and again as a kid, [Madoff] was spurned and humiliated for what was perceived to be his inferior intellect. . . . But he excelled at making money, and with it came the stature that once had eluded him. When he couldn't generate as much money as he wanted or needed, he simply invented it."[226]

Madoff didn't seek money as a reward for his competence—he sought money to prove to others that he was competent. He aimed, not to build a great business, but to manufacture a reputation as a great businessman. He didn't want to use his intelligence to create wealth, but to steal wealth in order to dupe others into thinking he was intelligent.

Madoff, you might say, wasn't greedy, but needy: he needed to feel like a big shot because, in reality, he felt like a nobody.

Madoff recounted a telling episode to *New York* magazine in 2011: "The chairman of Banco Santander came down to see me, the chairman of Credit Suisse came down, chairman of UBS came down; I had all of these major banks. You know, [Edmond] Safra coming down and entertaining me and trying [to invest with Madoff]. It is a head trip. [Those people] sitting there, telling you, 'You can do this.' It feeds your ego. All of a sudden, these banks which wouldn't give you the time of day, they're willing to give you a billion dollars."

Madoff went on: "It wasn't like I needed the money. It was just that I thought it was a temporary thing, and all of a sudden, everybody is throwing billions of dollars at you. Saying, 'Listen, if you can do this stuff for us, we'll be your clients forever.'"

Madoff took the money and created false statements indicating to his investors that he was making incredible 15 percent returns. In reality, his returns were nothing close to that, but Madoff refused to face the facts and admit to his investors that he had failed to meet their

---

225. Andrew Kirtzman, *Betrayal: The Life and Lies of Bernie Madoff* (New York: Harper, 2010), p. 22.

226. Ibid., p. 9.

expectations. "I was too afraid," he said.[227]

Madoff had first arrived on Wall Street with a chip on his shoulder. "I was upset with the whole idea of not being in the [Wall Street] club. I was this little Jewish guy from Brooklyn."[228] Once "the club" started giving him the attention he so desperately craved, he was unwilling to let reality get in the way.

In It for the Money?

It's hard to imagine someone truly concerned with reaping profits over the long term behaving this way. Take a tour through Silicon Valley and it becomes apparent that the genuine profit-seeker makes mistakes and acknowledges them. He views mistakes and failures as part of the process of success. After studying successful entrepreneurs, business expert Peter Sims concluded that most "understand (and come to accept) that failure, in the form of making mistakes or errors, and being imperfect, is essential to their success."[229] Mistakes are inevitable, and they are an indispensable part of how a person learns and improves. But Madoff's goal wasn't to become a skilled investor; it was to project a certain image, to maintain the illusion that he was infallible. Whenever that illusion was threatened by reality, well, so much the worse for reality.

Much later, as Madoff stood at his sentencing hearing, he told the court, "I believed when I started this problem, this crime, that it would be something I would be able to work my way out of, but that became impossible. . . . I refused to accept the fact, could not accept the fact, that for once in my life I failed. I couldn't admit that failure, and that was a tragic mistake."[230] (Kirtzman notes that Madoff was spinning the facts even then: "He was not an overachiever who'd failed at something; he was an underachiever who had succeeded by lying."[231] In either case, the underlying motive was the same: Madoff wanted to create the illusion of ability, and so the facts were dispensable).

It is impossible to overstate how different Madoff's motives were

---

227. Steve Fishman, "The Madoff Tapes," *New York* magazine, February 27, 2011, http://nymag.com/news/features/berniemadoff-2011-3/.

228. Fishman, "The Madoff Tapes."

229. Peter Sims, *Little Bets* (New York: Free Press, 2011), pp. 35–36.

230. Kirtzman, *Betrayal*, p. 267.

231. Ibid., p. 267.

from those of genuinely successful businessmen, who thrive and prosper over the long run through their productive exploits. Steve Jobs, for instance, explained that his "passion has been to build an enduring company where people were motivated to make great products. Everything else was secondary."[232]

That included money. In an interview for the PBS documentary "Triumph of the Nerds," Jobs explained that "I was worth about over a million dollars when I was 23 and over 10 million dollars when I was 24, and over 100 million dollars when I was 25 and it wasn't that important because I never did it for the money."[233]

Madoff pursued money to prove he was a big shot. Jobs? In his words, "Sure it was great to make a profit, because that was what allowed you to make great products. But the products, not the profits, were the motivation."[234]

A library of business biographies testifies to the fact that the reason genuine profit-seekers get out of bed in the morning is because they love creating things: they love producing new products, improving old ones, finding better ways to do things, building a business into something great, and making a fortune in the process. They are at heart producers.

Underneath all its complexities, production is the process of transforming the material world for the benefit of human life. Human beings figure out the potentialities of the things around us and then we rearrange them to create something even better.

In this regard, the financial industry is no different from the tech industry. Again, the history of Apple is illustrative. A critical factor in its success was attracting an early financial supporter, Mike Markkula, who invested $91,000 and extended Apple a $250,000 line of credit.[235] Markkula's great virtues were his ability to see Apple's potential at a time when its future greatness was by no means apparent and his willingness to risk a significant portion of his personal wealth on that assessment. His decisions helped create one of the most productive companies in history. In one way or another, that is what all financiers do: they direct capital to what they judge to be its most productive uses, and so help make

232. Ibid., p. 567.

233. Interview in the PBS documentary *Triumph of the Nerds: The Rise of Accidental Empires* (1996).

234. Walter Isaacson, *Steve Jobs* (New York: Simon & Schuster, 2011), p. 567.

235. Jeffrey S. Young and William L. Simon, *iCon* (Hoboken, N.J.: Wiley, 2005), p. 45.

possible the creation of every sort of good and service on the market.

When a businessman—a real businessman, not a con artist with a business card—grows rich, it's not by taking from others and leaving them with less, the way a criminal does. It's by creating more and more wealth, of which his income—however large—represents only a fraction of what he created. He grows rich by making others richer. This is what led the late success guru Steven Covey to include "Think Win/Win" among his "Seven Habits of Highly Effective People." Whereas win/win relationships foster long-term profits, Covey observes, "Win/Lose is not viable because, although I appear to win in a confrontation with you, your feelings, your attitudes toward me, and our relationship have been affected. If I am a supplier to your company, for example, and win on my terms in a particular negotiation, I may get what I want now. But will you come to me again?"[236]

Alas, some businessmen do share Madoff's desire to prove they are "somebody," but it's clear that goal is actually at odds with the profit motive. To the extent that a businessman is driven by the challenge of creating value, his work brings not only material rewards, but intense spiritual challenge, meaning, and satisfaction. On the other hand, to the extent an individual is driven, as Madoff was, by a desire to feel like a big shot, the effort to avoid acknowledging his weaknesses and mistakes will divert him from the productive process. In the long run, that's a recipe for failure.

Jobs said it well. As he told the Stanford graduating class of 2005, "I'm convinced that the only thing that kept me going was that I loved what I did. You've got to find what you love. And that is as true for your work as it is for your lovers. Your work is going to fill a large part of your life, and the only way to be truly satisfied is to do what you believe is great work. And the only way to do great work is to love what you do."[237]

That hardly seems to have been the case with Madoff. Far from loving his job, he fled from it whenever he could. According to Kirtzman, "The [Madoff] family members were often on vacation and came and went as they pleased. Weeks would sometimes pass without a sighting of Bernie and Ruth."[238]

Whenever we classify creators such as Jobs and destroyers such as

236. Stephen R. Covey, *The 7 Habits of Highly Effective People* (New York: Simon & Schuster, 2004), p. 211.

237 Stanford University, "Steve Jobs' 2005 Stanford Commencement Address," *YouTube*, March 07, 2008, https://www.youtube.com/watch?v=UF8uR6Z6KLc.

238. Kirtzman, *Betrayal*, p. 117.

Madoff as greedy or selfish, we equate polar opposites. A creator creates new wealth, is motivated by the process of creating wealth, and deals with other people by trading his creations for theirs, win/win style. Madoff wasn't a producer, but a predator. He did not make money—he appropriated and ultimately destroyed it. In terms both of his motives and his means, Madoff was essentially different from profit-seeking businessmen. But he fit the pattern of other criminals to perfection.

Inside Madoff's Criminal Mind

In February 2009, Dr. Stanton Samenow, a distinguished criminal psychologist, told an interviewer, "I'll make you a bet that Mr. Madoff and others like him all say they're good people; they by no means regard themselves as evil. I've interviewed serial killers who, despite leaving dead bodies in their own view, say they are good people."[239]

Samenow would have won that bet. Less than a month later, *New York* magazine published its interview with Madoff. "Everybody on the outside kept claiming I was a sociopath," Madoff told the magazine. "I am a good person."[240]

Going back and reading Samenow's groundbreaking 1984 book *Inside the Criminal Mind*, it's striking how well Samenow's description of the criminal personality fits Madoff—and how radically different it is from the picture one gets from studying the lives of creators such as Jobs.

According to Samenow, the criminal "adamantly refuses to acknowledge his own fallibility."[241] Madoff, recall, "couldn't admit . . . failure."[242] Creators embrace failure as a core component of success.

According to Samenow, "When doors do not open immediately to a criminal, he complains about lack of opportunity or discrimination."[243] Madoff saw Wall Street as "a business where you had to have an edge, and the little guy never got a break. The institutions controlled everything. . . . I realized from a very early stage that the market is a whole

---

239. http://sweeps.thirdingredient.com/wow/wowowow/post-whats-wrong-bernie-madoff-psychologist-stanton-samenow-184867.

240. Fishman, "The Madoff Tapes."

241. Stanton E. Samenow, *Inside the Criminal Mind* (New York: Time Books, 1984), p. 101.

242. Kirtzman, *Betrayal*, p. 267.

243. Samenow, *Inside the Criminal Mind*, p. 88.

rigged job. There's no chance that investors have in this market."[244] Creators don't pout about their lack of opportunity—on the contrary, they search tenaciously for opportunity and even create it.

According to Samenow, "When the doors of prison first lock behind them, some criminals temporarily are frightened, remorseful, and depressed. These emotions are not strange because criminals experience them occasionally on the street when they weary of the daily grind, tired of looking over their shoulders, and regret disappointing people who care about them. Even on the outside, there were moments when life seemed no longer worth living."[245] Madoff claims that he could have kept his scheme going but turned himself in because he "got tired."[246] He knew it was just "a matter of time" before he got caught. "It was almost like . . . I just wanted the world to come to an end. . . . The world would come to an end, and I'd be dead and everyone would be gone."[247]

Madoff's world did come to an end. It had to, because Madoff was fighting an opponent he could not beat: reality. The pattern that emerges from Madoff's life is one of systematically blinding himself and others to the facts of reality. The pattern of a creator is to ruthlessly face facts in order to deal with reality on a progressively higher level. "Face reality as it is, not as it was or as you wish," says former General Electric CEO Jack Welch. "[F]acing reality is crucial in life, not just in business. You have to see the world in the purest, clearest way possible, or you can't make decisions on a rational basis."[248]

Apple's iPhone, for instance, emerged from Jobs's relentless focus on facts—in that case, the uncomfortable fact that despite the preeminence of Apple's iPod in the portable music market, its days were numbered. As *Wired* explained, "[Jobs] saw millions of Americans lugging separate phones, BlackBerrys, and—now—MP3 players; naturally, consumers would prefer just one device. He also saw a future in which cell phones and mobile email devices would amass ever more features, eventually challenging the iPod's dominance as a music player. To protect his new product line, Jobs knew he would eventually need to

---

244. Fishman, "The Madoff Tapes."

245. Samenow, *Inside the Criminal Mind*, p. 141.

246. Henriques, *The Wizard of Lies*, p. 337.

247. Henriques, *The Wizard of Lies*, p. 337.

248. Quoted in Edwin A. Locke, *The Prime Movers* (New York: AMACOM, 2000), p. 44.

venture into the wireless world."[249] Many an enterprise has gone from bankable to bankrupt thanks to a failure to face unpleasant realities. Jobs faced them and Apple flourished.

To place criminals and creators in the same moral category is to commit an error probably best captured by William F. Buckley: it's equal to "saying that the man who pushes an old lady into the path of a hurtling bus is not to be distinguished from the man who pushes an old lady out of the path of a hurtling bus: on the grounds that, after all, in both cases someone is pushing old ladies around."[250]

Both a Madoff and a Jobs in some sense pursue their desires. But that is a superficial similarity hiding a fundamental difference. Madoff blindly pursued his desires in defiance of reality, and as a result achieved nothing but destruction. Creators think about what they want and the real-life requirements for achieving it. They see their interests as consisting in facing facts, in production, and in win/win trade.

Madoff's crimes were not an indictment of businessmen, the profit motive, or the profit system. But the widespread claim that Madoff illustrated what's wrong with American businessmen? That was an indictment of us.

249. Fred Vogelstein, "The Untold Story: How the iPhone Blew Up the Wireless Industry," *Wired*, January 9, 2008, http://www.wired.com/gadgets/wireless/magazine/16-02/ff_iphone?currentPage=all.

250. Linda Bridges and John R. Coyne, *Strictly Right: William F. Buckley Jr. and the American Conservative Movement* (Hoboken: John Wiley & Sons, 2007), p. 182.

PART 2

The "Inequality" Attack on Finance

Turning the Tables on the Inequality Alarmists

By Don Watkins and Yaron Brook

Here's the familiar narrative on inequality: the American Dream is vanishing. The rich are getting richer, while the rest of us are struggling to keep our heads above water, and unless the government fights economic inequality through tax hikes on "the rich," a larger welfare state, and a "living wage," things are going to get much worse. "The rich" will not only continue to amass huge (and usually undeserved) fortunes, but they will use their power to game the political system for their own ends. Fighting this alarming trend of rising economic inequality, in President Obama's words, is "the defining challenge of our time."

What's been the response from those who reject this narrative?

Some challenge the statistics behind these claims, and argue that economic inequality really isn't as bad as the inequality alarmists suggest. Others challenge the solutions advocated by the alarmists. They say that the best way to achieve economic equality is to embrace market-oriented policies rather than higher taxes and higher government spending.

But both of these approaches commit a deadly error: they grant the inequality alarmists the moral high ground by conceding that economic equality is the ideal. This allows the alarmists to present themselves as idealists who are trying to move this country in the direction of equality by pursuing an agenda of economic leveling, and it allows them to paint their opponents as "deniers" who are trying to delude Americans into believing that leaving CEOs free to make tens of millions of dollars a year will somehow make us more equal.

Ceding the moral high ground to the alarmists is a losing strategy. The fact is, if economic equality is an ideal, then free-market capitalism is immoral. Free markets don't lead to economic equality. They make it possible for each individual to rise as far as his ambition and ability will take him: some will make huge fortunes, most will make a good living, and some will make a mess of their lives. Freedom provides us with economic opportunity—not economic equality.

But how do we go about challenging the moral ideal of the inequality alarmists? Some have argued that they are sacrificing liberty to equality. The alarmists' problem, they say, is that they care too much about equality to the detriment of other values.

But that's not the problem. The problem is that the inequality alarmists are the enemy of the only kind of equality that matters: political equality.

As we'll see, it is *political* equality that secures the opportunity that allows individuals to make the most of their lives—and it is the slow erosion of political equality that is threatening to turn the American Dream into a fading memory.

Political Equality: the Foundation of the American Dream

Before the creation of the United States, every system of government had taken for granted that some people were entitled to rule others, taking away their freedom and property whenever some allegedly "greater good" demanded it. Such systems were rigged against any outsider or innovator who wanted to challenge convention, create something new, and rise by his own effort and ability rather than through political privilege. But building on the achievements of thinkers like John Locke, the Founding Fathers established a nation based on the principle, not of economic equality, but of *political equality*.

Political equality refers to equality of *rights*. Each individual, the Founders held, is to be regarded by the government as having the same rights to life, liberty, and the pursuit of happiness as any other individual. When the Founders declared that "all men are created equal," they knew full well that individuals are unequal in virtually every respect, from intelligence to physical prowess to moral character to wealth. But in one respect we *are* equal: we are all human beings, and, despite our differences, we all share the same mode of survival. Unlike animals that have to fight over a fixed amount of resources in order to survive, human survival is achieved by using our minds to *create* what we need to live. We have to think and produce if we want to live and achieve happiness, and as a result we must have the *right* to think and produce (and to keep what we produce) if we are to create a society where individuals can flourish.

What can violate those rights? What can stop us from exercising the thought and productive effort human life requires? Basically, just one thing: physical force. The only way human beings can coexist peacefully is if they "leave their guns outside" and agree to live by means of production and voluntary trade rather than theft and brute violence. This is the purpose of government: in Locke's words, to protect the rights of the "industrious and rational" from violation by "the quarrelsome and contentious."[251]

By making the government the guardian of our equal rights rather than a tool for the politically privileged to control and exploit the rest of society, the Founders transformed the state from an instrument of oppression into an instrument of liberation: it liberated the individual so that he was free to make the most of his life.

It's important to keep in mind that the Founders failed to fully implement the principle of equality of rights, above all by failing to end slavery. And although that doesn't change the essential issue, it is worth noting that the opponents of slavery mounted their moral opposition to "the peculiar institution" by appealing to the principle of political equality, and to the way in which slaves were treated unequally by being deprived of their right to property. In Frederick Douglass's words, the slave "can own nothing, possess nothing, acquire nothing, but what must belong to another. To eat the fruit of his own toil, to clothe his person with the work of his own hands, is considered stealing. He toils that another may reap the fruit; he is industrious that another may live in idleness; he eats unbolted meal, that another may eat the bread of fine flour."[252] This was the ultimate form of political inequality because, as Abraham Lincoln put it in his debates with Stephen Douglas, it is precisely "in the right to eat the bread, without the leave of anybody else, which his own hand earns, [that the slave] is my equal and the equal of Judge Douglas, and the equal of every living man."[253]

To the extent it was realized, then, political equality was the foundation of the American Dream. The reason America became a land in which there was "opportunity for each according to ability or achievement," as James Truslow Adams put it when he coined the phrase "the American Dream," was because political equality ended the exploitation of the individual by the politically powerful. If you wanted to make something of your life, nothing would be given to you—but no one could stop you. In place of the guild systems, government-granted monopolies, and other strictures that had stifled opportunity in the Old World, the New World provided an open road to the visionaries, inventors, and industrialists who would transform a virgin continent

---

251. John Locke, *The Second Treatise of Government* V, sec. 34.

252. Frederick Douglass, "Lecture on Slavery, No. 1."

253. Abraham Lincoln, "Abraham Lincoln, First Debate with Stephen A. Douglas at Ottawa, Illinois, August 21, 1858 (excerpt)," http://mason.gmu.edu/~zschrag/hist120spring05/lincoln_ottawa.htm.

into a land of plenty.

Political equality is a moral ideal because it is the foundation of economic progress, it is the foundation of economic mobility—and it is the foundation of fairness in political and economic affairs.

Why Political Equality Leads to Economic Inequality

Political equality and the opportunity it unleashes have always gone hand-in-hand with enormous economic inequality. There is no contradiction in that fact. Political equality has to do with how individuals are treated by the government. It says that the government should treat all individuals the same—black or white, man or woman, rich or poor. But political equality says nothing about the differences that arise through the voluntary decisions of private individuals. Protecting people's equal rights inevitably leads to enormous differences in economic condition, as some people use their freedom to create modest amounts of wealth while others reach the highest levels of success.

It also leads to differences in *opportunity*. To be sure, political equality does provide a level playing field, in the sense that everyone plays by the same rules. Each of us is free to use our talents and resources to pursue happiness and success, without interference by others. But it is obviously true that some people will find the struggle to succeed harder than others. If you're born to loving, educated, and affluent parents, you will likely find it easier to achieve your aspirations than someone born in less desirable circumstances.

But that does not mean we should pursue an agenda of "equality of opportunity," as some advocate. As the critics of economic inequality are the first to point out, the only way to equalize opportunity is to equalize outcomes. "Inequality of outcomes and inequality of opportunity reinforce each other," writes economist Joseph Stiglitz.[254] Every time a person achieves a successful outcome, such as finishing college, that opens up a new range of opportunities—opportunities not enjoyed by those who haven't achieved the same outcome. When parents rise from poverty to become affluent, their outcomes translate into unequal opportunities for their children, who can now enjoy better health care, go to better schools, and afford to take prestigious but

---

254. Joseph E. Stiglitz, "Equal Opportunity, Our National Myth," Opinionator, *New York Times*, February 16, 2013, http://opinionator.blogs.nytimes. com/2013/02/16/equal-opportunity-our-national-myth/.

low-paying internships. "What it all comes down to," writes economist Paul Krugman, "is that although the principle of 'equality of opportunity, not equality of results' sounds fine, it's a largely fictitious distinction. A society with highly unequal results is, more or less inevitably, a society with highly unequal opportunity, too." And so, argue the critics, to achieve genuine equality of opportunity, the government needs to equalize results: in education, in health care, in wages, in wealth. "If you truly believe that all Americans are entitled to an equal chance at the starting line," concludes Krugman, "that's an argument for doing something to reduce inequality."[255]

The key thing to keep in mind is that the opportunities enjoyed by some people don't hold others back. On the contrary, part of the reason why people flock to the United States is precisely because it is a land where other people are wealthier, better educated, and more productive than in their home countries. It is infinitely easier to prosper as a cab driver in the Hamptons than in Havana. If the greater opportunities enjoyed by some actually held back those with fewer opportunities, then instead of foreigners immigrating to America, Americans should be immigrating to places like Mexico and India, where they would be among the wealthiest and best-educated people in the country. The reason almost no one does that is because we know in some terms that we aren't locked in a zero-sum battle for success, where we have to conquer opponents in order to achieve victory. In reality, we succeed by producing values and trading them with other producers, in exchanges where *both* sides win—and the more others have to offer, the easier our success becomes.

If we genuinely care about opportunity, we need to reject the concept of "equality of opportunity," and put the focus squarely back on equality of rights and the freedom it gives us to take advantage of life's limitless opportunities.

Is Economic Inequality Unfair?

So if economic inequality necessarily emerges from political equality, is that fair? To answer that question we need to start by realizing that the inequality alarmists have tried to smuggle into the discussion a perspective on wealth that tacitly *assumes* that economic inequality is unjust.

---

255. Paul Krugman, *The Conscience of a Liberal* (New York: W.W. Norton & Company, 2009), p. 249.

The "fixed pie" assumption. The alarmists often speak of economic success as if it were a fixed-sum game. There is only so much wealth to go around, and so inequality amounts to proof that someone has gained at someone else's expense. Arguing that "the riches accruing to the top have come at the *expense* of those down below," Stiglitz writes:

> One can think of what's been happening in terms of slices of a pie. If the pie were equally divided, everyone would get a slice of the same size, so the top 1 percent would get 1 percent of the pie. In fact, they get a very big slice, about a fifth of the entire pie. But that means everyone gets a smaller slice.[256]

What this ignores is the fact of *production*. If the pie is constantly expanding, because people are constantly creating more wealth, then one person's gain doesn't have to come at anyone else's expense. That doesn't mean you *can't* get richer at other people's expense, say by stealing someone else's pie, but a rise in inequality per se doesn't give us any reason to suspect that someone has been robbed or exploited or is even worse off.

Inequality, we have to keep in mind, is not the same thing as poverty. When people like journalist Timothy Noah complain that "income distribution in the United States is now more unequal than in Uruguay, Nicaragua, Guyana, and Venezuela," they act as if it's irrelevant that almost all Americans are rich compared to the citizens of these other countries. Economic inequality is perfectly compatible with widespread affluence, and *rising* inequality is perfectly compatible with a society in which the vast majority of citizens are getting richer. If the incomes of the poorest Americans doubled while the incomes of the richest Americans tripled, that would dramatically increase inequality even though every single person would be better off. Inequality refers not to deprivation but *difference*, and there is nothing suspicious or objectionable about differences per se.

The "group pie" assumption. In a famous speech denouncing economic inequality, President Obama said, "The top 10 percent no longer takes in one-third of *our* income—it now takes half."[257] (Emphasis

---

256. Joseph E. Stiglitz, *The Price of Inequality* (New York: Norton, 2013), p. 8.

257. Barack Obama, "Remarks by the President on Economic Mobility."

added.) This sort of phraseology, which is endemic in discussions of inequality, assumes that wealth is, in effect, a social pie that is created by "society as a whole," which then has to be divided up fairly. What's fair? Economists Robert Frank and Philip Cook start off their book on inequality with a simple thought experiment. "Imagine that you and two friends have been told that an anonymous benefactor has donated three hundred thousand dollars to divide among you. How would you split it? If you are like most people, you would immediately propose an equal division—one hundred thousand dollars per person."[258] If the pie belongs to "all of us," then absent other considerations, fairness demands we divide it up equally—not allow a small group to arbitrarily "take" a third of "our" income.

But although we can speak loosely about how much wealth a society has, wealth is not actually a pie belonging to the nation as a whole. It consists of particular values created by particular individuals (often working together in groups) and belonging to particular individuals. It is not distributed by "society": it is produced and traded by the people who create it. To distribute it, "society" would first have to *seize* it from the people who created it.

This changes the equation dramatically. When individuals *create* something, there is no presumption that they should end up with equal shares. If Robinson Crusoe and Friday are on an island, and Crusoe grows seven pumpkins and Friday grows three pumpkins, Crusoe hasn't grabbed a bigger piece of (pumpkin?) pie. He has simply created more wealth than Friday, leaving Friday no worse off. It is dishonest to say Crusoe has "taken" 70 percent of "the island's" wealth.

It's obvious why these two assumptions about wealth would lead us to view economic inequality with a skeptical eye. If wealth is a fixed pie or a pie cooked up by "society as a whole," then it follows that economic equality is the ideal, and departures from this ideal are *prima facie* unjust.

But if wealth is something that individuals *create*, then there's no reason to expect that we should be anything close to equal economically. If we look at the actual individuals who make up society, it is self-evident that human beings are unequal in almost every respect: in size, strength, intelligence, beauty, frugality, ambition, work ethic, moral character. Those differences will necessarily entail huge differences in economic condition—and there is no reason why those

---

258. Robert H. Frank and Philip J. Cook, *The Winner-Take-All Society* (New York: Free Press, 1995), p. vii.

differences should be viewed with skepticism, let alone alarm.

If we keep in mind that wealth is something individuals *produce*, then there is no reason to think that economic equality is an ideal or even that economic inequality is something that requires a special justification. On the contrary, it is an inevitable byproduct of the ideal of political equality.

But as the above analysis suggests, differences in productive achievement aren't the only source of economic inequality. Economic inequality *can* result from injustices. To think clearly about inequality, we have to be able to distinguish between the *earned* and the *unearned*.

What does it mean to say that someone "earned" his income? In short, that he *produced* it. If Robinson Crusoe builds a spear and uses it to catch a fish, he earned that fish—he produced it, it belongs to him, and it would be wrong for Friday to come along and take it. By the same token, we can earn values *indirectly*, by trading what we produce for the things that others produce. If Crusoe chooses not to eat his fish, but exchanges it with Friday for a coconut Friday chopped down from a tree, then Crusoe earned that coconut by obtaining it through the voluntary consent of Friday in a value-for-value trade.

In a division of labor economy, the principle is the same, but its application is less obvious. We don't produce and trade concrete items like fish and coconuts, as people do in barter economies. Instead, we produce in exchange for money, and we exchange money for the things that others produce. What determines how much money we receive for our productive efforts, and what we are able to buy with that money? The voluntary consent of the people we exchange with. To earn something, in a division of labor context, is to acquire it through production and voluntary exchange. What we merit is the economic value we create, *as judged by the people who voluntarily transact with us.*

It's a mistake to view economic rewards as payment for merit as such. We do not get paid in proportion to the laudable qualities we display—virtues such as diligence, integrity, and effort. Bill Gates worked hard to build Microsoft, but he's not a billionaire because he worked 20,000 times harder than the average American. To be sure, when a person is enormously successful, this almost always indicates virtue on his part. But the essential issue is that what a person merits or earns or deserves, in an economic context, is that he is able to reap whatever rewards he can achieve through productive effort and voluntary exchange.

In 1997, J.K. Rowling published the first book in her Harry Potter series. Over the course of the next decade, she published six more

Harry Potter books. Millions of delighted readers willingly paid about $10–$20 for each one, making Rowling a billionaire.

One of the highest paid CEOs over the last decade was Steve Jobs, who took home several billion dollars (mostly in the form of stock options). But over the course of his tenure as CEO, Jobs not only saved Apple from bankruptcy, but helped grow it from $3 billion in market capitalization to $347 billion—all through creating products that improved the lives of millions of customers, who happily paid hundreds or thousands of dollars for their Macs, iPods, iPhones, and iPads.[259]

Warren Buffett is the wealthiest investor of all time, with a net worth of about $60 billion. That's a lot of money, but Buffett helped grow his company, Berkshire Hathaway, from $22.1 million in market capitalization to more than $300 billion. Put another way, a $20.50 investment with Berkshire Hathaway in 1967 would be worth more than *$200,000* today—a track record no one else even comes close to.[260] Buffett's net worth came from using his genius to identify opportunities that no one else could see, putting resources into companies that created an enormous amount of value for their customers and shareholders, standing by those companies through thick and thin, and helping guide them so that they could prosper.

These men and women of extraordinary ability achieved their fortunes through merit. They *deserve* their riches. The insignia of deserved rewards is that they don't come at other people's expense. Bill Gates's billions didn't make anyone else poorer. He *created* billions of dollars of value by producing products that fueled the prosperity of his customers, suppliers, software makers, and that played a pivotal role in the Internet revolution. His $50 billion gain is puny in comparison. However great the fortunes earned by the most successful creators, they represent but a fraction of the total value they create.

To fully grasp this point, the thing to ask about these billionaires is why, since every dollar they earned came from the voluntary consent

---

259. Jay Yarow and Kamelia Angelova, "CHART OF THE DAY: Apple's Incredible Run Under Steve Jobs," *Business Insider,* August 25, 2011, http://www.businessinsider .com/chart-of-the-day-apples-market-cap-during-steve-jobs-tenure-2011-8.

260. JPL, "A Look at Berkshire Hathaway's Annual Market Returns from 1968–2007," *AllFinancialMatters.com,* blog, April 2, 2008, [https://web.archive.org/web/ 20080412003318/] http://allfinancialmatters.com/2008/04/02/a-look-at- berkshire-hathaways-annual-market-returns-from-1968-2007/ (accessed May 28, 2015); "Berkshire Hathaway Inc. (BRK-A)," Yahoo! Finance, May 28, 2015 http:// finance.yahoo.com/q?s=BRK-A.

of other people, so many people were willing to give them so much money. In short, it's because what they got in return was even *more* valuable. This is the key to understanding how inequality arises under freedom—and why it should.

In 1996, J.K. Rowling's net worth hovered somewhere in the neighborhood of nothing. She grew rich through a massive number of voluntary transactions. Because millions of individuals chose to pay $20 for a copy of one of her books, inequality increased: her income and wealth rose, her fans' income didn't budge and their wealth fell slightly. But the net result was that everyone involved in these transactions was *better off.* The readers valued the book more than the $20; Rowling (and her publisher) valued the $20 more than that copy of the book. They were win/win transactions, and the totality of those voluntary, win/win transactions meant that Rowling joined the ranks of the top 0.1 percent of earners. Inequality increased, and the world was a better place as a result.[261]

If the insignia of deserved rewards is that they emerge from voluntary, win/win transactions, then the insignia of undeserved gains is that the relationship is involuntary and win/lose. Someone gains at someone else's expense. There is no question that there are a lot of people who have achieved undeserved gains today, above all through the rising trend of cronyism. And there is no question that it is becoming harder and harder for Americans to earn their way to success. These facts have created an opening for the inequality alarmists to make Americans care about economic inequality—and to endorse their program for fighting it.

Political Equality and the State of the American Economy Today

Historically, Americans haven't cared about economic inequality, and it continues to be low on our list of concerns. But that is starting to change. Why?

The inequality alarmists have crafted a narrative that claims that inequality threatens the American Dream. It claims that incomes for all but the very rich are stagnating, and that mobility is declining: if you're born poor, you're going to stay poor, and if you're born rich, you're going to stay rich. What's responsible for this situation,

---

261. Robert Nozick famously gives a similar analysis using the example of Wilt Chamberlain in *Anarchy, State, and Utopia* (New York: Basic, 1974), pp. 160-64.

according to this narrative? The rich have used their power to pervert democracy so that the government works for "the 1 percent" rather than "the 99 percent." As just one piece of evidence, the alarmists point to the fact that "the rich" who allegedly created the 2008 financial crisis got bailed out, while poor Americans (supposedly) saw the social safety net pulled out from under them. The game is rigged in favor of the already-rich, and the result is a vicious circle: high inequality gives "the rich" more power to stack the deck in their favor, leading to further inequality, ad infinitum.

Americans *are* concerned about the state of opportunity today—and rightfully so. When the alarmists say that the American Dream is on life-support, their arguments often resonate because, in many instances, the problems they are pointing to are real (if sometimes exaggerated). In some ways, the road to success is *not* as open as it once was. Progress *is* slower than it should be. There *are* people getting their hands on money they do not deserve. But not in the way, or for the reasons, that the inequality alarmists say.

There are genuine barriers to opportunity, and the deck *is* becoming stacked against us—but not because "the rich" are too rich and the government is doing too little to fight economic inequality. The real threat to opportunity in America is increasing *political* inequality.

In a land of opportunity, an individual should succeed or fail on the basis of merit, not political privilege. You deserve what you earn—no more, no less. Today, however, some people are being stopped from rising by merit, and others are getting the unearned through political privilege. But the real source of this problem is that we have granted the government an incredible amount of arbitrary power: to intervene in our affairs, to pick winners and losers, to put roadblocks in the way of success, to hand out wealth and other special favors to whatever pressure group can present itself as the face of "the public good." Some of these injustices *do* increase economic inequality, but it isn't the inequality that should bother us—it's the injustices.

When a bank or auto company that made irrational decisions gets bailed out at public expense, that *is* an outrage. But the root of the problem isn't their executives' ability to influence Washington—it's Washington's power to dispense bailouts. When an inner-city child is stuck in a school that doesn't educate him, that *is* a tragedy. But the problem isn't that other children get a better education—it's that the government has created an educational system that often doesn't educate, and that makes it virtually impossible for anyone but the affluent to seek out alternatives.

The same goes for countless other ways the government gives special privileges to some people at the expense of others:

- **Cronyism**—whether in the form of bailouts, subsidies, government-granted monopolies, or other special favors—benefits some businesses at the expense of competitors and buyers.

- **Occupational licensing laws** in fields as varied as hair-braiding and interior decorating protect incumbents from competitors by arbitrarily preventing individuals from freely entering into those fields.

- **The minimum wage** raises some people's incomes at the expense of employers and customers as well as other low-skilled workers, who are priced out of the labor market and thrown onto the unemployment rolls.

- **The welfare state** openly deprives some people of their earned rewards in order to give other people the unearned.

- **The Federal Reserve**, through its control over the banking system and manipulation of the money supply, transfers massive amounts of wealth mainly into the hands of financial insiders.

Of course people will try to influence a government that has so much arbitrary power over their lives, and *of course* those with the best connections and deepest pockets will often be the most successful at influencing it. The question is, what created this situation, and what should we do about that? The inequality alarmists tell us that the problem is not *how much* arbitrary power the government has, but *whom* the government uses that power *for.* They say that by handing the government even more power, and demanding that it use that power for the sake of "the 99 percent" rather than "the 1 percent," everyone will be better off.

We believe that only when the government is limited to the function of protecting our equal rights can people rise through merit rather than government-granted privilege, and that the cure for people seeking special favors from the government is to create a government that has no special favors to grant.

What's required to save the American Dream is not to wage war on economic inequality, but to recommit ourselves to the ideal of political equality. We need to liberate the individual so that each of us is equally free to pursue success and happiness.

The alarmists' program to fight economic inequality will only make that harder. Whether it is dramatically raising taxes, doubling down on the bloated regulatory state, capping CEO pay, raising the minimum wage, or giving more political power to unions, their agenda consists of propping up those at the bottom and chopping down those at the top—always at the expense of the person who desires the opportunity to build a successful life for himself through his own thought and effort. The alarmists don't oppose people gaining the unearned or losing what they have rightfully earned—they merely want to change who gets sacrificed and who gets unearned rewards so as to make us more economically equal. This is what they refer to as "social justice."

The Importance of Challenging Immoral Ideals

In recent years, some defenders of free markets have started to realize the importance of not ceding the moral high ground to the inequality alarmists. But with few exceptions, their strategy has been to repackage their own agenda in the alarmists' moral language—to say that free-market supporters are the true champions of economic equality and social justice. This is a mistake. It implies that they agree with the alarmists at the level of values and disagree with them only about the means of securing these values. This has the paradoxical effect of taking the debate *off* of the moral issues and quibbling over data and economic theory.

When it comes to the debate over economic inequality, the real clash *is* a clash of values and the purpose of a moral argument is to make clear what values are at stake.

Americans today face a choice between two moral views. One view upholds *justice*: it says that each individual has an equal right to pursue his own happiness and success, and that whatever wealth, income, and opportunities he earns in that pursuit belong to *him*.

Another view upholds "social justice": it says that the government must restrict our freedom to make us economically equal, and that if one person produces "too much," his hopes and dreams should be sacrificed for the sake of those who haven't produced.

Either we're all equal in our rights or some people are to be met with burdens and others with special privileges. That is the choice.

The worst error we can make is to endorse an ideal we disagree with. To say, as some on the right have, that "our policies will truly make Americans more equal economically" comes off as insincere— and, in the end, it is suicidal. Because the fact is that if economic equality is a moral ideal, then economic freedom *is* immoral. If it's wrong for some people to make huge fortunes while others don't, then the government *should* prop up the bottom and chop down the top.

The American Dream is under attack today, but the threat is not economic inequality. It is the war on political equality. To win this debate, *that* is the ideal we need to champion.

Luck Is Overrated

By Don Watkins

"I think I just won a million dollars," Hubert Tang told a friend. The California bartender hadn't played the lottery in a decade, but after finding $20 outside of San Francisco International Airport, Tang bought two scratch-off tickets and walked away with a fortune.[262] That's some extraordinary luck. But to hear some of our leading politicians and intellectuals tell it, Tang's story isn't all that unique. The secret to success, in Barack Obama's words, is to become one of "society's lottery winners."[263]

It's a theme Obama kept returning to throughout his presidency. During his 2016 Howard University commencement address, the president underscored the importance of not taking too much credit for your own achievements: "[Y]es, you've worked hard, but you've also been lucky. That's a pet peeve of mine: People who have been successful and don't realize they've been lucky. That God may have blessed them; it wasn't nothing you did."[264]

This notion—that success is in large part the result of luck, and that successful individuals stubbornly deny it—has become one of the central themes of economic inequality critics like Obama. Last year, for instance, Cornell economist and inequality critic Robert H. Frank released his latest book, *Success and Luck: Good Fortune and the Myth of Meritocracy*, arguing that "chance events play a much larger role in important life outcomes than most people once imagined."[265] In a similar vein, *New York Times* columnist Paul Krugman writes, in a column condemning income inequality, that it would be "foolish" to "deny that great success in business (or, actually,

262. "Million Dollar Lottery Winner Bought Ticket in Millbrae with $20 Bill He Found on Street," CBS San Francisco, August 29, 2015, http://sanfrancisco.cbslocal.com/2015/08/29/million-dollar-lottery-winner-bought-ticket-in-millbrae-with-money-he-found-millbrae.

263. Barack Obama, "Obama Dismisses Wealthy Americans as 'Society's Lottery Winners'," DC Vids, YouTube, May 12, 2015, https://www.youtube.com/watch?v=rBmQiFs8ihw.

264. Barack Obama, "Obama's Full Remarks at Howard University Commencement Ceremony," *Politico*, May 7, 2016, http://www.politico.com/story/2016/05/obamas-howard-commencement-transcript-222931#ixzz48O4gSveQ.

265. Robert H. Frank, *Success and Luck: Good Fortune and the Myth of Meritocracy* (Princeton, NJ: Princeton University Press, 2016), p. xi.

anything else) has a strong element of luck—not just the luck of being the first to stumble on a highly profitable idea or strategy,"—not create, stumble—"but also the luck of being born to the right parents."[266]

Why does this matter? As Frank complains, "overlooking luck's role makes those who've succeeded at the highest levels feel much more entitled to keep the lion's share of the income they've earned."[267] But if Americans become convinced that they are not the authors of their own success but the beneficiaries of luck, then they will be much less opposed to the various wealth redistribution and other "social justice" schemes critics of economic inequality favor. When people don't believe they built that, it's much easier to take that.

But if some are guilty of ignoring the role of luck in success, the inequality critics are guilty of wildly exaggerating it in order to push their egalitarian agenda.

Today's greatest symbol of spectacular success has also become today's greatest symbol of spectacular luck. Bill Gates is the oft-cited illustration of the fact that it isn't talent and effort that matter most when it comes to attaining affluence: it's luck.

In his 2008 mega-blockbuster *Outliers*, Malcolm Gladwell sums up the then-standard story of Gates's rise: "Brilliant, young math whiz discovers computer programming. Drops out of Harvard. With his friends, starts a little computer company called Microsoft. Through sheer brilliance and ambition and guts builds it into the giant of the software world."[268] But according to Gladwell, this story papers over the real tale—that at every step of the way, Gates's success depended on good fortune.

The pivotal thing that allowed Bill Gates to become Bill Gates, Gladwell explains, was the countless hours he had spent programming computers. Citing the "10,000 hour rule" that *Outliers* would popularize, Gladwell argues that success is chiefly the result of unique circumstances that allow a person to put in the 10,000 hours of practice supposedly required to achieve mastery in a domain. Gates was able to spend his youth learning to program before virtually anyone else his age had access to computers. That wasn't Gates's achievement. He

---

266. Paul Krugman, "Is Vast Inequality Necessary?," *New York Times*, January 15, 2016, http://www.nytimes.com/2016/01/15/opinion/is-vast-inequality-necessary.html.

267. Frank, *Success and Luck*, p. 93.

268. Malcolm Gladwell, *Outliers: The Story of Success* (New York: Back Bay Books, 2008), p. 50.

lucked out. In fact, he lucked out multiple times—nine, by Gladwell's count—in ways that gave him the unparalleled advantage of becoming a master programmer before most of his peers had so much as touched a computer. In short, what distinguishes Gates, Gladwell tells us, is not his "extraordinary talent" but his "extraordinary opportunities."[269]

Robert Frank thinks Gladwell understates the role of luck in Gates's success. "Bill Gates would not have gone on to become one of the wealthiest people in the world if he had not achieved such deep mastery at writing software. But even coupled with his appetite for sustained hard work, that expertise does not fully explain his success." Frank goes on to describe one of the turning points in Microsoft's rise: its early deal to provide the operating system for IBM's first personal computer. It's a topsy-turvy tale that involves Gates securing a deal with IBM that was initially pitched to a company called Digital Research but fell through for reasons that remain murky, and a contract that gave Gates what, in retrospect, turned out to be insanely favorable terms. "In short," concludes Frank, "most of us would never have heard of Microsoft if any one of a long sequence of improbable events had not occurred."[270]

There is another way of looking at Gates's story, however—one that neither denies that chance events played a role nor treats Gates as a lottery winner. "Consider these questions," Jim Collins and Morten Hansen write in their book *Great by Choice*:

> Was Gates the *only* person of his era who grew up in an upper middle-class American family?
>
> Was Gates the *only* person born in the mid-1950s who attended a secondary school with access to computing?
>
> Was Gates the *only* person who went to a college with computer resources in the mid-1970s?
>
> Was Gates the *only* person who read [a seminal] *Popular Electronics* article?
>
> Was Gates the *only* person who knew how to program in Basic?
>
> No, no, no, no and no.[271]

---

269. Gladwell, *Outliers*, p. 55.

270. Frank, *Success and Luck*, pp. 34–35.

271. Jim Collins and Morten T. Hansen, *Great by Choice* (New York: HarperCollins, 2011), p. 162.

In their book, Collins and Hansen investigate what distinguishes ultra-successful companies from all the others. One possibility, they concede, is that it's all just a matter of luck. But whereas authors like Frank and Gladwell think that you can make that case merely by pointing to lucky events enjoyed by the successful, Collins and Hansen observe that the question isn't whether luck plays *some* role in success—but whether it plays a *differentiating* role. Life is filled with events and circumstances we can neither control nor predict. But to say that luck *explains* success (or failure) is to say that successful individuals (and companies) enjoy *more* good luck and *less* bad luck than the rest of us.

But when Collins and Hansen tried to investigate the matter, that is not what they found. What distinguished the most successful companies "wasn't luck per se but what they *did* with the luck they got."[272] This led the authors to formulate the concept of "return on luck."

> The difference between Bill Gates and similarly advantaged people is not luck. Gates was lucky to be born at the right time, but many others had this luck. And yes, Gates was lucky to have the chance to learn programming by 1975, but many others had this same luck. Gates *did* more with his luck, taking a confluence of lucky circumstances and creating a huge *return* on his luck. And this is the important difference.[273]

Collins and Hansen *aren't* saying that we all can be as successful as Bill Gates—that getting "return on luck" negates the influence of every other factor. If Gates had been born a peasant in Communist China during the Cultural Revolution, they point out, it's simply not true that he would have created Microsoft. What they are drawing attention to is something the "luck" advocates minimize: the decisive role of human agency.

Winning the lottery is a matter of luck because once you buy a ticket the outcome is not in your hands. No choice you make, no strategy you concoct, no effort you exert is going to increase your chances of hitting it big. You're at the mercy of the odds. That's why you don't see professional lotto players who support themselves by hitting the jackpot year after year. But we do see plenty of professional business

---

272. Collins and Hansen, *Great by Choice*, p. 160.

273. Ibid., p. 163.

leaders—people who build companies that lead the pack over the course of decades, or who start multiple successful companies, or who consistently (if imperfectly) invest in companies that achieve notable success. That is not what we would expect to see if luck were the sole or even primary driver of business success.

In his book on success and luck, *The Success Equation*, investment strategist Michael Mauboussin says a test for whether you're dealing with a game of pure luck is whether you can lose on purpose. If you can choose to lose on purpose, you're not dealing with a game of pure luck. If you've ever tried to let your kid win a game of *Candy Land*, you've experienced this firsthand: unless you cheat—and, hey, I'll admit to loading the deck to make sure my four-year-old triumphs—nothing you can do will ensure that your kid wins. It's all a matter of luck.

But failing in your career on purpose? Nothing could be easier. J. D. Vance, in his 2016 blockbuster *Hillbilly Elegy*, describes how he spent a summer working at a job that was great by local standards: decent pay, health insurance, high job security, and no degree required. Yet he watched as a couple badly in need of stable employment—they had a kid on the way—lost their jobs after consistently showing up late, taking multiple extra breaks throughout the day, and regularly missing work without advance notice. (When the boyfriend was fired, Vance notes, he blamed the manager: "How could you do this to me? Don't you know I've got a pregnant girlfriend?" As Vance goes on to observe, "There is a lack of agency here—a feeling that you have little control over your life and a willingness to blame everyone but yourself.")[274] You can *choose* to fail, and people do it all the time. But in what sense can you choose to succeed?

Actually, that's something we do all the time, too. We are constantly setting goals, gathering knowledge for how to achieve them, and then taking purposeful action to realize them, whether it's planning a dinner party, earning a college degree, or executing a project at work. And more often than not, our efforts pay off. We make choices that allow us to *succeed*. Not all goals are made equal, of course. They differ in timescale, complexity, importance, and the degree to which the factors relevant to our success or failure are within our control. But the basic *process* of success is always the same.

And this is true of career success as well. If you study the lives of successful individuals, what you inevitably find is that they set

---

274. J. D. Vance, *Hillbilly Elegy* (New York: Harper, 2016), pp. 5–7.

ambitious goals, relentlessly pursue knowledge relevant to their goals, and exercise dedicated effort in pursuit of their goals. Instead of passively waiting for success to find them, they actively chart a course that points them in the direction of the future they want.

The importance of setting clear goals for achieving success is not exactly a state secret. The business and self-help sections of any bookstore are filled with books explaining why goals are important, how to set them, and how to follow through on them. In one form or another, all successful people achieve success on purpose. They have a conception of what they're after that guides their actions. And that last part is important. A goal isn't just a desire or a wish. Plenty of people daydream about success. They would *like* it if they had money or a business or a better job, but those desires don't govern their day-to-day choices. A goal is a consciously selected purpose that guides your action. When someone says on New Year's Eve, "I'm going to lose 20 pounds," that's a wish. When they write out a plan, throw out their junk food, and show up at the gym the next day, losing weight is a goal.

"A computer on every desk and in every home." That was Bill Gates's vision for Microsoft. Today it's hard to appreciate how daring that vision was. Gates formulated his goal at a time when most computers were still too big to fit on a desk, and when only a few technically savvy hobbyists had computers at home. Nevertheless, that purpose became the organizing principle of Gates's life. It's *why* he left Harvard to found Microsoft. It's why he worked insane hours instead of taking it easy or starting a family. It's why he kept on growing Microsoft long after he could have sold the company and retired to an island.

We aren't born with goals. Many people spend their entire lives governed by routine and short-range concerns. But all of us have the ability, during any waking moment, to go from passive to purposeful: to define what we want and to start to move toward it. That's not luck. That's choice. And while pursuing a goal doesn't guarantee success, not pursuing success as a goal guarantees failure. You can point to Gates's "lucky breaks" all you want, but at minimum what you can say is that Gates put himself in a position where luck could find him. And in reality he did a whole lot more than that.

If a goal is an action-guiding purpose, then the discovery of knowledge and dedicated effort are the basic kinds of actions that lead to its achievement.

It is striking how seldom the luck advocates discuss the role of knowledge in success. For them, success is either about luck or "talent and hard work." They ignore that most of what successful individuals do to succeed is restlessly seek out knowledge. We survive by gathering and using knowledge. It's how we grow food, it's how we build airplanes, it's how we write software code, it's how we create successful companies that outdo competitors year after year. Every goal we want to achieve requires knowledge, and the quest for knowledge is a major part of successful action. Gates is a case in point.

"I'm not an educator, but I'm a learner," Gates has said about himself.[275] It's a self-assessment that not even Gates's critics have dared to challenge. His success depended, not on sheer hard work, but on effort that was directed by an incredible depth of knowledge of programming, of business, of tech trends—as well as an incredible breadth of other knowledge. Psychologist Edwin A. Locke sums it up this way:

> Bill Gates can be described as an information-gathering, information-integrating, superpowered vacuum. His idea of a vacation is to study physics, history, literature, biology, and biotechnology. He also reads widely in the field of software technology, goes through hundreds of e-mail messages daily, reads business magazines, talks with the best minds in his company and many outside it, and pushes Microsoft relentlessly to develop new products and improve the ones it already has.[276]

Recognizing that knowledge is the fuel that feeds success, Gates fostered a culture of learning at Microsoft. In the best study of Microsoft's success, the 1995 book *Microsoft Secrets*, researchers Michael A. Cusumano and Richard W. Selby devote an entire chapter to how Microsoft succeeded through superior learning, or what they called improvement *"through continuous self-critiquing, feedback, and sharing."*[277] For example, the authors note that Microsoft received huge numbers of questions and complaints from customers, and analyzed that information "more thoroughly than any other company we have seen. It then channels this information quickly and directly to the product development groups."[278]

---

275. Janet Lowe, *Bill Gates Speaks* (New York: Wiley, 2001), p. 43.

276. Edwin A. Locke, *The Prime Movers* (New York: AMACOM, 2000), p. 54.

277. Michael A. Cusumano, *Microsoft Secrets* (New York: Free Press, 1998), p. 327.

278. Cusumano, *Microsoft Secrets*, pp. 328–29.

The goal was to avoid making the same mistakes over and over again—mistakes that competitors would have been all too happy to capitalize on. They conclude:

> The principles of learning that we see in Microsoft we also see in other successful companies. Good firms everywhere critique their processes and products in order to learn from past successes as well as past failures. They measure and benchmark what they do. They study customers. And they try to get different parts of the organization to cooperate and share components, as well as product and process knowledge more generally. Particularly for a PC software company, however, we feel Microsoft is distinctive in the degree to which it now emphasizes these principles.[279]

Much of that is applicable to Gates and to all successful individuals. Their thirst for knowledge leads them to be extremely self-critical, and to squeeze as many lessons from success and from failure as they can. And all of that is a *choice*—a choice that most people don't make, at least not consistently. It's painful to admit mistakes, and it takes time and self-discipline even to learn from successes. Yet that is what successful individuals and companies do. They don't want to hear how great they are—they want to know the truth about their strengths and weaknesses. Nothing less will get them to their goals.

But knowledge on its own doesn't lead to success. You need knowledge plus action. We often sum up this sort of action as "hard work." But that's potentially misleading. Success doesn't come from physical toil but from mental achievement—from conceiving of value-creating ideas, cultivating the knowledge required to realize those ideas, and implementing that knowledge through deliberate action. What is true is that success is difficult. Namely, it is a long-range endeavor requiring *dedicated effort*. Dedication is the commitment to do whatever it takes to achieve your goals, no matter the obstacles, no matter how long it takes.

According to Gates:

> When I was in my 20s and early 30s, I was fanatical about software. By "fanatical" I mean that I was so focused on my vision of putting a computer on every desk and in every

---

279. Cusumano, *Microsoft Secrets*, p., 328.

home that I gave up a normal existence. I didn't take vacations or weekends off. I wasn't interested in getting married. (Obviously, that changed when I met Melinda!) My colleagues and I at Microsoft took tremendous pride in being the first to arrive at work and the last to leave. It was an incredibly fun chapter of my life.[280]

Most high earners work far more hours than low earners.[281] But Gates was in a league of his own. From 1978 to 1984, he spent a grand total of fifteen days not working.[282] Most of us hit the fifteen-day mark in two months. And you can be sure few if any of those workdays started at 9 and ended at 5.

Dedication is hard. In some ways, harder than physical effort. If you're digging ditches, it is painful and exhausting, but you know that you're making progress, and when it's time to clock out, you can go home and disconnect. Dedicated effort to a long-term goal is different. It can involve working without any external reward for months, years, and even decades. It can be impossible to know if you're making progress or spinning your wheels. It can be tempting to give up—in part because sometimes you *should* give up. And for many goals, you're always on call. If you're trying to create a business and your server crashes or your best engineer leaves or your sales are falling short, you can't say, "Hey, I put in my eight hours, I want to relax." Not if you want to succeed.

And it's not just time. One *Huffington Post* contributor called it "shockingly obtuse to suggest that an hour spent in a comfortable office doing a job you love is even remotely comparable to an hour spent in a sweltering kitchen flipping burgers."[283] What's shockingly obtuse is to suggest that mental effort is not real effort. It's true that most successful individual enjoy their jobs—it's why they fought so hard to be

280. Bill Gates, "A Year to Remember," *gatesnotes*, blog, December 20, 2016, https://www.gatesnotes.com/media/GN_Newsletter_Archive/TGN-Newsletter-Online-V12202016.html.

281. Robert Frank, "Do the Wealthy Work Harder Than the Rest?," *Wall Street Journal*, August 27, 2012, http://blogs.wsj.com/wealth/2012/04/27/do-the-wealthy-work-harder-than-the-rest/.

282. Lowe, *Bill Gates Speaks*, p. 37.

283. Anthony W. Orlando, "The Rich Aren't Rich Because They Work Harder. They Work Harder Because They're Rich," *Huffington Post*, February 14, 2014, http://www.huffingtonpost.com/anthony-w-orlando/the-rich-arent-rich-becau_b_4791626.html.

successful. But speaking as an author who spent his early years doing the equivalent of burger flipping, I can say that, when you are struggling with creative work, physical comfort is little comfort indeed. You are often in a position where you *have* to solve a problem and you don't know how to solve it—but you are the only one who *can* solve it. For business leaders, the pressure is compounded because your success or failure often has consequences not just for you and your family, but to hundreds or even thousands of people who depend on you: your investors, your customers, your employees. No wonder entrepreneurs experience more stress, anxiety, and depression than other workers.[284]

Dedication means subjecting yourself to fear, discomfort, fatigue, failure, and even anguish over and over again in order to achieve a goal worth achieving. It's a price very few people are willing to pay. Most don't try, and most who do give up. The continual choice to forge ahead, to accept the pain, and to do so when success might never come—all of that is ignored and discounted by comparing successful men and women to "lottery winners."

The larger point in all of this is that human beings have the power to set goals, to accumulate knowledge relevant to our goals, and to purposefully move toward those goals, even in the face of obstacles. We act in a world where countless factors are outside of our control—and yet this doesn't mean *we* are out of control. We can try to predict and prepare for chance events. When we encounter good luck, we can act to capitalize on it. When we encounter bad luck, we can search for another route to our goal, sometimes even turning negatives into positives. And, perhaps most important, we determine the trajectory of our lives by deciding which goals to pursue and by choosing how (and how hard) to pursue them. Bill Gates could not have predicted his exact path or the level of his ultimate success—but he set his general course, and maintained it over decades in the face of challenges and obstacles. That is what the luck advocates label a "lottery winner."

In the lottery, your success or failure is determined by luck. In life, your success or failure is determined by the choices you make—including what you do in the face of luck. In fact, the best way to think about your life isn't through the prism of luck at all. It's to think in terms of challenges and opportunities. Luck leaves us passive—challenges and

---

284. Jessica Bruder, "The Psychological Price of Entrepreneurship," *Inc.*, September 2013, http://www.inc.com/magazine/201309/jessica-bruder/psychological-price-of-entrepreneurship.html.

opportunities set a context for action.

Bill Gates may have had opportunities that most people didn't, but he chose to capitalize on them—despite the challenges he encountered, despite the fact that many people enjoying similar opportunities did not capitalize on them, despite the fact that Gates himself could have made different choices. He could have chosen not to take advantage of his school's computer. He could have stayed at Harvard. He could have frittered away the IBM deal, as Digital Research did. He could have worked a normal work week and been surpassed by the competition. But he didn't. Facing his unique set of challenges and opportunities, he made choices that led him to become one of the most successful businessmen in history. That is what it means to choose to succeed.

But scratch beneath the surface and it's clear that the luck advocates have a very different conception of what it would mean to choose to succeed. For them it's not enough that we be able to exercise choice in the face of our circumstances, over time moving ourselves to a better state of affairs. No. To have control over (and deserve credit for) our success requires having *total* control over our life outcomes—outside factors can play no role. How else to make sense of their claim that because we can identify specific lucky events in the lives of people like Gates we can conclude that luck *explains* their success? In their telling, Bill Gates may have made choices that, given the circumstances he faced, led to the creation and triumph of Microsoft. But he gets no credit for that—simply because we can imagine circumstances he did *not* face where he wouldn't have created one of the most valuable companies in history.

This is rewriting reality. We form our conception of what it means to deserve something, not by comparing ourselves to a god who can guarantee whatever outcomes he wants by a sheer act of will, whatever the circumstances. We form it by observing that a person, facing alternative paths in life, can make choices that move him toward a desired result or make choices that lead to failure.

But "what about the many talented and hardworking people who never achieve much material success?" Robert Frank wonders.[285] The idea is that if talent and hard work—the closest he comes to discussing things open to an individual's choice—lead to failure just as often as success, then it's senseless to say that we have a substantial impact on our own success.

---

285. Frank, *Success and Luck*, p. 7.

Frank follows that question with the story of Birkhaman Rai, a young man from Bhutan who cooked for Frank in Nepal. "To this day, he remains perhaps the most enterprising and talented person I've ever met. . . . If he had grown up in the United States or some other rich country, he would have been far more prosperous, perhaps even spectacularly successful." Yet he didn't, so he wasn't.[286]

But Frank's example proves only too much: to whatever extent Rai lives in a country where he has the freedom to exercise and benefit from his productive efforts, his "talent and hard work" surely make him more successful than he would be if he was lazy and incompetent. And although he would almost certainly be far wealthier had he been born in a wealthy country, this doesn't show the inefficacy of talent and hard work. It shows only that the particular *scale* of success is determined in part by the economic context a talented and hardworking person is operating in. Frank is in effect arguing that because Dan Marino never won a Super Bowl, that means talent and hard work aren't efficacious in football, whereas the reality is, Marino's talent and hard work made him and his team more successful than they otherwise would have been—even if, applied in the context of a better team, his ability would have brought home the trophy.

What Frank wants us to believe is that a country like America is teaming with individuals who have set success as a genuine goal, who have exerted the same ambitious pursuit of knowledge and demonstrated the same dedicated effort as Bill Gates, but experienced unremitting failure. But is that really true? Neither Frank nor Gladwell nor Obama—no one, really—has provided evidence to support that.

The most they could plausibly claim is that there are a lot of ambitious, productive people who fail to become billionaires. True enough. Some ambitious people deliberately choose not to go into fields that are especially remunerative. Others may have to settle for making a low six-figure salary, which would make them among the richest people in the world and in human history. But the idea that luck is keeping a significant number of those who choose to do what is necessary to succeed poor—poor across the whole of their lives? That's more myth than reality.

I think the luck advocates get that. They know that most people fail because of the *choices* they make. And that's why many of them go on to deny that we make *any* genuine choices. According to many luck advocates, human beings are puppets who lack free will: things

---

286. Ibid.

happen to us—we don't make things happen. Frank, for instance, although he spends page after page arguing that luck, not talent and skill, is the key to success, also tells us that bickering over whether Bill Gates succeeded through talent and hard work or by cashing in on various contingencies, such as access to a computer, is really beside the point. Even talent and hard work, he says, are outside of our control, but instead "spring from some combination of genes and the environment." And so, Frank writes:

> if you have such qualities, on what theory would it make sense for you to claim moral credit for them? You didn't choose your parents, nor did you have much control over the environment in which you were raised. You were just lucky. . . . In short, even if talent and hard work alone were enough to ensure material success—which they are not—luck would remain an essential part of the story. People with a lot of talent and an inclination to work hard are extremely fortunate.[287]

(One can't help but think of poor Birkhaman Rai. Is Frank saying we shouldn't admire the gentleman for his work ethic since he was simply "extremely fortunate?")

Obviously if human beings don't make choices, if we're essentially robots without free will and self-direction, then the luck narrative wins. But if that's the case Frank wants to make, then he should write a treatise on the perennial debate between free will and determinism—not waste his time hammering away at why skill and hard work don't matter. Then again, if we don't make any genuine choices, why bother offering us any advice about what we *should choose* to believe and which political policies we *should choose* to enact?

But if we do make choices, then the luck narrative is not simply wrong: it is vicious.

Unless you think that all choice is an illusion, it is obvious that the choices we make are at the heart of our success or failure. The people who have succeeded at making something of their lives did so by setting their course and—however long it took, however difficult the obstacles—building the life they wanted. The luck narrative looks at these people and says we should think of them as drunks in Vegas who put

---

287. Frank, *Success and Luck*, p. 8.

their life savings on lucky number 13 and hit it big. What does that sort of image do to a human being who accepts it?

I remember years ago, when I lived in Fairfax County, a well-to-do suburb of Washington D.C., talking to the father of my girlfriend. He had grown up in a small Kentucky town but had gone on to have a successful career. He wasn't making millions or anything, but he certainly would have skewed his hometown's mobility statistics upward. I asked him how the people he grew up with viewed his success. He said he encountered a fair deal of jealousy. The phrase he heard again and again was "You're getting too big for your britches," which was striking because he was if anything excessively humble. And yet the attacks stung. He was successful, but instead of feeling proud of his success, it was a source of conflict and guilt. At the time, I found that to be tragic. I still do.

Resentment and envy of success are real and more widespread than most of us would like to admit. From the stereotypical schoolyard bully who beats up the straight-A student to the political blowhard who caricatures affluent individuals as devious moustache-twirling villains, there is a deep undercurrent in our culture that looks at success without admiration or celebration, but with contempt—as if poverty and failure was a morally superior state. They want to see rich people become poor, or at least feel guilty about being rich. For those who view pride in earned success as the enemy, the luck narrative is one of their chief weapons.

That's not speculation. For all intents and purposes, that's the premise of Robert Frank's book: that people's belief they have earned their success is a problem to be solved so that the government can take more of their money and spend it on whatever Frank and his cronies believe is good for society. I find that deeply disturbing. Unearned guilt is corrosive, and to try to instill it in people who do not have it? I think of my own kids. I want them to be successful in whatever they choose as their life's work. I want them to make something of themselves. And if they succeed, I want them to enjoy their success. The idea that they should feel defeated if they fail and guilty if they succeed is repugnant.

If there is anything more tragic than the effect of the luck narrative on those who have succeeded, it's the effect on those who have yet to succeed. My friend Jeremiah grew up in an abusive home, or rather, with abusive parents who often didn't have a home, but marched Jeremiah around to homeless shelters until he was sent off to foster care. Instead of escaping into drugs or crime, Jeremiah escaped that entire world by developing an intense focus on education and a savage work ethic. Now ask yourself: what sort of moral evaluation would you pass on someone who had said to him, when he was struggling to rise out of hell, "Don't bother kid—it's all a matter of luck, and if you're born poor, you're probably going to stay poor"? And what sort of tragedy would it have been if Jeremiah had listened?

There are people who believe that success is a matter of luck, and who live accordingly. Not the luck advocates themselves, who are nothing if not ambitious. Rather, it's those who devote their mental efforts to ferreting out all the reasons why life is unfair, why the deck is stacked, why it's not their fault, why they are indeed a helpless victim of fate. And in a sense, they are. If we choose *not* to set demanding goals, and to pursue them through unflagging thought and effort, then our course will be determined by chance. Only we were not helpless in the matter: we could have chosen otherwise.

We human beings are not gods who determine our own destiny through an omnipotent act of will. But neither are we pawns moved by the hands of fate. We are prime movers: we do not control everything, but we control our thoughts and actions, and that gives us an incredible power to shape our lives. Sweeping all that aside, the luck narrative fosters passivity and fatalism among those who have yet to succeed, and stokes resentment and envy at whoever has succeeded.

And that's its purpose. It is not a corrective aimed at those unwilling to acknowledge the role of outside factors in their success. It is a rallying cry for those who seek to tear down the successful, materially and morally.

The Trouble with "Rent Seeking"

By Don Watkins

In our book *Equal Is Unfair: America's Misguided Fight Against Income Inequality*, Yaron Brook and I argue that one of the problems with the concept of "economic inequality" is that it lumps together two fundamentally different things: inequality that reflects differences in productive achievement and inequality that reflects some people's ability to gain unearned wealth. Package-deals like this lay the groundwork for injustice.

For example, you'll often hear critics of economic inequality point to instances of cronyism—people getting rich through government privileges like subsidies—in order to justify "fighting inequality." But then they propose solutions that would penalize every successful person, including the Jeff Bezoses of the world who get rich by creating enormous amounts of value.

There's a fundamental moral distinction between voluntary trade and physical force, and so if you are using a concept that treats those as the same, there's something wrong with your concept.

Another concept that comes up again and again in the inequality debate, and which also commits this error, is "rent seeking."

Most free-market-leaning thinkers treat rent seeking as synonymous with cronyism. Here, for example, is how economist David Henderson describes it:

> People are said to seek rents when they try to obtain benefits for themselves through the political arena. They typically do so by getting a subsidy for a good they produce or for being in a particular class of people, by getting a tariff on a good they produce, or by getting a special regulation that hampers their competitors. Elderly people, for example, often seek higher Social Security payments; steel producers often seek restrictions on imports of steel; and licensed electricians and doctors often lobby to keep regulations in place that restrict competition from unlicensed electricians or doctors.
>
> But why do economists use the term "rent"? Unfortunately, there is no good reason. David Ricardo introduced the term "rent" in economics. It means the payment to a factor of production in excess of what is required to keep that factor in its present use. So, for example, if I am paid $150,000 in

my current job but I would stay in that job for any salary over $130,000, I am making $20,000 in rent. What is wrong with rent seeking? Absolutely nothing. I would be rent seeking if I asked for a raise. My employer would then be free to decide if my services are worth it. Even though I am seeking rents by asking for a raise, this is not what economists mean by "rent seeking." They use the term to describe people's lobbying of government to give them special privileges. A much better term is "privilege seeking."[288]

In Henderson's description, rent seeking can consist of gaining money through voluntary exchange and making money through government coercion. True, Henderson says that economists "use the term to describe people's lobbying of government to give them special privileges." But that unfortunately is not always the case.

Here's a recent example from columnist Megan McArdle, who argues that finance and academia are benefiting from rent seeking.

> The next question is, "How are these guys managing to capture so much rent?" The classic answer is "barriers to entry," which means pretty much what it sounds like: aspiring entrepreneurs might like to compete with your products, but there's some reason it's hard for them to do so.
>
> It's hard to start a new college or a new investment bank. There are regulatory barriers, but there are also market factors. In both cases, customers are often paying for the reputation of an institution. Reputations are hard to amass, and that protects banks and colleges from competition. Thus shielded from new entrants, bankers can collect multi-million dollar fees and colleges robust tuitions to fund a bloated and top-heavy institutional form that has, if anything, seen falling productivity while the rest of the world races ahead.[289]

Get that? On the one hand, financiers can capture rents when the

288. David R. Henderson, "Rent Seeking: *The Concise Encyclopedia of Economics*," Library of Economics and Liberty, 2008, http://www.econlib.org/library/Enc/RentSeeking.html.

289. Megan McArdle, "Banks and Colleges Are Wasting Our Money," *Bloomberg View*, September 13, 2016, https://www.bloomberg.com/view/articles/2016-09-13/banks-and-colleges-are-wasting-our-money.

government uses its coercive power to restrict freedom of competition in finance. On the other hand, financiers can capture rents by earning a good reputation that makes it more difficult for newcomers to successfully compete.

The lesson that most people draw from this sort of view is that sometimes we'll have to fight rent seeking by reducing government intervention—but other times we'll have to fight it by increasing government intervention in the name of "promoting competition." (See Ayn Rand on why using coercion to "promote competition" is a contradiction in terms.[290])

I don't mean to pick on Megan. Hers is really the standard view. Joseph Stiglitz, a Nobel Prize-winning economist and one of the leading critics of economic inequality, rests his case for fighting inequality on the claim that rent seeking is responsible for much of the high incomes we observe among "the 1 percent."

Is that because they're all running to Washington and asking for special privileges? Nope. According to Stiglitz, "Not all rent seeking uses government to extract money from ordinary citizens." The "private sector can excel on its own," e.g., by creating "entry barriers. . . . such as maintaining excess capacity, so that an entrant knows that, should he enter, the incumbent firm can increase production, lowering prices to the point that entry would be impossible."[291]

The lesson here is that to speak of "rent seeking" (or "barriers to entry" or "economic inequality") is to blur the distinction between voluntary trade and physical force. But if we are trying to create a moral, just system, then no distinction can be more important.

---

290. "Competition," *Ayn Rand Lexicon*, accessed June 10, 2017, https://campus
.aynrand.org/lexicon/competition.

291. Joseph Stiglitz, *The Price of Inequality* (New York: Norton, 2013), pp. 50, 54.

The Corrupt Critics of CEO Pay

By Yaron Brook and Don Watkins

Since the start of this crisis, we've been regaled with stories of CEOs receiving lavish bonuses. Well-paid executives have been vilified as reckless and greedy. *L.A. Times* columnist Patt Morrison captured the mood when she declared: "I want blood."

But this is nothing new.

Long before the current crisis, Warren Buffet, John McCain, President Obama, and many other critics condemned (supposedly) outrageous executive pay. "We have a [moral] deficit when CEOs are making more in ten minutes than some workers make in ten months," Obama said during the presidential campaign.

With today's government entanglement in business affairs, many Americans are open to attempts by Washington to slash CEO pay. Apparently hoping to exploit that opportunity, the chairman of the House Financial Services Committee, Barney Frank, recently floated the idea of extending the TARP executive pay caps to every financial institution, and potentially to all U.S. companies.

It's understandable that taxpayers think they should have some say in how bailed-out businesses are run, which is one reason why Washington should never have bailed out those companies in the first place. But why have the critics been so intent on dictating to shareholders of private companies how much they can pay their CEOs?

It's not because the supposed victims, shareholders, have been demanding it. A few ideologically motivated activists aside, most shareholders in the years leading up to the crisis weren't complaining about CEO pay packages. Virtually every time they had a chance to vote on a "say on pay" resolution, which would have given them a non-binding vote on CEO compensation, shareholders rejected the measure. Even if they had been given a say, there is no reason to expect they would have put the brakes on high pay. In Britain, for instance, shareholders had a government-mandated right to vote on management compensation, yet CEO pay still rose unabated.

So what has the critics all riled up?

They allege that, despite appearances, executives were not really being paid for performance. Pointing to CEOs who raked in huge bonuses while their companies tanked, the critics say that executive pay was driven not by supply and demand, but by an old boys' network that placed mutual back-scratching above shareholder welfare. As Obama put it last year, "What accounts for the change in CEO pay is not any market imperative. It's cultural. At a time when average workers are experiencing little or no income growth, many of America's CEOs have lost any sense of shame about grabbing whatever their . . . corporate boards will allow."

It was a compelling tale, but this account of rising pay just doesn't square with the facts. To name a few: (1) the rise in CEO pay was in line with that of other elite positions, such as professional athletes; (2) the rise in pay continued even as fewer CEOs chaired their board of directors; (3) the companies that paid CEOs the most generally had stock returns much greater than other companies in their industries, while companies that paid their CEOs the least underperformed in their industries.

The critics of CEO pay ignore all of this. They take it as obvious that executives making millions are overpaid. "It turns out that these shareholders, who are wonderfully thoughtful and collectively incisive, become quite stupid when it comes to paying the boss, the guy who works for them," Barney Frank has said. But what kind of compensation package will attract, retain, and motivate the best CEO is a complicated question. Companies have to weigh thousands of facts and make many subtle judgments in order to assess what a CEO is worth.

What should be the mix between base salary and incentive pay? What kind of incentives should be offered—stock options, restricted stock options, stock appreciation rights? How should those incentives be structured; over what time frame and using which metrics? And what about a severance plan? What kind of plan will be necessary to attract the best candidate? And so forth and so on.

The mere fact that people make their living as executive-pay consultants illustrates how challenging the task is. Central planners like Frank cavalierly dismiss this and declare that they can somehow divine that lower pay for executives will not hinder a company.

Of course, a free market doesn't eliminate mistakes. A company can hire an incompetent CEO or structure a pay package that rewards executives for short-term profits at the expense of the company's long-term welfare. But a company suffers from its mistakes: shareholders earn less, managers need to be fired, and competitors gain market share.

There is, however, something that can short-circuit this corrective process and help keep highly paid incompetents in business: government coercion.

Take the Williams Act, which restricts stock accumulation for the purpose of a takeover, for example. In a truly free market, if poor management is causing a company's stock to tank, shareholders or outsiders are incentivized to buy enough shares to fire the CEO and improve company performance. But the Williams Act, among other regulations, makes ousting poor management more difficult.

And while the critics have tried to scapegoat "overpaid executives" for our current financial turmoil, the actual cause was, as past editions of *Fusion* have indicated, coercive government regulations and interventions. Far from vindicating the denunciations of "stupid" shareholders and "inept" CEOs, the recent economic downturn shows what happens when the government interferes with economic decision-making through policies such as the "affordable housing" crusade and the Fed's artificially low interest rates.

If the critics' goal were really to promote pay for performance, they would advocate an end to all such regulations and let the free market work.

But that's not what they advocate. Instead, they call for more regulatory schemes, such as government-mandated "say on pay," massive tax hikes on the rich, and even outright caps on executive compensation. They do not want pay to be determined by the market, reflect performance, or reward achievement—they just want it to be lower. Frank stated the point clearly when he threatened that if "say on pay" legislation doesn't sufficiently reduce CEO compensation, "then we will do something more." Another critic, discussing former Home Depot CEO Robert Nardelli, confessed that "it's hard to believe that those leading the charge against his pay package ... weren't upset mainly by the fact that Nardelli had a $200 million pay package in the first place—no matter how he had performed."

The critics want to bring down CEO pay, not because it is economically unjustifiable, but because they view it as morally unjustifiable. Prominent opponent of high CEO pay, Robert Reich, for instance, penned a *Wall Street Journal* column titled "CEOs Deserve Their Pay," where he defended CEO pay from an economic standpoint, but denied that it was justified ethically. Insisting that wealth rightfully belongs to "society" rather than the individuals who create it, the critics maintain that "society" and not private owners should set salary levels. Many critics go so far as to regard all differences in income as morally unjust and the vast disparity between CEOs and their lowest-paid employees as morally obscene.

But it's the attack on CEO pay that's obscene.

Far from relying on nefarious backroom deals, successful CEOs earn their pay by creating vast amounts of wealth. Jack Welch, for instance, helped raise GE's market value from $14 billion to $410 billion. Steve Jobs's leadership famously turned a struggling Apple into an industry leader. Only a handful of people develop the virtues—vision, drive, knowledge, and ability—to successfully run a multibillion-dollar company. They deserve extraordinary compensation for their extraordinary achievements.

In smearing America's great wealth creators as villains and attributing their high pay to greed and corruption rather than productive achievement, the critics want us to overlook the virtues that make CEOs successful. In demanding lower executive pay, despite the wishes of shareholders, the critics aim to deprive CEOs of their just desserts. In denouncing CEO pay for the sole reason that it's higher than the pay of those who haven't achieved so much, the critics seek to punish CEOs because they are successful.

Ultimately, how to pay CEOs is a question that only shareholders have a right to decide. But in today's antibusiness climate, it's vital that we recognize the moral right of successful CEOs to huge rewards.

They earn them.

Some CEO Pay Ratios that Actually Matter

By Don Watkins

The SEC recently mandated[292] that most public corporations pub-lish the ratio between the pay of its top executives and the medi-an pay of its employees. It's a totally meaningless ratio that has no pur-pose other than to shame highly paid CEOs.

But in his recent book, *The Inequality Trap*, Canadian economist William Watson gives us some ratios that do matter—ratios that, in this case, contrast what JP Morgan Chase head Jamie Dimon earned and the value his company created.

> At the end of 2011 [Jamie Dimon's] bank had $2.1 trillion in assets under management, larger than Canada's GDP for that year (US$1.73 trillion). The bank's net income was $18.98 billion on revenue of $97.2 billion. Jamie Dimon's 2011 com-pensation of $23.1 million was therefore 0.12 per cent of the bank's net income, just a little over one-tenth of 1 per cent. Between 2010 and 2011 that net income had risen by $1.606 billion. The increase in Dimon's compensation (from $20.8 to $23.1 million) was just 0.14 per cent of that increase. . . . [The relevant question is, did] he manage in 2011 to raise his com-pany's income and profits by one-tenth of 1 per cent?[293]

In the end, what a company pays its executives is nobody's busi-ness but the shareholders. They're the ones that foot the bill, and if they think a CEO is overpaid, they can either fight for lower compensation or sell their shares.

But I do think it's important for the public to have some sense of why successful CEOs are paid so much. (It's precisely because they don't have that sense that the attacks on CEO pay have been success-ful.) Comparing a CEO's pay to his employees' pay doesn't shed light on that issue. Comparing his pay to the value the company creates, does.

---

292. Victoria McGrane and Joann S. Lublin, "SEC Approval of Pay-Gap Rule Sparks Concerns," *Wall Street Journal*, August 5, 2015, https://www.wsj.com/articles/sec-set-to-approve-final-ceo-pay-ratio-rule-1438783961.

293. William G. Watson, *The Inequality Trap: Fighting Capitalism Instead of Poverty* (Toronto: University of Toronto Press, 2015), p. 36.

PART 3

Financial Controversies

You Can Take My Index Fund When You Pry It Out of My Cold Dead Hand

By Don Watkins

How should you invest if you're not a Warren Buffett-level stock picker? Take Warren Buffett's advice:

> My advice . . . could not be more simple: Put 10% of the cash in short-term government bonds and 90% in a very low-cost S&P 500 index fund. (I suggest Vanguard's.) I believe the . . . long-term results from this policy will be superior to those attained by most investors—whether pension funds, institutions, or individuals—who employ high-fee managers.[294]

Index funds are passive investment funds: instead of having researchers try to pick stocks that will perform better than the overall market, which is difficult and expensive, these funds try to match the market by buying all of the securities in the S&P 500 or some other index. Thanks to their low cost and difficult-to-top returns, index funds have become increasingly popular in recent years.[295]

So of course some people want to make them illegal.

A recent *New York Times* op-ed by Eric Posner, Fiona Scott Morton, and Glen Weyl argues that the institutional investors like Vanguard who run large index funds are violating the Clayton antitrust act, since by design they own stakes in many or all of the competitors in certain industries.

> Vanguard and BlackRock are the largest owners of Apple and Microsoft, and among the top three owners of CVS, Walgreens and Rite Aid. If you zoom down to, say, the market in cooking stoves, you will see that the largest owners

---

294. Austin Smith, "Warren Buffett's 15-Minute Retirement Plan," *USA Today*, June 21, 2016, https://www.usatoday.com/story/sponsor-story/motley-fool/2016/06/21/warren-buffetts-15-minute-retirement-plan/85979746/.

295. Victor Reklaitis, "5 Charts Show How Index Investing Is Beating Stock-Picking," MarketWatch, June 24, 2015, http://www.marketwatch.com/story/5-charts-show-how-index-investing-is-beating-stock-picking-2015-06-24.

of two of the three major competitors—GE, Whirlpool and
Electrolux—are Vanguard, BlackRock and State Street. The
same patterns appear in airlines, soft drinks, you name it.

Economic theory tells us that when a single investor owns
large stakes in competing firms, the investor will want
firms to keep prices high and wages low. Price and wage
competition lowers profits and stock values.[296]

In other words, firms typically compete for market share. But if
those firms are owned by the same people, then the owners don't care
if Pepsi gains a bit on Coke—they want Coke and Pepsi to maximize
their overall returns, possibly by charging higher prices for soda than
they otherwise would.

The evidence this is happening is not exactly overwhelming, coming from all of two academic papers looking at a single industry each
(airlines and banking, respectively). But that doesn't stop the authors
from offering a solution to this supposed problem that would dramatically curtail our investing choices: have the government end indexing
as we know it.

[T]he government should enforce the Clayton Act against
institutional investors while recognizing a safe harbor for
those that either take a small stake in an oligopolistic industry (less than 1 percent of each company) or invest
in no more than one company per industry. BlackRock
could own a large stake in United or Delta or American or
Southwest, but not all of them.[297]

In other words, institutional investors like Vanguard could keep
indexing so long as they . . . started picking stocks. Which would
mean research and trading whenever their assessments change. Which
would raise their costs and make it less likely their returns would track
the market. Which would be an index fund . . . how?

Nor is this just an attack on index funds. It's an attack on any

296. Eric Posner, Fiona Scott Morton, and Glen Weyl, "A Monopoly Donald
    Trump Can Pop," *New York Times*, December 7, 2016, https://www.nytimes.
    com/2016/12/07/opinion/a-monopoly-donald-trump-can-pop.html.

297. Ibid.

institutional investor who owns large stakes in companies—and a call for government to micromanage how they invest. I could explain how this sounds an awful lot like central planning, and how central planning has devastated every economy in which it has been tried. But what's really galling is the sheer injustice of it all.

When Vanguard's Jack Bogle created the first index fund forty years ago, he faced skepticism and even derision. It was only after a long struggle and proving that he was right—that Vanguard's index funds did offer a superior value to customers—that Bogle's company achieved its current dominance.

And now, because he succeeded on such a grand scale, a few professors waving studies want the government to declare the business model he pioneered illegal. Why? Because their models show that sometimes, in some industries, indexing will lead companies to conclude that it's not to the interests of their shareholders to compete as hard on price, causing their customers to pay somewhat higher prices.

Well, maybe. But so what?

There's a moral premise underlying antitrust that businesses exist to serve consumer (and sometimes worker) satisfaction. Everything a business does—raise or lower prices, offer new products, lay off employees, merge with other businesses, make a profit—has to be justified by showing that it maximizes the well-being of consumers.

This means that businessmen like Jack Bogle and Steve Jobs have a duty to come up with new ideas for amazing products or services, risk their time, money, and reputations trying to make those ideas successful—and, if they do succeed, endure the indignity of having their business decisions second-guessed by the representatives of "the consumer," i.e., of anyone who has attained the exalted status of having contributed nothing to the creation of their business.

Such a view is demeaning to businessmen and patronizing to their customers.

Ayn Rand offered an alternative moral framework for thinking about the relationship between businessmen and their customers—what in *Free Market Revolution* Yaron Brook and I have called[298] "a fellowship of traders."

On this view, buyers and sellers are seen as independent equals pursuing their own self-interest through voluntary exchange. Neither

---

298. Yaron Brook and Don Watkins, *Free Market Revolution: How Ayn Rand's Ideas Can End Big Government* (New York: Palgrave Macmillan, 2013).

is serving the other: they are trading value-for-value. Each side has the right to decide the terms on which he'll trade. Sellers decide what to produce, how to produce it, and what prices to offer—and buyers decide whether to accept the deal or, if they don't like the terms, go their own way. A seller no more has to justify his pricing by proving that it maximizes the well-being of the buyer than the buyer has to justify his decision by proving that it maximizes the well-being of the seller. (No, that doesn't lead to "monopolists" holding buyers hostage.[299])

The *New York Times* authors end by asserting that their plan to destroy indexing would "raise living s tandards while making American companies more competitive." But if we really want businesses to thrive and Americans to prosper, we aren't going to get there by crippling passive investing—it's to actively oppose central planning technocrats who think they're entitled to control businesses they did nothing to create.

---

299. Search results for "Antitrust," Ayn Rand Institute, accessed June 10, 2017, https://ari.aynrand.org/search-results?search=antitrust.

Insider Trading: The Rule of Unreason

By Don Watkins

In 1962, Ayn Rand wrote:

> It is a grave error to suppose that a dictatorship rules a nation by means of strict, rigid laws which are obeyed and enforced with rigorous, military precision. Such a rule would be evil, but almost bearable; men could endure the harshest edicts, provided these edicts were known, specific, and stable; it is not the known that breaks men's spirits, but the unpredictable. A dictatorship has to be capricious; it has to rule by means of the unexpected, the incomprehensible, the wantonly irrational; it has to deal not in death, but in sudden death; a state of chronic uncertainty is what men are psychologically unable to bear.[300]

She goes on to observe, "The American businessmen have had to live in that state for seventy years."[301] Rand was talking about antitrust laws. But she could just as easily have been talking about laws that punish insider trading.

Yesterday, the Supreme Court heard arguments in *Salman v. United States*, a case that illustrates the vague, arbitrary, and capricious nature of insider trading "laws."

Insider trading laws restrict people's ability to buy and sell securities based on "material nonpublic information."[302] But what the government considers insider trading is often so nebulous that it amounts to ex post facto law: in many cases, it is impossible to know whether you've committed a crime until the government says you committed one.

Take the Salman case, in which Bassam Salman was convicted for trading on information he got from his brother-in-law, Mounir Kara, who got it from his brother, Maher Kara, who obtained the information

---

300. Ayn Rand, Leonard Peikoff, and Peter Schwartz, *The Voice of Reason: Essays in Objectivist Thought* (New York: Meridian, 1990).

301. Ibid.

302. Stanislav Dolgopolov, "Insider Trading: *The Concise Encyclopedia of Economics*," Library of Economics and Liberty, 2008, http://www.econlib.org/library/Enc/InsiderTrading.html.

from his work in the health care investment banking group at Citigroup.

Although no one disputes that Salman traded on information passed down from his brother-in-law, it's hardly an open-and-shut case. It's not always illegal for an outsider to trade on a tip from an insider. If a stranger who worked at Citigroup had revealed the information during a casual chat at a bus stop, Salman would not have been committing a crime trading on the information. But an outsider can be considered an insider by the law under certain circumstances. A 2014 federal appeals court ruled that the recipient of insider information can be penalized if he knew that the individual providing the tip was revealing confidential information in exchange for a "personal benefit."[303]

The question in the Salman case, then, is whether Maher received a personal benefit when he revealed information he learned at Citigroup. Maher did not trade on the information, nor did he receive any material benefit from his brother's and brother-in-law's trading activities. But a lower court held that because Maher passed along the information to help out the people he loved, that was enough of a personal benefit to make the action criminal. This led Cato's Thaya Brook Knight to quip, "If they had loved each other less, would Salman still be facing prison?"[304]

But what's outrageous here is not that the government is treating satisfaction from helping a family member as a personal benefit—it's that everyone agrees that the law did not clearly spell out that Salman's action was illegal. According to accounts[305] of Wednesday's oral arguments, America's greatest legal thinkers are struggling to define what counts as a "personal benefit" rendering a trade criminal—and yet Americans are being sent to prison for failing to divine the whims of regulators and prosecutors.

Don't make the mistake of thinking this particular case is somehow unique. In case after case what you find is twisting, changing, expanding definitions of what insider trading is—definitions that are

---

303. Ben Protess and Matthew Goldstein, "Appeals Court Deals Setback to Crackown on Insider Trading," *New York Times*, December 10, 2014, https://dealbook. nytimes.com/2014/12/10/appeals-court-overturns-2-insider-trading-convictions/.

304. Thaya Brook Knight, "Supreme Court Has a Chance to Clarify Insider Trading," *The Hill*, October 4, 2016, http://origin-nyi.thehill.com/blogs/congress-blog/ economy-budget/299049-supreme-court-has-a-chance-to-clarify-insider-trading.

305. Tim Ryan, "Justices Tackle Blurry Insider-Trading Lines," *Courthouse News*, October 5, 2016, http://oldarchives.courthousenews.com/2016/10/05/justices-tackle-blurry-insider-trading-lines.htm.

only made explicit after the government's axe has fallen.

Just one example. (You can find many more in Daniel Fischel's excellent book *Payback: The Conspiracy to Destroy Michael Milken and His Financial Revolution.*[306]) One of the most important Supreme Court insider trading cases, *Dirks v. SEC*, started when security analyst Raymond Dirks received a tip about fraud going on at the Equity Funding insurance company. Dirks tried to bring the fraud to the attention of the press and the government, but when no one paid attention, Dirks told his clients, who sold their shares in Equity Funding.

The fraud eventually came to light, Equity Funding's stock collapsed, and—you can guess what happened next—the SEC went after Dirks for illegal insider trading since he got the initial tip about the fraud from Ronald Secrist, a former Equity Funding employee. According to the SEC, securities laws "require equal information among all traders"—which must have come as news to traders like Dirks, who made a living in large measure by digging up more information than their rivals.

The case eventually went to the Supreme Court, which ruled in Dirks's favor, rejecting the SEC's "equal information" notion. But the very fact that Dirks was targeted to begin with reveals how "flexible" insider trading laws are. And make no mistake: the government likes things that way. As the *Wall Street Journal* points out:

> Congress has never clearly defined insider trading. The Securities and Exchange Commission could define it more clearly, but it resists doing so because the ambiguity benefits regulators and prosecutors who can make up their own standard case by case. The result is arbitrary enforcement that aggrandizes prosecutors at the expense of the rule of law.[307]

All of this would be bad enough if insider trading laws were just lousy attempts to define a legitimate crime. But in reality what they criminalize is voluntary behavior that violates no one's rights.

The stock market exists so that people can buy and sell securities in the pursuit of their self-interest. A trade involves a buyer bidding for a

---

306. Daniel R. Fischel, *Payback: The Conspiracy to Destroy Michael Milken and His Financial Revolution* (New York: HarperBusiness, 1996).

307. "Insider Trading Hits the High Court," *Wall Street Journal*, October 4, 2016, https://www.wsj.com/articles/insider-trading-hits-the-high-court-1475622944.

security and a seller accepting or rejecting the bid. Both sides are acting on their knowledge and judgment about the value of the security, and neither presumes that their knowledge and judgment is identical to their counterparty's. On the contrary, most trades occur precisely because people have different beliefs about the value of a security, and each party enters the transaction knowing he might be wrong. The fact that one person has inside knowledge makes absolutely no difference to the nature of the transaction. There's no fraud involved. No deception. It's completely voluntary.

Take the Salman case. We don't know whom he bought his stock from. What we do know is Salman didn't take anything from them, except an unexpected windfall they no doubt regretted missing out on. But missing out on a rising stock price isn't a harm, let alone a rights violation.[308] It's a risk you assume whenever you trade.

A proper legal system has one function: to protect individual rights. That means barring force and fraud. If someone wants to argue that some of the actions that currently fall under "insider trading" involve rights violations, then I'm all ears. But often those who argue for criminalizing insider trading don't bother trying to identify a victim whose rights have been violated. Instead, they appeal to various government "interests," such as maximizing market efficiency, bolstering investor confidence in markets, or putting the small investor on a level playing field with professionals.

These are bad arguments even on their own terms, but they all miss the point.[309] The government has an awesome power—the power to legally use physical force—and that power should be used only to protect the freedom of its citizens. To throw people in prison in the name of "efficiency" or "investor confidence" is the real crime.

---

308. Charles L. Hooper, "Who Is Harmed by Insider Trading?," Library of Economics and Liberty, March 2, 2015, http://www.econlib.org/library/Columns/y2015/Hooperharmed.html.

309. Henry G. Manne, "The Case for Insider Trading," *Wall Street Journal*, March 17, 2003, https://www.wsj.com/articles/SB104786934891514900; Daniel R. Fischel and Dennis W. Carlton, "The Regulation of Insider Trading," *Chicago Unbound*, 1982, http://chicagounbound.uchicago.edu/cgi/viewcontent.cgi?article=2424 &context=journal_articles; Stephen M. Bainbridge, "Insider Trading: An Overview," UCLA School of Law, October 24, 1998, https://papers.ssrn.com/sol3/papers.cfm?abstract_id=132529; Charles L. Hooper, "Insider Trading Turned Inside Out," Library of Economics and Liberty, June 2, 2014, http://www.econlib.org/library/Columns/y2014/Hooperinsidertrading.html.

No, Taxpayers Are Not Subsidizing Banker Bonuses

By Don Watkins

If I were to make a list of the most abused words in the English language, "subsidize" would almost certainly make my top ten.

Here's *Merriam-Webster*: "Subsidize, *vb*: to aid or promote (as a private enterprise) with public money."[310] When the government takes money from some people and gives it to others—say, solar and wind companies—it's subsidizing those others. "Subsidize," then, is just a fancy word for redistributing wealth.

But according to some commentators, when the government takes less of someone's wealth, it is giving him a subsidy.

Exhibit A: "This simple cartoon shows how US taxpayers help make rich bankers even richer."[311] That's from *Vox*, and if you think they're referring to bank bailouts—which most certainly were a subsidy—well, you're giving them too much credit.

> From 2012 to 2015 [Wells Fargo CEO John Stumpf's], salary was $2.8 million a year. But Wells Fargo also gave him $155 million in stock options and bonuses that were tied to the company's performance.
>
> The reason Wells Fargo paid him this way is because the government doesn't tax performance-based pay for Stumpf, or any other top bank executive[312] in America.
>
> Unlike regular salaries—where the government takes out taxes to pay for Medicare, Social Security, and all other sorts of things—US tax code lets banks deduct the big bonuses they give to their executives.

---

310. "Subsidize," *Merriam-Webster*, accessed June 11, 2017, https://www.merriam-webster.com/dictionary/subsidize.

311. Alvin Chang, "This Simple Cartoon Shows How US Taxpayers Help Make Rich Bankers Even Richer," *Vox*, September 6, 2016, https://www.vox.com/policy-and-politics/2016/9/6/12774760/ceo-bank-loophole-cartoon.

312. "26 C.F.R. § 1.162-27—Certain Employee Remuneration in Excess of $1,000,000," Legal Information Institute, 2015, https://www.law.cornell.edu/cfr/text/26/1.162-27.

That means taxpayers essentially subsidized $54 million of his pay.[313]

Scott Greenberg from the Tax Foundation explains why this is factually wrong. To wit: "Under the U.S. tax code, households are generally required to pay individual income taxes on the value of the stock options and bonuses that they receive. This means that Mr. Stumpf was likely required to pay an individual income tax rate of up to 39.6% on the performance-based pay that he received from Wells Fargo."[314] (There's much more that's good in Greenberg's article, so do read the whole thing.)

What *Vox* is presumably referring to, Greenberg goes on to say, is the fact that corporations can deduct performance pay from their taxable income, the same way they can deduct—again, contrary to *Vox*—compensation paid to other employees. Like every other business, corporations are taxed on their profits, i.e., what they make after their expenses are subtracted from their revenues.

So where's the subsidy? Back to *Vox*:

> We've long known that bank executives get massive bonuses. But a new report from the Institute for Policy Studies[315] shows just how much money Americans lose out on because of this policy, which allows banks to write off certain kinds of executive compensation.
>
> From 2012 to 2015, the top five executives at the 20 largest US banks earned about $2 billion in performance-based pay that their companies could deduct.
>
> The report found that it caused the the [sic] federal government to lose more than $725 million in revenue from 2012 to 2015—enough money to hire 9,000 elementary school teachers.[316]

313. Ibid.

314. Scott Greenberg, "The Tax Code Does Not Subsidize CEO Pay," Tax Foundation, September 7, 2016, https://taxfoundation.org/tax-code-does-not-subsidize-ceo-pay.

315. Sarah Anderson and Sam Pizzigati, "The 23rd Annual Executive Excess Report: Wall Street CEO Bonus Loophole," August 31, 2016, http://www.ips-dc.org/wp-content/uploads/2016/08/IPS-report-on-CEO-bonus-loophole-embargoed-until-Aug-31-2016.pdf.

316. Chang, "This Simple Cartoon."

Get that? The government is "subsidizing" bankers at the expense of Americans (presumably *Vox* doesn't count bankers as Americans) because if it took more money from bankers it could give away more money to taxpayers.

By that logic, a thief is subsidizing you whenever he doesn't take your wallet.

What this really illustrates is that, far from being opposed to subsidies, the critics of CEO pay are angry because—as Yaron and I argue in our book *Equal Is Unfair*—they object to high pay for CEOs, as such, and want to see a massive increase in how much wealth is seized from affluent Americans and redistributed to less affluent Americans.

But since open wealth confiscation tends to leave a bad taste in the mouths of most Americans, critics of CEO pay try to paint their vendetta as a crusade for justice. After all, if CEOs (bankers, no less!) are getting richer through special favors from the government, then even the most devoted advocate of laissez-faire will want to see the practice end.

This is why *Vox* focuses specifically on bankers, even though their argument would apply equally to all corporate executives. There is a case that some bankers have gotten rich through special favors from the government, including, as *Vox* notes, the bailouts that followed the financial crisis. That arguably doesn't apply to Wells Fargo, though, which was basically forced to take TARP money[317] against its will, and promptly repaid it.[318]

Setting aside Wells Fargo, however, the solution to cronyism[319] is never to give the government more power to control American businesses, but to limit its already immense power so that it no longer acts as the great dispenser of special privileges. No subsidies for anyone: rich, poor, or anywhere in between. That should be the goal.

Such an agenda, however, would not achieve the goals of critics of CEO pay: to penalize the successful for being successful.

---

317. Damian Paletta, Jon Hilsenrath, and Deborah Solomon, "At Moment of Truth, U.S. Forced Big Bankers to Blink," *Wall Street Journal*, October 15, 2008, https://www.wsj.com/articles/SB122402486344034247.

318. Elinor Comlay and John Wallace, "Wells Fargo Repays Government Bailout," Reuters, December 23, 2009, http://www.reuters.com/article/us-wells-tarp-idUSTRE5BM2U720091223.

319. Steve Simpson, "Bernie Sanders Is the Cause of Cronyism," *Voices for Reason*, blog, Ayn Rand Institute, October 19, 2015, https://ari.aynrand.org/blog/2015/10/19/bernie-sanders-is-the-cause-of-cronyism.

John Allison on How Dodd-Frank Is Smothering Small Business Lending

By Doug Altner

We have heard several prominent business leaders—such as Home Depot co-founder Bernie Marcus and Subway founder Fred Deluca[320]—state that they could not have started their amazingly successful businesses if they had to do it in today's regulatory environment. This is alarming, and it is important to get a concrete sense of how regulations are killing the potential Home Depots and Subways of tomorrow.

To learn more about one significant regulation in this respect, I asked John Allison—the president of the Cato Institute and the former CEO of BB&T bank—about the Dodd-Frank Act[321] of 2010, the 2,000+ page bill of sweeping financial regulations. He was kind enough to take a few minutes of his time, at the recent annual meeting of the Academy of Management, to talk to me about one of the ways in which the Dodd-Frank Act is smothering entrepreneurial activity in America:

> Dodd-Frank and the related regulatory reaction have caused a tightening of lending standards for small businesses. This is because Dodd-Frank and the regulators' interpretation of it mean that bank loans are based totally on mathematical formulas.

> Small business lending is part science and a lot of art. If banks cannot practice the art, the only thing banks can do is tighten their lending standards. Lending standards for small businesses are the tightest that they have ever been in my 40-year career.

---

320. Paul Toscano, "Subway 'Wouldn't Exist' If Started Today Due to Regulations: Founder DeLuca," CNBC, February 27, 2013, http://www.cnbc.com/id/100501700.

321. "Dodd-Frank Wall Street Reform and Consumer Protection Act," *Wikipedia*, June 9, 2017, https://en.wikipedia.org/wiki/Dodd%E2%80%93Frank_Wall_Street_Reform_and_Consumer_Protection_Act.

. . . . There are thousands and thousands of promising businesses that simply could not get a bank loan today that could have gotten one ten years ago.

Mr. Allison is drawing from decades of experience in commercial banking, nearly half of which he spent as a CEO. As CEO, he successfully grew BB&T from $4.5 billion to $152 billion in assets.[322] We should take what he says seriously.

How many great businesses may never be started because they cannot get the initial credit that a bank would otherwise be free to lend them were it not for the Dodd-Frank Act?

---

322. John A. Allison, "John A. Allison," Cato Institute, October 3, 2016, https://www.cato.org/people/john-allison.

EPILOGUE:

An Interview with Yaron Brook

Don: Yaron, tell us a bit about your background.

Yaron: Sure. I got interested in finance while getting my MBA at the University of Texas in Austin in the late1980s, and went on to get a PhD in finance from the University of Texas. I later taught finance at the university level, and did some consulting and other related things in the field until I joined the Ayn Rand Institute as its executive director in 2000.

What appealed to me about finance was how scientific and reality-oriented it was. Unlike the other subjects I studied, which struck me as wishy-washy, in finance, I enjoyed that I was actually learning something about the real world—and that it touched on both economics and business, which were two subjects I was already interested in. In addition to all that, I realized how important finance was, both as a subject and as an industry. Simply put, you cannot understand our world today—you can't understand why advanced economies are so prosperous or why we keep encountering economic difficulties—without understanding finance and financial markets.

The financial industry is really the allocator of capital in the economy. Capital in this context refers primarily to money and credit that is being deployed for productive uses: to build factories, to pay people's salaries, to buy equipment. It's money spent for the sake of producing wealth rather than consuming wealth. The primary role of financial markets in the economy is to allocate money in ways that enhance production—to put money into the hands of the Apples and Ubers of the world, rather than the Pets-dot-coms.

The analogy I sometime use is the circulatory system of the body. Finance is in effect the heart and the veins and the arteries of the economy: they make sure the blood (the capital) gets to where it is most needed. A healthy economy, like a healthy body, depends on a well-functioning circulatory system. Economic progress and economic prosperity require a robust, functioning, vibrant, and politically *free* financial system that fosters the accumulation and efficient use of capital.

Don: And yet finance is one of the most reviled, demonized, and regulated industries in the economy. Why is that?

Yaron: The attacks actually begin in Greece, and even Aristotle is critical of money-lenders, who were the financiers of the time. Now, the Greek's objection to finance really comes down to not understanding its productive role, which was understandable at the time. Aristotle, for instance, talks about money as barren: money doesn't produce more money. If I give you seeds, you can plant the seeds, and they grow into something. But if you plant money in the ground, nothing happens. And so there's this perception that financiers are not doing anything useful or productive—they're just transferring money around between people. Now, think of the implication of that. Why are money-lenders getting rich by receiving interest when they aren't doing anything useful? It struck many thinkers at the time as unjust.

If that were the only objection to finance—a mistaken conclusion that financiers aren't productive—then those attacks would have faded hundreds of years ago, when it became clear to economists that finance plays a crucial role in the production of wealth. But it was not the only objection. You also have a view that comes out of Christianity that says it's our duty to help others with no expectation of a return. This is what you can call the altruistic objection. The idea is that someone needs a loan, and our job is to help him—not try to profit off his back. We should be happy we're even getting the principal back.

So these two ideas fuse into the belief that financiers are immoral parasites: they profit, not by doing something productive, but by exploiting people in need when their actual duty is to help those people without any expectation of profit.

Here's an anecdote that captures this whole attitude. The Christians believed so deeply that lending someone money at interest was bad for the borrower, that they *encouraged* lending to their enemies like the Muslims because they thought that they would hurt them by charging them interest. They just couldn't grasp that money-lending can allow people to enhance their productivity.

Today, and really for the last few hundred years, most leading thinkers have grasped the productive value of finance. But they and the rest of us have never shed the moral perspective that condemns profiting via finance—by making money from money. That altruistic perspective remains and so on the news and throughout the culture we talk about greedy Wall Street paper-pushers who are just out for themselves at the expense of the little guy, or evil payday lenders who exploit the worst-off members of society.

And that moral perspective, it turn, makes it very hard to convince people of the productive role of finance. The idea that a billionaire hedge fund manager could be doing something so productive that he creates value far beyond his personal income just doesn't mesh with what people have heard again and again. This is why the culture, on the whole, has no better grasp of finance's role than the Greek's, despite the fact that every serious economist and business leader understands it. Most people still view finance as a zero-sum, if not a negative-sum, game, where bankers and speculators are getting rich at other people's expense.

Don: And so the prevalence of that view makes it plausible to people that financiers are to blame for all the problems in the economy. People think, "That's what you'd expect from bad guys."

Yaron: Yes, and it's our intellectual and political leaders who cash in on that plausibility by blaming every crisis, disaster, or problem on finance, such as the financial crisis of 2008. They never place the blame on the true source of the problems: central bankers, political intervention, government regulations.

Something we always have to keep in mind is that we do not have a free market in finance. On the contrary, it is arguably the most regulated industry in America. And this is not something that started with Dodd-Frank. It actually goes back to the founding era. I cannot overstate my respect for the Founding Fathers, but many of them had a real distrust of banking and finance.

In part this distrust came from the same sources I mentioned earlier: a failure to grasp the productive role of finance and a moral suspicion of financiers. But there was another element that has played a large role throughout American history: a distrust of "bigness." Banks, especially big banks, were seen as incredibly powerful, and therefore in need of being reined in by government.

Now, certainly banks can be powerful, but the power they hold in a free market is *economic*, not *political*. They have the power to offer people values—not to coerce them or deprive them of values. Economic power is in fact something positive, not something threatening that needs to be curtailed. The only time bankers had political power was when the government gave it to them, when the government gave them privileges they would not have had on a fully free market: the power, for instance, to restrict competition from other banks.

But because there wasn't a clear understanding of the difference between economic and political power, and because banks from the start were intertwined with government, they were also controlled and regulated by the government. And if you look at economic theory and at history, what becomes clear is that the tendency is for government intervention to make banks and the financial system unstable.

Just to give one example, branch banking was largely prohibited during the 19th century, which meant that it was very hard for banks to diversify. So if your local farmers had a bad crop yield, your local bank could quickly become insolvent, and the result could be a financial panic. But who took the blame for those panics? The government, for restricting branch banking? No: greedy bankers and our "free-market" banking system.

So it comes down to this. We have a negative view of the financial industry because of wrong ideas: about the productivity of the industry, about the morality of the industry, and about the power of the industry. That is unjust toward the men and women in finance, and it is destructive for the country as a whole—because our standard of living and the future of economic progress depend on a free and vibrant financial industry.

Don: Okay, let's talk more about the productive role of finance, starting with the stock market, which is something most people are familiar with. What value does the stock market provide?

Yaron: Why is the stock market important? One indication that it *is* important is the fact that you will not find a developed economy without a healthy, thriving stock market. And the primary reason is straightforward: the stock market allows companies to raise huge amounts of capital, which is crucial for many productive endeavors. How did Apple grow within a number of years from two kids in a garage to the leading personal computer company in the world? By raising a ton of money in the stock market. Why has Uber been able to grow at lightning speed? It hasn't gone public yet, but you can be sure that the reason investors have been willing to pour hundreds of millions of dollars into the company is because they know they will ultimately be able to make a whole lot more when the company goes public.

So that's the primary role of the stock market: to give businesses access to capital. But intimately related to that is a secondary purpose of the stock market: it plays a key role in allocating capital across the economy. Stock markets help decide *which* businesses and industries are going to thrive and which are going to fail.

Take the horse and buggy industry a hundred years ago. Once it became feasible that automobiles could become the primary means of transportation, there was a need to shift capital away from the horse and buggy industry and into the new industry. The stock market made that possible, and in fact the first sign that the horse and buggy industry's future was in trouble would have been when the leading buggy manufacturers saw their stock prices declining as investors started selling off horse and buggy stocks and buying auto stocks.

The stock market is a powerful information tool, because stock prices reflect the best judgment of the smartest people about the future prospects of a given company or industry. Everyone has an opinion, but a stock price arises when people are willing to put their money where their mouth is, where those with the best judgment have the most influence (since they see their fortunes rise) and those with the worst judgment have the least (since they lose money and go broke). As a consequence, the tendency is for the stock market to give the best estimate possible about where various businesses are headed.

That information is incredibly useful: it guides managers, who can use the feedback of the stock market to assess whether they are headed in a good (i.e., profitable) direction or a bad (i.e., unprofitable) direction, and above all, it guides the decisions of financiers about where to supply capital. It is very important, then, that stock prices reflect the most and best information available. Anything that undermines that process—any government control or regulation that distorts or stifles the reliability of stock prices—hampers economic progress.

Don: Let's turn now to a different financial institution: hedge funds. Most people have a sense that the stock market is important, but few people understand what hedge funds are and what they do, and to the extent people are familiar with them, there is a widespread perception that they allow a few managers to make huge amounts of money with virtually no risk to themselves, and with virtually no benefit to anyone else.

Yaron: What is a hedge fund? It's a fund that pools financial resources from investors and invests them to make a profit. In that sense, they aren't fundamentally different from a mutual fund. But there are some distinctive features of hedge funds that make them unique. First of all, they are taking money in from accredited investors—investors with a lot of money and knowledge about financial markets. Second, they are often using tools like short-selling, leverage and derivatives to maximize profits, which is more complex than simply investing in stocks and bonds. Third, they are typically using really sophisticated investment strategies. And fourth, they are less regulated than other financial intermediaries like mutual funds. All of these factors give them certain advantages over traditional mutual funds: in particular, it makes it possible for investors to "hedge" against the direction of stocks and bonds, thus the name.

Now, what you're referring to when you suggest that hedge fund managers can supposedly make money without personal risk is the way in which their compensation is structured. They get a management fee, and then they get a percentage of the fund's profits: typically you'll see something like a 1.5–2 percent fee and 15–20 percent of all the profits.

Now, there's nothing unusual or nefarious about a guaranteed fee for service. A lawyer gets a fee even if he does a lousy job for you. But if he does do a lousy job, what happens? You fire him, and you tell other people not to hire him. The same thing holds true for hedge funds. It's a fickle business, and if a hedge fund manager does a bad job, he loses his reputation and investors will quickly move their money away from him to managers who have a better track record.

And what about receiving a percentage of the profits? This, of course, acts as a powerful positive incentive for hedge fund managers to do a good job: to maximize profits. It helps align the interests of the investor and the manager. In fact, unlike the mutual fund business, where past performance does not predict future performance, in the hedge fund business past performance *does* tend to predict future performance. That is, good performers tend to continue to be good performers. And this has to do with the fact that hedge funds are less regulated than mutual funds: hedge funds attract the best managers because they can pay their managers better due to less regulation. So this is in reality a business that's based on merit.

Now, what is the productive contribution of hedge funds? In essence, it's the same as any other investor. Hedge funds consist of very smart people trying to figure out what different financial assets are really worth, and by doing so make markets more efficient. Through their buying and selling, they help make sure that prices reflect the real value of the assets they're pricing, whether derivatives, bonds, or any other security. They play a key role in making prices meaningful.

Who benefits from that? Well, again, everyone. Not only do we all gain from a market that quickly and accurately reflects the best information, but hedge funds also increase liquidity. They make it easier for everyone else to buy when they want to buy and sell when they want to sell. And here's something else that's worth noting: many of the people who criticize hedge funds are *in* them: most pension plans have a hedge fund allocation. So when unions go out there and blast hedge funds, they are demonizing the people who are helping them retire one day.

Don: You've mentioned several times the importance of speed: of making sure prices reflect new information quickly. Why is that important? Why does it make a difference whether the price adjusts within five seconds versus, say, five minutes or five hours?

Yaron: Well, the general value of speed is pretty obvious. To the extent that it takes longer for new information or better information to show up in, say, a stock price, people will make worse decisions. If stock prices only adjusted quarterly, they would often be completely out of touch with reality. You couldn't rely on them to make decisions about where to invest or whom to lend to, and management couldn't rely on them to assess how good of a job they were doing. So we want to see prices reflect the most and best knowledge fast.

It is inherent in financial markets, where people profit by having better information, that the first person to act on that information will reap the benefits, regardless of whether they do so a few seconds before others or a few months. It's a value to be a few seconds faster than others *to* the person who is a few seconds faster.

Now, let me say something though about financial innovation and regulation, and this leads into the discussion of high frequency traders. Much of the financial innovation that has happened over the last fifty years is a response to regulation. Government regulates the financial industry in many, many ways—and those regulations have been growing. And they grew even during the era of so-called deregulation. These controls don't protect people from engaging in fraud, which has always been illegal. Instead, they stop people from taking *productive* actions that government doesn't approve of. The government tries to control the way financiers allocate capital.

It is inevitable that financiers are going to respond to those regulations by trying to find ways around them. If there's a real need for a particular kind of product, or for capital, and you can't get there because the government has put these restraints on you, you're going to try to build a tunnel underneath the wall. As long as there's money to be made from allocating capital to a productive function, financial markets will usually find a way to allocate the capital there. It might require convoluted financial instruments, it might require huge amounts of money—but as long as they can do all this and still be profitable, at the end of the day they will do it.

Just one example: money market accounts. They were created to get around regulations that prohibited banks from paying interest on checking accounts. Instead of getting interest on your account, what you get is interest on instruments that the bank buys at the end of the day and sells the next morning. That's just a game; it's just moving stuff around. But there's a whole money market industry now as a consequence of this game, which arose to meet a totally legitimate need that government regulation had interfered with. And there are thousands of examples like this.

High frequency trading is one more example: in part it's a response to regulation. My understanding of the regulation is that, in the old days, the New York Stock Exchange stocks traded under the New York Stock Exchange, NASDAQ stocks traded on the NASDAQ. A few years ago, the SEC decided that that didn't make sense because all trading was now electronic: why couldn't the NASDAQ trade NYSE stock and why couldn't the NYSE trade NASDAQ stock, and so on? So you can now trade the same stocks in many different locations. But it turned out there would be slight price discrepancies between the markets lasting for a few milliseconds, and so there was money to be made by using super-fast computers to take advantage of these discrepancies.

Now is that serving an incredibly productive function? No, but there's money on the table; somebody is going to take advantage of it, somebody is going to make it. But it's an artificial thing created by regulation. If we had kept the exchanges separate, it probably would never have arisen. Now, I can't see any negative aspect to it—prices are reflecting information a little bit faster—but it's not a huge positive as far as I can see, and I doubt it would have come up, in this form, absent regulation.

Don: We'll come back to derivatives in a second when we turn to the 2008 financial crisis, but I would take one more broad issue, and that's the debate on economic inequality. The financial industry has been targeted as a real source of inequality, especially by Occupy Wall Street. Do you think the financial industry has contributed to rising inequality and if so, what do you make of that?

Yaron: So, first why is finance such a target of the left and of Occupy Wall Street? In part, because it's an easy target. Americans still believe that economic inequality is okay if it reflects productive achievement. If Steve Jobs made billions, well, good for him: he created amazing products. But Americans do not understand the productive role of finance, and so they wonder, why are all these paper shufflers making millions or billions of dollars? Add that to the fact that finance takes the blame for legitimate problems caused by government intervention, and to the fact that government intervention has encouraged genuine evils on the part of some financiers, such as cronyism, and of course the opponents of capitalism are going to target finance.

What about economic inequality? It's true that some financiers make a lot of money, it's true that they contribute to whatever rise there's been in inequality, and it's true that some of the money they make is the result of cronyism or other forms of government intervention, such as the activities of the Federal Reserve. But some—I would say *most*—of the money made by financiers is earned through genuine productive achievement. And so the problem isn't inequality—it's the injustice of government intervention. To fight inequality by taxing or regulating financiers, including financiers who honestly earned their wealth, is unfair. Instead, we need to end the injustice. We need to fight cronyism, get the government out of banking and finance, and establish a truly free market, where there are no opportunities to use the government to get your hands on unearned wealth.

I want to make one additional point here. Although the critics of inequality will often point to the prevalence of cronyism in order to justify their attacks, cronyism is *not* why they hate financiers. And the proof here is their attacks on the less regulated parts of the financial industry, such as hedge funds and private equity. Hedge funds and private equity firms make lots of money, and it's clearly not as a result of cronyism. What the inequality critics object to, at the end of the day, is not unjust success, but success as such. In their view, if you're far richer than other people, you've done something wrong.

But it's exactly the opposite. Hedge fund managers and other financiers who earn lots of money as a result of productive achievement have done something *right*. They are the ones making markets efficient and directing capital to where it's most needed. They're making money for themselves and their clients and helping to make sure that innovators like Steve Jobs and Jeff Bezos can provide us with all of the amazing things that make up our incredible standard of living.

Don: Let's turn to the financial crisis. We've written on this in our book *Free Market Revolution*, and our friend John Allison devoted an entire book to this subject, but can you at least give us an overview of what you think caused the crisis, and contrast your view with the contemporary narrative that blames greedy Wall Street bankers for blowing up the economy?

Yaron: Fundamentally, I believe the financial crisis was caused by two government policies. One is a policy of keeping interest rates very, very low in order to avoid the pain of recession following the dotcom bubble and September 11th. The economy was going into a recession and then-Fed chair Alan Greenspan engineered what was called at the time a "soft-landing." He lowered interest rates below the rate of inflation, thus flooding the markets with cheap money so that people would continue to invest, even though one could argue that there had been a lot of malinvestment leading up to that point that needed to be corrected. So, Greenspan kept interest rates very, very low for two and a half years, which I think created massive malinvestments, mainly in housing.

Why did that money go into housing? That leads to the second piece of the puzzle, which is government housing policy. The government attempted to increase home ownership in America, in many different ways but especially through Freddie Mac and Fannie Mae. Freddie and Fannie became these monstrously large organizations. They were basically buying up mortgages, securitizing them, and selling those securities on the marketplace. And because they had a mandate to buy up mortgages with lower-income Americans, they didn't discriminate in terms of the quality of the mortgages they were willing to buy—they were effectively willing to buy junk and sell the securities to people who thought, "These are coming from Freddie and Fannie, how bad can they be?" Well it turned out they could be very bad. Lending standards had been lowered. It used to be that Fannie and Freddie would only purchase 20 percent down, 30-year fixed mortgages. But by the mid-2000s, they were buying 3 percent down and they were doing so on a huge scale.

Now, this creates a really bad incentive for investment bankers to compete with Fannie and Freddie in a securitization business that seems very lucrative—even though it's all predicated on an assumption that housing prices will continue to rise and defaults on mortgages will remain very low. And they did—not very wisely from a long-term view, although it's easy to say that in hindsight.

But why were so many bankers so short-sighted? Well, one reason is another government policy: that the big investment banks were "too big to fail." For decades the government had been bailing out big financial institutions that made mistakes, rather than allowing them to go bankrupt. That policy had a huge effect on bondholders, the people who provide capital to banks. Typically bondholders are the people most concerned about excessive risk, but when the government protected them on the downside, that concern was effectively eliminated. They could make a lot of money loaning to banks that were engaged in very risky behavior, knowing that if things went bad, they would be protected.

Now, you can't blame all this on greed. John Allison likes to say that Wall Street is always greedy—people there are always trying to make money. And in a free market that's a very healthy thing, since the way you make money is to direct capital to productive uses (and to protect yourself from excessive risk, since you'll pay the price if things don't work out).

But when you have such a regulated marketplace distorted by Fed-engineered interest rates, now the signals you're getting from the market are not accurate. And that encourages you to be short-term—how can you act long-term in a situation where interest rates are determined by which side of the bed Ben Bernanke wakes up on that morning?—and to take destructive actions that would not appear prudent absent government interference.

Even with all that, what actually led the crisis to turn into a serious recession was the government's response to the crisis. And here I don't mean the fact that Lehman was allowed to go bankrupt. What I mean is the panic and uncertainty created by the government, its unpredictable bailouts, and Treasury Secretary Hank Paulson going on television and saying, in effect, "If Congress doesn't give me approval to be financial dictator (which is what the $700 billion TARP measure amounted to) the economic world will end." I mean, that's scary. The Lehman bankruptcy? Financial markets could have easily dealt with that. But when the Secretary of the Treasury and the chairman of the Federal Reserve Bank, the most powerful economic institution in the world, panic, people lose trust in the financial system, they stop lending, they rush to cash, and *that's* when you get a genuine economic catastrophe.

So that, I would say, is the briefest overview of what happened. Let me add that there's still a lot of debate by economists about the details of what went wrong. The one thing that is undeniable, however, is that this was a crisis created by government. Absent government's enormous intrusion into housing and the financial system, it could not have happened.

Don: I wonder if you could expand on one part of this story, specifically, the role of derivatives. And, more broadly, do you think derivatives are a valuable, productive innovation, or a useless and dangerous one?

Yaron: There a lot of different types of derivatives out there and, in one form or another, they have been around for hundreds of years. And they serve an incredibly important, productive function.

The classic example here is farmers, who use derivatives to lock in prices for, say, wheat or corn. If the price of corn goes up, they don't get the benefit of that rise in price, but by the same token, if the price of corn goes down, they won't take the hit. Same goes for oil companies. The price of oil recently dropped from about $100 to something like $45 a barrel. Oil companies use derivatives to hedge the price. For a year or so, oil companies didn't take a financial hit from the price of oil going down and could prepare over that time for the change in oil prices, say, by shifting production away from its more higher-cost wells. Derivatives, then, give them time to adjust to the new economic reality.

The broader point is that derivatives play a crucial role in helping producers deal with risk. Companies can use interest rate swaps to lock in different interest rates and different types of interest rates (i.e., you can swap out a fixed interest loan for a variable one). Or, you can control for currency risk. So what derivatives do is allow producers and bankers to adjust the level of risk they are comfortable with over time. And to allocate risk, from those who are unwilling or incapable of handling it, to those who can and will. You cannot have robust financial markets and institutions without derivatives. They are incredibly productive and incredibly important economically.

That said, some derivatives are consequences of regulation or government policy. For example, many derivatives that are linked to interest rates, probably wouldn't exist in a free market, because in a free market there wouldn't be as much volatility and uncertainty about interest rates as there is today, thanks to the Federal Reserve. So, a lot of derivatives are created in order to deal with the uncertainty and the risk created by government.

There are a lot of derivatives in the background of the financial crisis, because all these mortgages were securitized, and these securities are basically derivatives. What does "derivative" mean? It means that the securities' value is derived from not an asset that it has a direct claim on, but a derivative claim on. So a derivative security on a pool of mortgages, gets its value comes from the performance of mortgages on the homes in the pool.

Now, the existence of mortgage-backed securities is fantastic. The fact that we can take loans in mortgages and divvy them up and create these pieces of paper that millions of people or institutions can hold, provides a real benefit: some people can make money off the mortgages while providing more liquidity to banks, which allows them to give out more mortgages and potentially at lower rates. If this market were healthy, if it weren't regulated and distorted by government, this would be a positive phenomena that would reduce risk and increase lending. But in a situation where the government is encouraging poor quality mortgages, and where too-big-to-fail is undercutting concern for risk, they can be disastrous. But the problem isn't the derivatives—it's the government distortions.

The same is true of the CDSs, or credit default swaps. CDSs provided insurance on bonds: in the end, they were nothing more than an insurance policy. The idea that credit default swaps would wipe out the economy was a ludicrous idea. It shows a complete ignorance of how swaps and derivatives more broadly work. Yes, if AIG had gone bankrupt there would have been a lot of messiness and some companies might have gone bankrupt, but the world would not have ended. And again, in a healthy, unregulated market, these things are productivity enhancers and risk reducers.

Don: So you mentioned how regulated these markets are several times. That's contrary to everything that we've heard since the crisis, which is that these markets were *not* regulated—that they had been deregulated and that's precisely why we had the problems we did.

Yaron: It's important to understand that financial regulations, as I said before, existed from the founding of the country. The first financial regulations come right after the Constitutional Convention and they're basically state regulations, controlling things like how much capital the banks needed to have, whether banks could branch out and diversify. Then in the 1930s, there were massive regulations on banks. Glass-Steagall and other securities and banking regulations were imposed on banks, along with the government providing banks with deposit insurance, which ultimately became the main inspiration for banking regulations.

Deposit insurance basically says that the government, through the FDIC, will insure depositors up to some cap. Initially that cap was low, because the goal was supposed to be to protect small investors, although today the FDIC insures up to $250,000. I don't know of any small investors who have $250,000 in cash in their checking account, but by definition, you're not a small anything if you have $250,000 in cash in your bank account. But that's what deposit insurance evolved to be: from protecting unsophisticated moms and pops to protecting everybody. So as deposit insurance grew, the regulators got more antsy and said: "Oh, wait a minute. If we're insuring all this stuff, we need a lot more control over the bankers, because they might do stupid things that will cost the government money."

Ultimately, by the time of this financial crisis, almost every aspect of a bank's functioning was regulated. For a good illustration of this, consider what's involved in starting a bank. To start a bank, you have to first get government approval. And that approval is based on submitting a business plan, which has to be approved by regulators, who will negotiate with you on the business plan. You have to provide a list of the officers: CEO, Chief Credit Officer, Chief Financial Officer, which all have to be approved by the regulators. Your Board of Directors has to be approved by the regulators. And your investors have to be approved by the regulators. So that's when you start. Then, every quarter, the regulators come in and examine your books and supposedly make sure you're giving the kind of loans that you said you would give, that you've rated them at the appropriate risk level, and that you're not taking too much risk.

Or look at this another way: How many different regulatory agencies regulated a bank, pre-2008? You have the FDIC, which is deposit insurance. You have the OCC, or Office of the Comptroller of the Currency. Then the Federal Reserve. And if you're a publicly traded company, you've got the SEC. Add to all that, you've got state regulators. Today, we've added to that with the Consumer Protection Agency, and, if you're very big, there's the Systemic Risk Commission. This is what we call an unregulated, free market? It's nuts.

Now, it's true that certain aspects of banking had been deregulated. For example, the interest that banks could pay you on your checking account had been set by government, via Regulation Q, and that was eliminated in the 1970s. A lot of little stuff like that was de-regulated, but the big pieces of regulation were still there. Then in 1999 one aspect of the Glass-Steagall Act was changed (not, as we're often told, eliminated). Glass-Steagall had separated commercial and investment banks, and in 1999 that was altered so that now commercial banks and investment banks could merge, so long as they had all sorts of firewalls and met various reporting requirements.

Or to take another example: derivatives. People point out that Congress wanted to regulate the derivatives market but that Alan Greenspan made a famous speech in front of Congress and argued against regulating the derivatives. And that's true. Basically what Alan Greenspan said is, "Regulators are not smart enough to regulate the derivatives market, so you better leave it alone." And on this point Greenspan was right. There is no reason to think that Congress would have made things better had they regulated derivatives. First of all, the government generally approved of what was going on pre-crisis, and second of all, the whole history of financial regulation shows that regulations create more problems than they solve. That said, the overall trend during the time was an intensification of financial regulations, not deregulation.

So, going into the Financial Crisis, every one of the major banks was heavily regulated. Around that time, Lehman Brothers and Goldman Sachs and the investment banks wanted to increase their leverage to 30:1, and of course they needed government permission for that. So it wasn't deregulation that allowed them to lever up: it was government policy—and government policy is what caused the financial crisis and every one of its aspects.

Following the financial crisis, of course, regulation intensified dramatically even before Dodd-Frank, most obviously through forcing banks to take TARP—even healthy banks who didn't want to take TARP were forced to accept it and then pay the money back with interest. As a result, the government made a positive return off TARP, but at the expense of the rest of the economy.

Then you've got Dodd-Frank, which is this massive bill which regulates every aspect of banks, to the point that I consider banks today to be basically public utilities. They're private in name only—the government is to a large extent controlling every aspect of how they operate. For example, every day about a hundred and fifty regulators go to work *at the offices* of JP Morgan. One consequence of all this regulation is that it becomes very hard to analyze finance, to figure out what controls are responsible for what effects, to distinguish what are the productive actions of banks from what are unproductive actions. What you can say is that, overall, the market is far less efficient and productive, and that's one reason why the economic recovery has been so slow.

Don: You've been very critical of how regulated finance is, but didn't the Bernie Madoff scandal prove that, not only do we need regulations, but that if we had had more regulations we might have been able to catch him earlier?

Yaron: What Bernie Madoff did was commit fraud; a classic pyramid scheme. Fraud has always been illegal—it's not something you need the regulatory state to outlaw. Nor can you regulate fraud away. Fraudsters by definition operate by breaking laws and trying to get around laws. Regulations can cause them to change *how* they perpetrate their crime—it can't stop the crime before it occurs. Indeed, note that Madoff was friends with many of these regulators, which arguably made it easier for him to get away with his scheme.

In terms of enforcing laws against fraud, this is not something you need a regulatory agency for. Perhaps just a division of the FBI responsible for financial fraud. You could take the SEC, scrap all of its regulatory functions, and restructure it so that all it did was catch fraudsters—the people who lie, cheat, and steal for a living.

I would actually argue that it took so long to catch Bernie Madoff because the SEC was too busy reading all of our financial statements. They were too busy reading my 13Gs and 13Ds, and all this stuff that non-criminals file. Who has time to go after a real crook?

In a free market, Madoff would've been caught quickly. The market first of all would have been suspicious of him. One of the reasons frauds can get away with this is because people are far less skeptical of crooks when they believe the government is looking after them. Why do our due diligence? Surely if Madoff was cooking the books the SEC would have discovered it. In a free market, people would be far more prudent because they know they have to be.

The bottom line is that regulations aren't the solution to fraud. Instead, they divert the government from the real crooks and make them focus on the good guys, which is *destructive*.

Don: You mentioned Federal Reserve several times. Explain what the Fed does, what its effects are, and what role, if any, you think it should play in the economy.

Yaron: The Federal Reserve is America's central bank, formed in 1913 by an act of Congress. It is theoretically a private bank, but it is controlled by the government's executive branch, and the President appoints the Chairman of the Board. The treasury receives any profits the Fed makes. So the Fed is for all intents and purposes a government institution. Its main responsibility is to manage the money supply in the United States in way that is supposed to control inflation and maximize employment.

There's a famous video of Milton Friedman on YouTube where he shows what an absolute disaster the Fed has been. He points out that the Fed started operating in 1914 and that since then it has been responsible for creating the financial crisis in 1920, for creating the recession of 1929, and then turning that recession into a Great Depression, and for creating the inflation of the 1970s. And then, as I've mentioned, I would argue that it played a major role in the Great Recession of 2008.

So the Federal Reserve, from the beginning, has been a destabilizing force, although it was set up, theoretically, to stabilize the banking system. But the banking system had been unstable because of regulation, especially because of state banking laws, which restricted branching and restricted diversification. As an aside, it's interesting to note that, since the founding of America, the United States has gone through twelve banking crises. Canada has had zero. Canada also has five big banks; we have 6,000 banks today and used to have three or four times that. This meant that our banks weren't diversified: they basically prospered or floundered along with the local economy. Again, this was the result of regulation—a free market would have never produced thousands of independent banks—and that is why you had this instability that the Fed was supposed to cure.

But the reality is that the Fed made things much worse. You had nothing like the Great Depression or the Great Recession before the Fed, and setting aside wartime, you had nothing like the inflation of the 1970s before the Fed. The lesson is that you cannot and should not have the government try to control the money supply. Central planning doesn't work: not when it comes to producing clothing and cars, and not when it comes to the money supply and interest rates. All of that should be determined by the market. The banking system should be free, and currencies should be private, which historically has meant a gold standard.

This has been tried historically and it works—it's not just economic theory, although the theory of free banking is sound too. The best work here has been done by economists George Selgin and Lawrence H. White, and I highly recommend their works for what is an important, complicated, and widely misunderstood issue.

So, to sum it up, the Federal Reserve has no productive function in the economy. It can only distort things and cause problems. As long as we have a Fed, we can debate how it should operate so that it leads to the least amount of harm. Certainly a rule-based approach is better than what we have now, where the Fed does whatever Bernanke or Yellen feels like doing. And there might be some rules that are better in some respect than other rules. But in the end all of it is central planning, and all of it is bad. I would like to see our best economists coming up with plans for getting rid of the Federal Reserve—not for making it somewhat less destructive.

Don: As we start to wrap up, I'd like to go a little deeper. Most people view the financial industry as fundamentally immoral. But you take the opposite view: not just that it isn't monstrous but that it's actually a morally good industry. Why do you say that?

Yaron: Finance is fundamentally a moral industry *because* it is productive—productive on a grand scale. My standard of morality is what promotes human life and happiness, and a key component of that is producing the material values that human life requires. Well, as I've tried to indicate in this interview, virtually all of the material values that make our lives so rich and amazing today depend on finance and financiers.

Financiers helped create Silicon Valley. Financiers help us buy the homes we live in and the cars we drive. Financiers help us send our kids to college and save for old age. Financiers help millions of small-business men and women achieve their dreams. They prosper by engaging in these productive, win/win relationships that have made America the wealthiest nation in history.

If you care about a rational individual's well-being, then the only conclusion you can draw is that finance is a moral endeavor.

But the problem is that not everyone holds human life and happiness as their moral standard. The dominant moral code in our culture is altruism—the idea that morality consists, not of creating the values your life and happiness require, but of sacrificing yourself to others. Placing others above yourself.

Well, financiers don't sacrifice, they make money. They create wealth and get really, really rich. And this is true of businessmen more widely. They are obviously not sacrificing themselves to others: they are pursuing profits. And so that is supposed to taint them morally. According to altruism, they should be giving with no expectation of return.

But if you think about it, this is really an indictment of altruism—not of financiers. If what financiers are doing is prospering by creating enormous value and dealing with other people win/win, then I would say that any supposed moral principle that denounces them cannot truly be a moral principle. If financiers have helped us live longer, richer, more enjoyable lives, then any code of morality that condemns them is committing a horrific injustice.

We need to completely reorient how we think about morality. When we think about what it means to be moral, what should come to mind is not saints who wallow in the mud and champion poverty and suffering, but *producers*—people who pursue their own happiness by using their minds to create values.

Don: With that in mind, what is your view of how the industry defends itself today and how it *should* defend itself?

Yaron: Well, for the most part financiers don't defend themselves. They just stay quiet, and they spend a lot of time lobbying government, trying to get regulations off their back or trying to manipulate regulations in their favor. But they very rarely actually articulate a case for what they do. Instead, they give a lot of money to charity, they give a lot of money to political campaigns, they try to drive humble cars, they try to downplay their wealth. But you almost never hear of financiers talking about their value.

For a great example of this, look at Mitt Romney when he was running for president. Mitt was the COO of a very successful private equity fund. And private equity is relatively easy to explain, right? You go into a company that is not doing too well, you buy out the owners, you improve it, and then you sell it and you make a profit. You profit by making businesses better, and by putting resources to more productive uses. Mitt Romney could never articulate that. He never actually said that, and he spent his whole campaign on the defensive, trying to explain that he wasn't as evil as people thought he was, rather than helping people see that he was doing something admirable and enormously positive.

So, overall, I think what you see is a non-defense. When financiers do defend themselves, though, it's almost always in very abstract, economic terms: that they promote efficiency or help foster economic growth or job creation. But it's seldom very clear or compelling, and it's never put in moral terms.

In essence, I think there are a few steps required to change the way people think of finance.

First, you need to be explicit about the *moral* standards we should use. If the standard we're measuring financiers by is altruism, self-sacrifice, then of course they're immoral. Instead, you need to say, in effect, my standard is each individual's life and happiness. What's moral is for each individual to strive to make his life as happy and successful as possible through his own rational thought and productive effort—dealing with others through mutually beneficial, win/win relationships. No fraud, no force, no sacrifices.

Second, you have to make the broader case for business and the profit motive. You need to help people grasp that wealth creators are doing something noble: they are creating the wealth that has lifted us from the Stone Age to the digital age, with each individual profiting, according to the value that he creates.

Third, you have to explain the productive role of finance in terms that people can understand. For example, I would say that venture capital is probably the area in finance that most people have a positive view of. And that's because they can see the connection between what venture capital does and a positive result: here are the guys who are bringing us the Apples and Ubers of the world. Whatever your role is in finance, that's what you have to strive to do: to connect your function or your industry's function to people's existing values.

Finally, you need to be able to properly frame the real challenges that exist in your industry, above all, the way you need to be able to explain how government intervention causes genuine problems.

If you do that, you can change people's views of finance.

ABOUT THE CONTRIBUTORS

Yaron Brook

Yaron Brook is the executive chairman of the Ayn Rand Institute and host of *The Yaron Brook Show*. He travels extensively as ARI's spokesman. Brook can be heard weekly on *The Yaron Brook Show*, which airs live on the BlogTalkRadio podcast and on TheBlaze Radio Network. He is also a frequent guest on national radio and television programs.

An internationally sought-after speaker and debater, Brook also has published a number of books, including two with co-author Don Watkins: the national best-seller *Free Market Revolution: How Ayn Rand's Ideas Can End Big Government* and *Equal Is Unfair: America's Misguided Fight Against Income Inequality*. Brook is also contributing author to *Neoconservatism: An Obituary for an Idea*; *Winning the Unwinnable War: America's Self-Crippled Response to Islamic Totalitarianism*; and *Big Tent: The Story of the Conservative Revolution—As Told by the Thinkers and Doers Who Made It Happen*.

Brook was born and raised in Israel. He served as a first sergeant in Israeli military intelligence and earned a BSc in civil engineering from Technion-Israel Institute of Technology in Haifa, Israel. In 1987, he moved to the United States where he received his MBA and PhD in finance from the University of Texas at Austin; he became an American citizen in 2003. For seven years he was an award-winning finance professor at Santa Clara University, and in 1998, he cofounded BH Equity Research, a private equity and hedge fund manager, of which he is managing founder and director.

Brook serves on the boards of the Ayn Rand Institute, the Clemson Institute for the Study of Capitalism and CEHE (Center for Excellence in Higher Education), and he is a member of the Association of Private Enterprise Education and the Mont Pelerin Society.

Don Watkins

Don Watkins, a former fellow at the Ayn Rand Institute, is director of education at the Center for Industrial Progress. He is the author of *RooseveltCare: How Social Security Is Sabotaging the Land of Self-Reliance*. He is also co-author with Yaron Brook of *Equal Is Unfair: America's Misguided Fight Against Income Inequality* and of the national bestseller *Free Market Revolution: How Ayn Rand's Ideas Can End Big Government*.

Raymond C. Niles

Raymond C. Niles, a former Wall Street executive, is currently a PhD candidate in economics at George Mason University. Over a Wall Street career that spanned sixteen years, he worked as a stock analyst at Citigroup, Schroders, and Goldman Sachs, and as an investment manager. Mr. Niles is an expert in business cycle theory and monetary policy. He holds an MBA in finance and economics from New York University

Doug Altner

Doug Altner was an analyst and instructor at the Ayn Rand Institute between 2011 and 2014.

ACKNOWLEDGEMENTS

We wish to thank Onkar Ghate for his extensive comments, suggestions and feedback on this project and for editing the manuscript. Elan Journo edited many of the articles and essays in this collection. Steve Simpson provided valuable insight on the history, legality and morality of insider trading, and edited the essay "Insider Trading: The Rule of Unreason." Richard Salsman provided feedback on the essay "Finance Isn't Free and Never Really Was." For their help with bringing this book to press, we wish to thank Rikki Nedelkow, Simon Federman, Anu Seppala, Lew Hendrickson, Angela Dietrich, Chris Locke, and Duane Knight.

* * *

The Ayn Rand Institute acknowledges the generosity of our individual, corporate and foundation donors. We are grateful for their continuing support of our mission, and for sharing our vision for the future.

In the case of this book, we wish to especially recognize the support of Jeff Yass of Susquehanna Investment Group, without whom this project would not have been possible.

ABOUT THE AYN RAND INSTITUTE

The Ayn Rand Institute believes that your own happiness is the moral purpose of your life, that productive achievement is your noblest activity and that reason is your only absolute. ARI challenges people to rethink their convictions from the ground up and to call into question the philosophical ideas and moral ideals that dominate the world today. By increasing awareness of Ayn Rand and understanding of her revolutionary ideas, ARI continues to make significant strides toward the ambitious goal of creating a culture based in reason and individual rights.

Stay in Touch.

Subscribe to receive timely updates. You'll be the first to learn about our latest initiatives and program successes and how you can help ARI achieve its mission to spearhead a cultural renaissance of reason, rational self-interest, individual rights and laissez-faire capitalism. Now more than ever, it's an exciting time to engage with ARI.

AynRand.org/signup

54306849R00141

Made in the USA
San Bernardino, CA
13 October 2017